The Divine Hierarchy:

Popular Hinduism in Central India

LAWRENCE A. BABB

Columbia University Press
New York

The Andrew W. Mellon Foundation, through a special grant, has assisted the Press in publishing this volume.

Columbia University Press
New York   Chichester, West Sussex
Copyright © 1975 by Columbia University Press

Library of Congress Cataloging in Publication Data
Babb, Lawrence A
  The divine hierarchy: popular Hinduism in central India.

  Bibliography:
  1. Hinduism—Chhattisgarh, India. 2. Chhattisgarh,
India—Religious life and customs. I. Title.
BL1150.B29   294.5′0954′3   75–16193
ISBN 0–231–03882–8
ISBN 0–231–08387–4 (pbk.)

Printed in the United States of America

C 10 9 8 7 6 5 4
P 10 9 8 7 6 5 4 3

To Nancy

Contents

List of Illustrations

List of Maps

Preface to the Paperback Edition

It is naturally a source of great satisfaction to any author to have his or her work reissued in paperback. This book was originally published in 1975, the product of a first experience in the field. In the intervening years I have continued to study Hindu institutions, and, as one does, have come to understand this subject better. Since the early 1970s the field of South Asian anthropology has changed, and with this has occurred a very substantial deepening of anthropological understanding of Hindu institutions. It is now clear, for example, that the transactional analysis of ritual presented here is in need of substantial modification, which in fact I have supplied in subsequent publications of my own. Likewise, had I known what I know now, I would certainly have written my analysis of the role of the goddess in the pantheon with greater attention to finer modulations of her character—although I believe the essentials of my interpretation to have stood the test of time. Finally, it now seems clear to me that an analysis less focused on purity and more attentive to such principles as power and auspiciousness would have been a better one. In these and other matters my understanding has changed, and *The Divine Hierarchy* would be a very different book were I researching and writing it today.

Nevertheless, I believe the book continues to have value as a systematic portrait of popular Hinduism as a form of religious life, one that presents the tradition as a variegated but also internally consistent and interconnected whole. The Hindu world tugs irresistibly at the intellect and imagination. If this book imparts to students and other readers any sense at all of the tradition's inherent interest and appeal, then I am happy indeed to see it reappear.

Preface

The field research upon which this book is based took place between August 1966 and November 1967 in Raipur District, Madhya Pradesh, India. During this period I lived with my wife and later my daughter (who was born shortly after our arrival), in a residential colony on the outskirts of the city of Raipur. My initial purpose in going there had been to investigate the religious life of a particular sect, the Satnamis, but it became apparent that little could be understood about sectarian religious styles without taking into account the religious traditions of the Chhattisgarh region. I therefore broadened my research to encompass popular Hinduism in its regional dimensions, and in the end an understanding of popular religion in this extended sense became my principal goal. The fieldwork was not localized in the way that anthropological research often is, but instead took place in various settings in which important aspects of the religious life of the region are to be seen. Chief among these were the city of Raipur and a village I have pseudonymously designated Sitapur, but I also visited many other localities in Chhattisgarh, especially important temple or pilgrimage centers. The study does not pretend to be an ethnography, in the strictest sense, of the religious life of a region. Such a task would be completely beyond the capacities of any single investigator. Rather, I have sought to uncover certain basic conceptions in Chhattisgarhi Hinduism that are emergent in ritual activity as seen in selected contexts of observation. As will be seen, a regional frame of reference is essential to this type of analysis, but at the same time the religious life of the Hindus of Chhattisgarh combines sharply localized elements with traditions that are essentially pan-Indian in distribution. "Unity in diversity" is far more than a political slogan when applied to Indian civilization.

It would be impossible here to mention everyone in Raipur District who contributed to my study. Let me say only that my wife and I were received cordially and with every courtesy in virtually all areas of life in the region, and that with few exceptions we encountered an understanding of the aims of my project and a willingness to help. We were received with great kindness in many homes, and were allowed to enter temples, to take photographs, and to intrude into situations in which our presence must often have been an inconvenience, and occasionally a positive nuisance. A special word should be said concerning the villagers of Sitapur, who received an awkward stranger with kindness and tolerance; many displayed a sophisticated understanding of the purpose of my inquiries.

Certain individuals should be mentioned by name. Messrs M. S. Thakur, Nand Narang, Vimal Gideon, Lakhan Lal Verma, and Lakhan Lal Soni were friends, companions, and teachers. Eric and Pat Gass helped us establish ourselves in Raipur and were constant sources of friendship and counsel. Without their help the study could never have taken place. Many students and colleagues have helped me formulate my ideas about popular Hinduism, and rather than attempting to name individuals, let me express gratitude to all. I must, however, acknowledge debts of a special kind, though different in each case, to Arnold Green, Brenda Beck, and Alfred Harris. I also thank Mr. Leslie Bialler, my editor at Columbia University Press, for his indispensable role in shaping my original manuscript into a presentable book. Finally, I must express my debt to my wife, Nancy, who shared the difficulties of fieldwork with me, and who has been an unfailing source of encouragement and advice. Let me add, however, that although many people have helped me in the writing of this book, and in the research upon which it is based, all errors of reporting and interpretation are mine alone.

I would also like to acknowledge the support of the Foreign Area Fellowship Program which, in addition to its generous financing of the fieldwork, also supported a year of area study prior to the fieldwork and an additional year for the writing of the dissertation from which this book has developed. Some of the material presented in the book has been previously published in *The Eastern Anthropologist, Ethnology,* and *Southwestern Journal of Anthropology* (Babb 1973, 1970b, 1970a). I thank the editors of these journals for their permission to reprint these materials.

The orthographic conventions followed in this book have been aimed at maximum simplicity and readability. Hindi terms are italicized but are presented without diacritic marks. Hindi plurals are indicated by the addition of the English *s*. Certain familiar Indian terms (such as bazaar) are given without italicization, as are personal names, place names, the names of deities, and the names of castes.

Introduction

The Hindu religious tradition is ancient and immensely complex. The vast number of books published on Hinduism attest both to the extraordinary interest the subject excites in the West, and to the wide latitude for variant interpretations this elusive subject allows. It is a many-faceted tradition, and one abounding in apparent contradictions. One such contradiction seems to override all others—the dual impression of unity and diversity the tradition leaves on the mind and eye of the observer.

The religious life of the Hindus presents itself initially as a bewildering clutter, a quilt work of seemingly unrelated rites, ideas, attitudes, and myths. Closer scrutiny, however, yields a very different impression. There are obvious connecting threads—the concern with purity and pollution, the importance of hierarchy, common ritual usages—which seem to point to a deeper continuity. The impression of unity is augmented by the fact that the Hindus themselves insist that it is there. Unity is indeed a premise the Hindu tradition employs when it scrutinizes itself; "many paths to the same goal" is a customary expression by means of which Indians interpret obvious differences both to themselves and to Westerners. Even so, while diversity is quite evident, the basic underlying principles in the tradition remain obscure.

It is the question of unity, the question of the connections between apparently unrelated aspects of religion, that constitutes the main focus of this book. In the broadest sense, of course, the problem of unity in the Hindu tradition is far beyond the scope of a single essay, however ambitious. In this book I shall not attempt to deal with the problem on a grand scale; instead, I shall reduce it considerably in scope and present it in what I believe to be a manageable form. What is at one level a problem of unity within a subcontinental tradition may be seen at another level as the problem of relationships between apparently diverse and unconnected aspects of popular Hinduism in a specific regional setting. The present study deals with the problem in this reduced and recast form.

The region is a rice-growing area of eastern Madhya Pradesh known as Chhattisgarh. Here, as elsewhere on the subcontinent, is seen a rich and complex religious life, which encompasses concepts and practices sanctioned in the sacred literature along with those having seemingly little or no relationship with the textual tradition. Here, as elsewhere, the salvationary concerns of philosophical Hinduism exist in incongruous juxtaposition with the pragmatic and magical elements of popular religion. Chhattisgarh is not the South Asian subcontinent, nor is Hinduism in Chhattisgarh the Hindu tradition in the most encompassing sense. Nevertheless, it seems clear that many of the analytical problems relating to the diversity of Hinduism are fully exemplified in the Chhattisgarhi setting, though on a far smaller and considerably more tractable scale.

My emphasis will be on systemic aspects of religion in Chhattisgarh. I shall try to show that despite the apparent lack of continuity, there are connections between the concepts and practices that constitute the religion of Chhattisgarh—connections that draw diverse elements into a coherent whole. In the course of my analysis it will become clear that Hinduism in Chhattisgarh

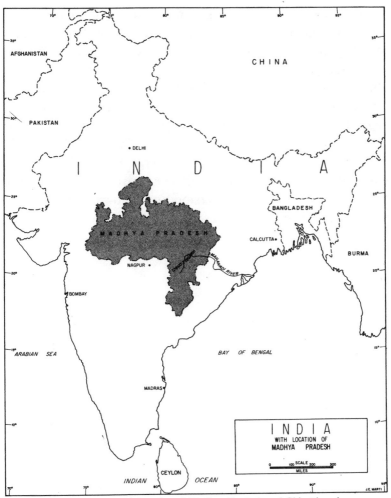

Map 1 India with location of Madhya Pradesh and Chhattisgarh

is related in the most intimate way to the social structure that forms its context. Nevertheless, my analysis is not primarily concerned with religion in relation to social structure, but rather is an effort to understand popular Hinduism as a system of concepts and practices in its own right, as an autonomous cultural domain which displays a pattern and consistency of its own. This is in no way intended to minimize the importance of connections

between religion and society in Chhattisgarh, nor is it to be construed as a denial of the anthropological canon that an understanding of social structure is a vital opening wedge to the
understanding of religion. Indeed, we shall see that nowhere is
this assumption more applicable than in Chhattisgarh, where a
single symbolic and conceptual paradigm underlies understand-
ings of human and divine hierarchy and supplies the structural
core of most if not all Chhattisgarhi ritual. Thus, in Chhattisgarh,
as elsewhere, religion and society converge. But the full implications of connections of this sort can be seen only when the
religious system itself is understood on its own terms. Such is
the goal of this book.

The Divine Hierarchy

1

The Ethnographic Setting

Chhattisgarh is far more than an arbitrarily drawn section on the map of Madhya Pradesh. It is an ethnographic and historical reality, a region distinct from those adjacent to it, with cultural traditions and a long dynastic history of its own. Its heart is the rice-growing plain drained by the upper Mahanadi river; the plain itself comprises some 10,000 square miles. Chhattisgarh in the most inclusive sense has usually been considered to consist of this nuclear plain and the immediately adjacent hilly areas. On the west it is separated from the Wainganga valley by an extension of the Satpura hills, and on the north it is bounded by the Maikal range. To the south it merges into the hill areas of the old Kanker and Bastar States. To the east Chhattisgarh is separated from Orissa by relatively hilly and inhospitable country. Accordingly, one of the principal historical facts about Chhattisgarh has been its relative degree of isolation from adjacent regions until rather recent times. It is also an area that has been very poorly described in the ethnographic and historical literature.

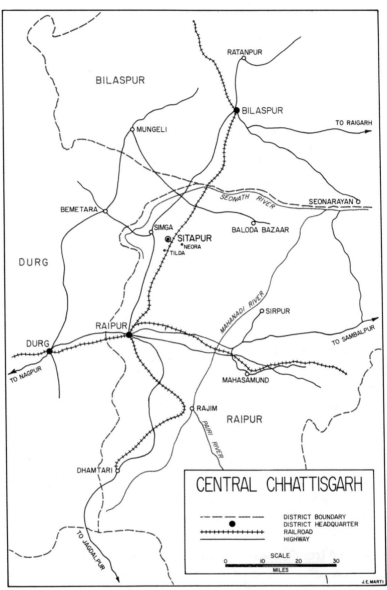

Map 2   Central Chhattisgarh

The early history of Chhattisgarh is obscure. On the basis of inscriptions,[1] the history of the region has been conventionally traced from about the fourth century of our era. At that time Chhattisgarh appears to have been a part of a "kingdom" known as Kosala, frequently designated Maha Kosala or Dakshin Kosala to distinguish it from another kingdom of the same name in North India. Reference to this kingdom is found in the Allahabad pillar inscription of Samudra Gupta, the Son of Chandra Gupta I, the founder of the Gupta dynasty at Patna. The inscription relates that on his great southern campaign Samudra Gupta marched southward through the region known today as Chota Nagpur and attacked Dakshin Kosala. He is said to have captured two kings of the region, Mahendra and Vyaghraraja, but to have later released them. From Dakshin Kosala he apparently marched as far south as the Krishna river, and he finally made his way home through the western Deccan. The *Bilaspur District Gazetteer* speculates that the kings of Dakshin Kosala acknowledged the suzerainty of the Gupta kings for as long as a century after the fall of the Gupta empire (Nelson 1910a:29). To what degree and for how long the Dakshin Kosala kings actually acknowledged the dominion of the Gupta kings is unclear, but the available evidence at least suggests that despite its southern location Chhattisgarh was in the sphere of North Indian cultural influence from relatively early times.

By the seventh century Dakshin Kosala had fallen under the rule of a Buddhist king whose capital was at Bhandak in the present Chanda District (Nelson 1909:39). Later, what appears to have been a branch of this dynasty became established at Sirpur (in the present Raipur District) and ruled the Chhattisgarh region as an independent kingdom (Nelson 1910a:30). Very little is known of the succeeding centuries until the coming of the Haihayas (or the Haihaibansis), a line of rulers who remained

---

[1] These materials were assessed by two men: Alexander Cunningham (1884) and Hira Lal. Hira Lal wrote the bulk of the historical chapter of the *Drug* (Durg) and *Raipur District Gazetteers* (Nelson 1909 and 1910b).

entrenched as the rulers of Chhattisgarh from about the tenth century until the Maratha conquest of 1745. The Haihayas regarded themselves as a branch of the dynasty of the Haihayas who ruled a kingdom called Chedi, to the north, from the city of Tripuri (or Tewar) near the present-day city of Jabalpur.

An inscription at Ratanpur, dated 1114, states that Kokalla, a Chedi king who ruled during the ninth century, had eighteen sons.[2] The eldest of these succeeded to the throne at Tripuri, while the others were given "subordinate estates" termed *mandalas*. The southernmost of these estates have been tentatively identified as Komo, Tuman, and Kosgain, located in the hills just north of the Mahanadi plain (Nelson 1910a:32). The inscription further relates that Tuman passed eventually to Kalingaraja, a descendant of the original grantee. According to the inscription, Kalingaraja "abandoned his ancestral land and acquired by his two arms the country of Dakshin Kosala." (Nelson 1910a:32) In fact it is likely that he only subdued parts of the northern portion of Chhattisgarh, as there are records of his descendants conquering other chiefdoms of the Chhattisgarh plain and, according to the inscription, he retained Tuman as his capital. At any rate, the whole of Chhattisgarh ultimately came under the rule of this house, and the dynastic capital was established at Ratanpur, where the remains of their royal architecture may be seen today. Later a junior branch of the line became established at Raipur from where it appears to have ruled the southern part of Chhattisgarh on a basis of partial autonomy. The divergence between the two lines has been estimated to have occurred in the fourteenth century (Nelson 1909:48), and the Raipur branch remained intact until it was ousted by the Marathas in 1758.

Although almost every vestige of the territorial organization of Chhattisgarh under the Haihayas was obliterated by the Maratha invasion and subsequent reorganization of the region, enough evidence remained for C. U. Wills (1919) to write a very intelligent, if speculative, account of the structure of the Haihaya kingdom. Wills finds evidence for a five-tiered system of terri-

---

[2] The number eighteen seems to be pure convention. See Sinha 1962:67.

torial organization. The smallest political units were the villages.
These in turn were grouped into larger units which, according to
convention, contained twelve villages each. These units were
called *barhons* (or *taluqs*) a word deriving from *barah*, "twelve."
The *barhons*, in turn, were grouped into still larger units which,
by convention, contained eighty-four villages each. These were
known as *chaurasis* or *garhs*, *chaurasi* meaning "eighty-four" and
garh meaning "fort." At the next level up were the Ratanpur and
Raipur kingdoms, perhaps better understood as "subkingdoms,"
located north and south of the Seonath (Shivnath) river. Each is
said to have contained eighteen garhs, and these units were consequently known as *atharagarhs* (*atharah* meaning "eighteen").
Finally, at the apex of the system was the Ratanpur kingdom as
a whole, all of which, both north and south, was at least nominally subordinate to the rulers at Ratanpur. Twice eighteen, of
course, is thirty-six, and the kingdom as a whole was accordingly
known as *chhattisgarh*, or "thirty-six forts."

The correspondence of the actual territorial organization
of the region to the numerical scheme described above is very
doubtful. The numbers clearly are purely conventional, and describe an ideal political order, which must have corresponded to
reality only poorly. Nevertheless, on the basis of the available
evidence there can be little doubt that the *barhons*, *chaurasis*, and
atharagarhs existed in some form as important political units
during the Haihaya period. As Wills remarks, the very neat
system represented by the numerical scheme must have been the
"theory . . . on which the system worked" (1919:199).

Whatever the nature of the organizational system of the
Haihaya kingdom, it is clear that by the eighteenth century the
kingdom was no longer well enough organized to withstand invasion from outside. In late 1740, Baskar Pant, a Maratha general,
entered Chhattisgarh while on his way to Chota Nagpur.[3]
Raghunath, the king at Ratanpur, either could not or would not
defend his dominions, and the Maratha forces were able to enter

---

[3] This reconstruction of events is based mainly on Nelson's account in the *Bilaspur
District Gazetteer* (Nelson 1910a).

Ratanpur after firing on the palace only briefly. Having taken Ratanpur, the general marched through the Chhattisgarhi countryside and succeeded in obtaining the allegiance of most of the petty chieftains. After the general had gone on to Chota Nagpur, Raghunath attempted to reestablish his independence, but he was ousted for good by Raghuji I, the Bhonsla ruler of Nagpur, in 1745. By 1758 Maratha rule was firmly established in Chhattisgarh, and gradually all traces of the old order began to disappear in the central Chhattisgarh plain, although the surrounding hill areas appear to have maintained a considerable degree of independence. The Maratha administration of these territories is said to have been extremely corrupt, and this has been blamed for the extreme degree of poverty in Chhattisgarh at the time the British took over. This view, however, may reflect an understandable bias in the British sources.

With the defeat of Appa Sahib in 1818 the Nagpur territories came under what amounted to British rule. From 1830 until 1853 Chhattisgarh, with the rest of the Nagpur territories, was administered by the Marathas under the supervision of the Nagpur residency. In 1853, following the death of Raja Raghuji III, the Nagpur territories reverted to the paramount power of the British. In 1854 Chhattisgarh was made a separate Deputy Commissionership with headquarters at Raipur. During the next few years revenue settlements were made on a triennial basis: 1855–57, 1858–60, 1861–62. It soon became apparent that Chhattisgarh was much too big to be administered efficiently as a single unit, and Bilaspur was formed as a separate district in 1861.

Surveys for the first regular revenue settlement were begun in 1862 and completed in 1868. The first settlement, and with it the establishment of proprietary rights in land, took effect in 1868. At the same time the special status of the *zamindars* (estate-holders) was defined. By 1909 it had become apparent that the Bilaspur and Raipur Districts were too large for efficient management, and in this year portions of each were incorporated into a

new district called Drug (now known as Durg). The British gave
the status of semi-independent "feudatory states" to the petty
chiefdoms of the hilly areas surrounding the central Chhattisgarh
plain. At the time of independence these were abolished, which
in turn entailed considerable reorganization of the Chhattisgarh
districts. Many of these territories were absorbed into the new
districts of Bastar and Raigarh, and various other territorial
adjustments were made, the details of which are not of direct
concern here. It is sufficient to note that Chhattisgarh, in the most
extended sense, includes the present-day Bilaspur, Surguja,
Raigarh, Raipur, and Durg Districts, and portions of northern
Bastar District as well. Its heartland is the plain drained by the
upper Mahanadi and its tributaries.

   The Chhattisgarh plain has been described as "a series of
gently undulating slopes running from ridge to streamlet and
from streamlet to ridge" (Nelson 1909:2). As one moves out in
any direction from this nuclear area the relatively flat plain gives
way to low hills. Generally a red lateritic soil is found on the
ridges of the plain, while the slopes consist of a yellow soil, which
merges with black in the lowest areas. Extremely fertile black
soil is found in the river valleys. The average yearly rainfall of
Chhattisgarh is about 49 inches, making it excellent country for
growing rice. Rice is usually grown without artificial irrigation
on the yellow and red soils that cover the better part of the plain.
Wheat is grown in some quantity in areas directly adjacent to
rivers, where black soil is found in abundance. Wheat, however,
has never been a major crop in Chhattisgarh.

   It is fair to say that the cultivation of rice constitutes the
governing factor in almost every dimension of life in the region.
The system of cultivation generally employed is an extremely
simple one. The paddy fields are small, and are bounded by water-
retaining walls made from earth. Planting usually starts in mid-
June with the coming of the monsoon season. The rice seedlings,
once established, are thinned by replowing, a procedure known
as *biasi*, which gives the Chhattisgarhi system of cultivation (the

so-called "*biasi* system") its name. A collection of fields forming one watershed is known as a *chak*. Usually a late-yielding variety of rice is planted in the middle and low fields of the *chak*, and earlier varieties in the outer and higher parts, so that the low and central fields may be harvested last. The harvesting, therefore, is staggered, lasting from late October to late November or early December. A winter (*unhari*) crop is often sown in the fields during the latter part of the summer growing season, and is sometimes sown on the earthen embankments. This crop might include any of the pulses (*urad, masur, batura, channa*) or linseed flax (*alsi*). An important subsidiary crop in the region is *kodon*,

The Fields

The Harvest

an inferior grain, eaten generally by poorer people, which can be grown on the poorest soils.

The main ethnographic break in Chhattisgarh is that between the central plain and the outlying hills, the latter characterized as "jungly" by the inhabitants of the region. Generally speaking these outlying areas are occupied by peoples conventionally classified as "tribal" (*adivasi*), while the plain itself is inhabited by a greater proportion of "caste Hindus." Caste Hindus are, of course, found in the hills, but are proportionally less significant. Groups of tribal origin are also present in central

Chhattisgarh, but here their tribal characteristics have tended to become submerged in the surrounding culture. The Gonds are an outstanding illustration. They are very numerous on the Chhattisgarh plain, but fit into local social systems as one caste among many; and, at least in central areas, they have no knowledge of the Gondi language.

It is crucial to determine in what sense or senses the region of Chhattisgarh constitutes an ethnographic entity. The answer is complex, for although Chhattisgarh has ethnographic as well as geographic reality, it is not a social or cultural isolate and never has been.

A degree of physical isolation has resulted in the development of certain cultural uniformities within Chhattisgarh which distinguish the region from adjacent areas of Central India. These cultural uniformities include certain features of dress, folklore, social structure, modes of cultivation, and the like. But of all these regional features the most important is language. Chhattisgarhi is a distinct dialect of Eastern Hindi, the other two being Avadhi and Bagheli. It is the vernacular of the entire Chhattisgarh plain, and is reported to extend into many of the surrounding tribal areas as well (Kavyopadhyaya 1921:iii). There are local differences in pronunciation and grammar, particularly on a north-south axis, but these differences are quite minor by comparison with the contrast between Chhattisgarhi and standard Hindi, much to the newly arrived visitor's dismay. It should be added that these days standard Hindi is widely spoken and understood even in rural areas.

Likewise, in terms of political structure the Chhattisgarh region has historically constituted an entity distinct from adjacent regions. We have seen that the region for many centuries has been (at least intermittently) a single political unit, though always, the available evidence suggests, a loosely structured one. The Haihaya kingdom appears at one time to have included the entire area, nuclear plain and surrounding hills, either as subordinate *garhs* or as tributary states. Of the fourteen feudatory states of the old Chhattisgarh Division, only one, Bastar, may possibly have remained independent of the Haihayas (De Brett 1909:9). It seems highly probable that the region was also a political unit in earlier times, but here the evidence is far from conclusive.

However, the most important sense in which Chhattisgarh is an identifiable and distinct ethnographic entity rests on a criterion far less tangible than the above—the inhabitants' strong sense of identity with Chhattisgarh, and with Chhattisgarhi things. While Chhattisgarhi villagers have scant knowledge of customs in other regions, they nevertheless speak of "Chhattisgarhi" ways of doing things. They have an easy familiarity with the geography of the region. They speak with assurance about the three major urban centers of Chhattisgarh—Raipur, Bilaspur, and Durg—but Nagpur and Jabalpur, the closest major cities outside the region, seem very distant indeed. On this regional scale Bombay, Delhi, and Calcutta could be at the ends of the earth. Above all, sacred geography provides a focus for Chhattisgarhi regionalism. There are several important pilgrimage centers in the region, places where at certain times of the year large numbers of people come to bathe in waters of special sanctity and to worship the deities in nearby temples. The most important sites are those at Rajim, Raipur, Ratanpur, and Sirpur, but there are many others of lesser significance. These places are very much a part of the regional identity of Chhattisgarh. People from the entire region know about the most important ones and make pilgrimages to them. But to people outside the region they are unknown, and would be of little religious importance even if they were.

However, if Chhattisgarh possesses ethnographic reality, it is by no means an ethnographic isolate. While it is true that to a degree the region has been insulated from the outside over the centuries, it is equally true that this insulation has never been complete, and Chhattisgarh has always been subject to outside influences, particularly from the north. This has been the case throughout the history of the region, and in more recent times Chhattisgarh has felt the full impact of changes resulting from its inclusion in the national life of the modern Indian state. Thus, although it is useful and proper to speak of "Chhattisgarhi culture" or "Chhattisgarhi society" in some contexts, it must be borne in mind that Chhattisgarh is connected to a larger subcontinental society by a dense social, political, and economic network, and that patterns of life in the region represent variations on cultural patterns of more general distribution in Northern and Central India, and even beyond. The language of Chhattisgarh may be treated as a distinct dialect, but it is nevertheless a variant form of a larger linguistic entity, Eastern Hindi. Just so, many other aspects of Chhattisgarhi life are continuous with broader patterns found elsewhere.

It is essential to distinguish between structural pattern and specific detail when examining aspects of Chhattisgarh life in relation to society and culture outside the region. As we have seen, for many centuries Chhattisgarh was governed by a regional political system and enjoyed a significant degree of political autonomy. But while this political system undoubtedly displayed certain regional peculiarities, in its overall structure it was quite similar to patterns of political organization found widely throughout Central India (see Sinha 1962). The same is true of caste. It is possible to say that certain very specific features of caste in Chhattisgarh are peculiar to the region. However, these peculiarities are for the most part the names and specific attributes of certain castes taken singly. But the structure of caste in Chhattisgarh, the system of relationships in which castes are mutually involved, exhibits the same principles of organization that operate in caste systems elsewhere on the subcontinent.

What, then, of religion? Essentially the same strictures apply. Patterns of religious life in the region exhibit local peculiarities, but at the same time the religion of Chhattisgarh draws upon subcontinental traditions and exhibits structural patterns consonant with patterns found in many other areas of India.

From these considerations it will be obvious that the regional focus of this study does not presuppose impermeable regional boundaries. Depending on how we look at it, Chhattisgarh is or is not an ethnographic unit; likewise the religion of Chhattisgarh. The Chhattisgarh region is a context of investigation, not a unit of study. The region is small enough to be manageable, and large enough to include important dimensions of popular religious life. It is, however, not a bounded unit. The Hindu tradition is, in a vital sense, subcontinental, and ignoring this fact would greatly distort the reality. Accordingly, my concern is not so much with "Chhattisgarhi Hinduism" as it is with "Hinduism in Chhattisgarh." My task is to show how religious ideas and practices are interconnected, and to the degree that subcontinental patterns intrude into the region, also to show how religion in Chhattisgarh is integrated with Hinduism in the broadest and geographically most inclusive sense.

No study that takes a regional perspective can be ethnographically omniscient. This study does not pretend to be. It is perhaps possible for studies of small, face-to-face communities at least to aim for something approximating totality of coverage, but in the present instance such a strategy would be unrealistic. Rather, it is necessary to focus the investigation on certain settings in which significant aspects of the religious life of the region are to be found. The problem is what these settings should be.

One possibility would be an intensive study of a village. It has long been known that the structure of Indian civilization is such that an examination of a single village yields relatively little unless the manifold connections between the village and its wider social and cultural contexts are taken into account. Nevertheless, Indian villages exist as physical and social realities, and as such can provide territorial settings for investigations of various aspects of Indian culture and social organization. If the village is only one aspect of Indian civilization, it is nonetheless a crucial one. With regard to the concerns of this book, however, the village cannot by itself provide an adequate observational base.

This is primarily because religion in Chhattisgarh is multilocational by its very nature. The village is an important context for ceremonial activity, but urban areas and pilgrimage centers are equally important. Taken in isolation, any one of these locales provides a glimpse of what is only part of a larger whole. Put simply, Hinduism in Chhattisgarh is never found *in toto* in any one place, and it is therefore not possible to examine it by resorting to the simple expedient of doing an ethnographic description of the religious activities of a single restricted territorial unit such as a village, or, for that matter, even a city.

Early in my fieldwork I found that there are essentially three settings of particular importance in which the religion of Chhattisgarh should be observed. One of these is the village, which is crucial. Another is the town or city, where equally important aspects of the cultural and social life of the region are to be found. The third context, and one of particular importance where religion is concerned, is that of the major temple and pilgrimage centers of the region. I attempted to use each of these settings as part of my observational base. I carried out most of the urban part of the investigation in the city of Raipur, though I had many occasions to visit other towns as well. In addition, during the period of fieldwork I visited most of the important temple centers in the region at least once. In the course of the fieldwork I visited many different villages, but I concentrated essentially on Sitapur (a pseudonym), a village located about thirty miles north of Raipur. Since Sitapur and Raipur were the most important locations for research, I shall sketch out a few of the most salient features of each of these communities.

Sitapur

It is difficult to say to what degree Sitapur is a typical Chhattisgarhi village. I chose it in part because it was easy to reach, but its accessibility makes it somewhat atypical. It is located on a major road and near a rural station on the Bombay–Howrah rail line. It is also close to the mission hospital complex at Tilda. In other respects Sitapur seems to fall closer to the norm. With a total population of something over 350 its size is somewhere near the lower middle range of villages. Its eighty-odd households are clustered in a pattern that is monotonously familiar in the Chhattisgarhi countryside: a nuclear area of houses cut by a few narrow lanes, an outlying cluster of houses inhabited by Untouchables, a nearby tank for bathing and water, the whole surrounded by fields. With the exception of a handful of full- or nearly-full-time artisans (three households of potters, a blacksmith, a shoemaker and a barber) most of the villagers are farmers or agricultural laborers. There are seven households of Kevants (fishermen) and three of Kandaras (basketmakers), but these people practice their caste-occupation only part-time.

All of the most important castes of Chhattisgarh[4] are found in Sitapur except three: the Telis (oilpressers), Mehetars (sweepers) and Brahmans. The constituent castes of Sitapur are listed in Table 1.1, arranged roughly in order of relative rank. The hierarchy represented in the table is based upon the responses of informants who were asked to rank a set of cards upon which symbols designating the various castes were drawn, and upon supplementary interviews. Within each rank category ("high," "highest," etc.) castes are arranged alphabetically.

The term Rajput denotes a cluster of castes that are accorded Kshatriya status in the *varna* system. Their heritage is royal and martial, and the one Rajput family of Sitapur stands at the apex of the local hierarchy. The term Bania is used generally for mercantile castes in North and Central India, and these castes are accorded Vaishya status in the *varna* system. The single Bania family of Sitapur is by far the richest of the village. The Rajputs and the Banias are the sole holders of twice-born *varna* status in the village; all others are Shudras or Untouchables.

[4] For a more complete enumeration and description of the castes of Chhattisgarh and adjacent regions see Russell 1916.

Table 1.1.   *The Constituent Castes of Sitapur*

	Caste Name	Traditional Occupation	No. of Households in Sitapur
Highest	Rajput	Rulers and Warriors	1
High	Bania	Businessmen	1
High Middle	Kevant	Fishermen	7
	Kurmi	Farmers	5
	Ravat (Jaria)	Cattle Herders	9
	Ravat (Kanaujia)	Cattle Herders	14
	Sonar (Soni)	Goldsmiths	1
Low Middle	Gond	Adivasis	20
	Kumhar	Potters and Tilemakers	3
	Lohar	Blacksmiths	1
	Marar	Gardeners	8
	Nai	Barbers	1
Low	Dhobi	Washermen	1
	Kandara	Basketmakers	3
	Painka	Watchmen	1
Lowest	Mehar	Shoemakers	1
	Satnami	Farmers (ex-leather workers)	7

The Kurmis are an agricultural caste of wide distribution in North and Central India. They have the reputation of being shrewd and industrious farmers. The Ravats are the cowherds of Chhattisgarh. As Table 1.1 indicates, two (endogamous) sub-castes of Ravats are present in Sitapur, the Kanaujias and the Jarias. The Kanaujias trace their origin to the ancient city of Kanauj, while the Jarias are supposed to be indigenous to Chhattisgarh. The Sonars are traditionally goldsmiths, but the one Sonar of Sitapur is a farmer. However, there are Sonars who practice their caste occupation in neighboring villages.

The Gonds I have already mentioned briefly. The Gonds of Sitapur do not speak Gondi, but they do retain certain distinctive features of religious life I shall again refer to later. The three families of Kumhars, the potters, moved to Sitapur within the last decade. Their main occupation is the making of rooftiles, not pots. The traditional occupation of the Marars is vegetable gardening, but in Sitapur only one Marar family follows this calling, and this on a part-time basis. The Nai and the Lohar perform their traditional tasks.

The single Dhobi, the washerman, practices his caste occupation as a sideline. The Kandaras make baskets, but, again, only part-time. The head of the one Painka family is the village watchman and a farmer as well. The Painkas are nominally Kabirpanthis but the Painkas of Sitapur participate fully in the religious life of the village, and a portrait of Sant Kabir in their family shrine is virtually the only mark of their sectarian identification.

The barrier between the castes of relatively low rank and the Satnamis and Mehars is an important one. In Sitapur, as in Chhattisgarh as a whole, these castes are regarded as untouchable (*achhut*). The Satnamis were originally Chamars (see Babb 1972), a caste of leatherworkers found virtually everywhere in North and Central India. During the last century most of the Chamars of Chhattisgarh became followers of a religious prophet, Ghasi Das, who was himself a Chamar. After a period of reflection in the wilderness he preached to his caste-fellows a new religion, which centered on the worship of one god of the "true name" (*satnam*), and he forbade activities and items of diet that symbolized the low status of Chamars. In particular he urged them to abandon their traditional occupation and to give up meat and liquor. Most of the Chamars of Chhattisgarh were converted to the new religion and are known as Satnamis today. Despite the reforms, the Satnamis of Sitapur are still considered untouchable by the other villagers. The villagers justify this by claiming that the Satnamis still eat carrion, their own claims to the contrary notwithstanding. For my part I have never seen the Satnamis of Sitapur engaged in scavenging, though it is possible that it is still done by them elsewhere. The Satnamis of Sitapur are farmers and casual laborers.

The Satnamis share their untouchability with the single household of Mehars (shoemakers) in Sitapur. In the general vicinity, though not in the village itself, are colonies of people belonging to two castes which the villagers say are even lower than the Satnamis and Mehars. These are the Mehetars (sweepers) and Devars (swineherds and beggars). Strictly speaking they are not a part of the village community, but they do appear for begging at certain ceremonial occasions.

The village of Sitapur may be considered a social unit in many senses—residentially, politically, administratively, and, as we shall see, ritually—but from a wider perspective it is obvious that the economic, social, and cultural life of Sitapur is only part of a much larger whole. The interactional patterns of the villagers extend outward in a variety of contexts. Village exogamy is observed in the great majority of marriages, with the result that kin networks branch out from the village over an extensive area of the countryside. The village is not economically self-sufficient. Many villagers have found employment outside the village, usually as laborers. Certain craft specializations are not found in Sitapur, and for these services the villagers must go elsewhere. The nearest rice mills are located in Neora, a small town about three miles from Sitapur, where the villagers market their surplus crop. In Neora the villagers purchase manufactured goods and sometimes foodstuffs that are not available in Sitapur. Near Neora is a camp for Sindhi refugees; the villagers sometimes go there to buy fabrics and other goods. Many villagers send their children to school in Neora, and village children who go to secondary school (by no means a remarkable occurrence any more) are usually sent to Raipur or Bilaspur. In sum, the world of the village is far larger than the village itself.

The same intermeshing between the village and the outside world is seen in the context of religious activities. Although there are many ceremonial events centering on the village itself—or on smaller social units within the village—religion generally tends to involve the villagers in interactional and cultural patterns extending far beyond village boundaries. For example, Sitapur has no Brahman priest in residence, and the villagers must engage someone from another community for the ritual services that require one. Non-Brahman exorcist–priests known as Baigas are present in Sitapur, but their reputation is not so high as that of a Baiga who lives at nearby Tilda Station, and many of the villagers go to the latter with their medical problems. The singing of devotional hymns (*bhajans*) is one of the most common forms of religious activity in Sitapur. These sessions almost always involve participants from nearby villages. Musicians and dancers are necessary for marriages and certain festivals. In Chhattisgarh the Ganda caste specializes in providing these services, and this caste is not to be found in the vicinity of Sitapur. Accordingly, it is necessary for the villagers to hire musical parties from some distance away, often from as far as the Bilaspur area. Finally, and perhaps of greatest importance, is the fact that the people of Sitapur participate in a pattern of temple-going and pilgrimage that extends to Chhattisgarh as a whole, and in some cases even beyond. The villagers go to temples at Neora and other nearby centers for certain festivals, and to major regional centers for occasional pilgrimages. Some have even been to Puri in Orissa for the great festival of *rath duj*. Visits of this sort to well-known temple centers are an important dimension of the religious life of rural Chhattisgarh, and it is quite likely that the pilgrimage pattern has contributed greatly to the formation of regional uniformities in Chhattisgarhi religion, and has provided the most important medium through which pan-Indian traditions have diffused through the Chhattisgarhi countryside. So it is, then, that the religious life of the villagers necessarily draws the villagers into a much wider social and cultural environment.

The outside world is easily accessible to the villagers and, as I have noted, for this reason Sitapur is probably atypical. Tilda station, on the Bombay–Howrah line of the Southeastern Railway, is less than a mile away. These tracks lead to Raipur in the South and Bilaspur in the North. The same cities are easily reached by bus. Of the two cities, Raipur, about thirty miles away, is the larger and more important. When the people of Sitapur speak of "the city," they are usually referring to Raipur.

Raipur

Raipur, with a population of 139,000 (1961 census), is the largest city in the region and unquestionably the major commercial and cultural center as well. Its commercial importance stems from its location at major rail and highway junctions. At Raipur's rail station the Bombay–Howrah line connects with a broad-gauge line to Vijianagaram in Andhra Pradesh, with connections there to points farther south. There is also a narrow-gauge line going south from Raipur to Rajim and Dhamtari, two rural towns in southern Chhattisgarh. Raipur is also situated on the Great Eastern Road, an important national highway running east and west. A national highway also connects Raipur with Jagdalpur in Bastar District to the south. Logs are trucked from Bastar to the many timber mills of Raipur. Other important commercial activities in the city include rice milling, *bidi* (country cigarette) manufacture, banking, light-metal industries, and dry-goods wholesaling.

Raipur's growth has been and continues to be very rapid. One important reason for this has been the construction of a steel mill at Bhilai, a few miles west of Raipur in Durg District. The mill is a startling sight to passers-by; it seems to spring up suddenly out of nowhere as if Gary, Indiana, had been miraculously transported to the rolling plains of Chhattisgarh. The construction of the mill has led to the development of numerous subsidiary industries and the stretch of the Great Eastern Road to the west of Raipur is lined with new manufacturing establishments. There can be no doubt that in years to come the presence of the industrial complex at Bhilai will have far-reaching effects on the Chhattisgarh region as a whole.

The heart of Raipur is the main bazaar, where mercantile activities of every conceivable sort take place. Along the main streets are open-fronted shops selling fabrics, clothing, hardware, radios, watches, provisions, drugs, and many other kinds of consumer goods. In front of these shops, on the edges of the street itself, are peddlers who sell petty merchandise of all descriptions. Sellers of fruits and vegetables compete with vendors of fountain pens, sunglasses, cheap clothing, religious paraphernalia, soft drinks, celluloid toys, herbs, amulets, sweets, and the like. The main vegetable market is located in an enclosure off the main street because of the problem of wandering goats and cattle. Adjacent to the vegetable market and discreetly hidden from the general view is a rather dark place, and for many a somewhat mysterious one: the meat market.

In the northeast quadrant of the city, perhaps half a mile from the central market area, is the Collectorate, an administrative center, which contains a court and the offices of various district officials. The District Hospital and the Raipur Jail are close by. Nearby too is an area known as the Civil Lines, a residential section where the city's elite live. The area presents a picture of well-regulated opulence, which contrasts in the most striking way with the sprawl and clutter of the rest of the city: large bungalows, neat and constantly tended gardens, and high compound walls.

Purani Basti, the oldest section of Raipur, lies to the south and west of the main market area. At one time it was apparently the center of the city. Most of the city's older and most important temples are located here, including many I shall have occasion to mention later: the Shitla temple, the Jagannath temple, the Mahamaya temple, and several others. The Dudhadhari Math, the city's most important temple complex and sacred center, is located just outside the city on the Purani Basti side.

The commercial and employment opportunities of Raipur have drawn many people from outside Chhattisgarh into the city. The result is a degree of ethnic mixture not to be found in the

Chhattisgarhi countryside. Since statistics on the ethnic composition of the city are unfortunately not available, all I can do here is sketch some of its main features. The largest part of the city's population is Chhattisgarhi, and Oriyas constitute another important element. Forced by economic conditions in their native Orissa to migrate westward into Chhattisgarh, they have become the menials of the city, the rickshaw-pullers and lowest-paid domestic servants. They tend to live in dense and unsanitary residential colonies at odd points throughout the city. Apart from a handful of Marathas, Bengalis, Madrasis, and others, the remaining important foreign groups in Raipur are four: the Panjabis, Gujaratis, Marwaris, and Sindhis. Together these groups constitute the core of the commercial life of the city and the region. Of the Panjabis, the Sikhs are especially prominent, and seem to have become the mainstay of the transport industries, though they are to be found in other commercial fields as well. It is said that in earlier days the commerce of the city was dominated by the Marwaris. The Gujaratis gradually gained prominance also, but the great transformation of Raipur's business life came as the result of the influx of Sindhi refugees after partition. By underselling the established concerns of the city, the Sindhis have managed to become one of the wealthiest communities of the city, and, in some circles, one of the most disliked as well. In general these business communities are materially far better off than the Chhattisgarhi residents of Raipur, and they increasingly tend to live in the newer, more expensive residential colonies on the outskirts of the city.

Raipur is by far the most important educational center in Chhattisgrah. Just to the west of the city on the Great Eastern Road is an educational complex which serves the region as a whole. Located here is Ravi Shankar University, an engineering college, a Sanskrit college, an allopathic medical school, and an Ayurvedic medical school and hospital. An agricultural college and two music colleges are to be found elsewhere in the city. These institutions have attracted a large number of students, and they have become a particularly volatile element in the political life of the city.

Likewise, Raipur is an extremely important religious center for the Chhattisgarh region. It is the site of a number of important temples, of which the Dudhadhari Math is the most prominent. It is also a distribution point for popular religious literature and the physical paraphernalia of popular Hinduism. Vernacular religious literature constitutes an important channel through which literary traditions are diffused into popular religion, and Raipur's bookstalls are full of Sanskritic popularizations, which find their way into the surrounding countryside. Indeed, one of Raipur's most important roles in Chhattisgarh's religious life is to provide a setting in which regional and extraregional religious styles and traditions come into direct juxtaposition and interaction.

The Problem of Levels

To students of South Asian culture no single problem has proven more difficult to resolve than that presented by the apparent existence of "levels" in Indian civilization. There is an apparent duality in Hinduism, a contrast between what Robert Redfield called the "great tradition of the reflective few" and the "little tradition of the largely unreflective many" (1960:41). The question is that of the nature of these two levels and their relationship with each other. Are they fundamentally different, or are they merely different aspects of the same thing? Do they compete in any sense, or are they functionally complementary? These and related questions contain the problem of levels.

In the literature on India various schemes have been employed in discussions of this cultural duality, but the most influential has undoubtedly been the contrast between "Sanskritic" and "non-Sanskritic" levels in Hinduism and the correlative notion of "Sanskritization"—ideas that appeared in systematic form for the first time in the work of M. N. Srinivas (1952). Srinivas' formulation continues to be influential today (see esp. Singer 1972), and accordingly any discussion of the problem of levels in Hinduism must begin at this point.

Although Srinivas distinguished between various levels in Hinduism—local, regional, peninsular, all-India—his master taxonomy consisted of a single basic dichotomy, that of Sanskritic and non-Sanskritic "systems of ritual and beliefs" (1952:212). According to this view, the unity of Indian civilization is to be found at the level of Sanskritic Hinduism, which is pan-Indian in distribution, transcending regional boundaries. Groups become a part of the larger whole of Indian civilization to the degree that their customs, rituals, and beliefs become "Sanskritized." "Sanskritic Hinduism," Srinivas wrote, "gives certain common values to all Hindus, and the possession of common values knits people together into a community. The spread of Sanskritic rites, and the increasing Sanskritization of non-Sanskritic rites, tends to weld the hundreds of sub-castes, sects, and tribes all over India into a single community. The lower castes have a tendency to take over the customs and rites of the higher castes, and this ensures the spread of Sanskritic cultural and ritual forms at the expense of others" (1952:208).

This idea has been one of the most useful ever produced by a social scientist for the study of Indian society and culture. There can be no doubt that the emulation of modes of behavior sanctioned by sacred literature has been an important dynamic in the evolution of Indian civilization, and because of this the Sanskritic–non-Sanskritic contrast has an important heuristic value, particularly in studies of detribalization and caste-mobility. As it stands, however this conceptual scheme is of questionable utility for an analysis of popular Hinduism. The difficulty is in part terminological, and in part of a more fundamental nature.

The term "Sanskritic" refers to the Sanskrit language, and what is called "Sanskritic Hinduism" is presumably the religion of sacred texts written in that language. However, as J. F. Staal has pointed out (1963: 264–65), some of the most influential sacred texts are written in languages other than Sanskrit. Certainly one of the most important textual influences in the Hinduism of Chhattisgarh is the *Ramayana*. However, this is not the Sanskrit epic, but rather the *Ramcharitamanas* of Tulsidas, which is written in Avadhi, and differs in substance and tone from the Sanskrit original. The religion of texts, then, is not necessarily the religion of Sanskrit texts.

Moreover, the use of the single term "Sanskritic" suggests that there is a definable and coherent Sanskritic tradition, located in Sanskrit texts, to which cultural elements either unambigiously belong or do not belong. However, taken as a whole the Sanskrit texts comprise an enormous body of sacred and secular literature, which has absorbed many elements that were almost certainly non-Sanskritic to begin with, and which sanctions many ideas and practices that seem at first glance to be non-Sanskritic today (Staal 1963:265–70). Which portions of the textual tradition, then, express "Sanskritic Hinduism"? Is it to be anything written in Sanskrit? If so, we shall find our net spread too widely, for there seems little doubt that some kind of textual paradigm, however remote or obscure, can be found for virtually every ritual practice associated with Hinduism. Alternatively, we could consider Sanskritic Hinduism to consist only of what is sanctioned by Brahman or high-caste practice. However, this would be hardly more satisfactory, for although certain values and ideas found in sacred literature are certainly embodied in standards of upper caste behavior, these are only a part of the Sanskritic tradition.

There is yet another difficulty. As Dumont and Pocock have pointed out (1959b: esp. 40–43), the Sanskritic–non-Sanskritic dichotomization as Srinivas formulated it seems, by its emphasis on the sacred literature as the universalizing level of Hinduism, to inject an awkward bias into attempts to understand unifying aspects of Hindu religious culture. While it is clear that Sanskrit texts have an important influence on Hinduism everywhere on the subcontinent, and that certain texts contain ideas and values that transcend structural and territorial boundaries, it is equally true that there are features of popular Hinduism that apparently do not derive directly from texts but that are nonetheless pan-Indian in distribution. The complementarity between the role of the Brahman priest and the non-Brahman curer–exorcist (below, ch. 6; Dumont and Pocock 1959c; Mandelbaum 1966) and the use of the symbolism of heat and cold in ritual (below, ch. 7; Beck 1969) are two apparent examples. If we assume that the unity of the Hindu tradition is found only in Sanskrit literature, we may be tempted to ignore what may turn out to be a more fundamental unity at another level (Dumont and Pocock 1959b:43).

Finally, from the standpoint of the concerns of this book there is another, even more crucial, difficulty: any model that radically dichotomizes Hinduism into categories such as Sanskritic and non-Sanskritic seems to carry with it the implication that in any ethnographic setting there will be two distinct "systems of belief and practice." It seems to imply that there is a clear break between a religious system defined by texts and a religious system of local origin, that since they are distinct from each other they are ultimately incompatible; accordingly one must in the end displace the other through the process of Sanskritization. The evidence from Chhattisgarh seems to support the opposite point of view. The evidence suggests that in this region we are dealing with one religious system, not two or more, and that cultural elements of both textual and local provenance are drawn into a single overall pattern of relationships.

Although these considerations do not dispose of the problem of levels, they nevertheless put it into perspective. While the Hinduism of Chhattisgarh is not divided into two distinct components, it is nevertheless clear that sacred texts, Sanskrit or not, play a more important role in some areas of religious life than in others. Certain ceremonials, for example, are conducted with a high degree of textual elaboration. They are directed toward deities who are described in texts, they are conducted in accord with ritual formulas found in texts, and they frequently involve the recitation of textual passages. Other rituals do not involve texts to the same degree or in the same sense. They center on parochial deities, and are carried out in accordance with ceremonial patterns defined by local custom. This is not to say that these are rigid categories; a particular ceremonial event may fall somewhere between the two poles. Nevertheless, the difference does exist, and any analysis of Chhattisgarhi religion must somehow deal with it.

I shall not deal with differences of this order as manifestations of different levels of Hinduism, but as differences of "style," or of "ritual dialect." Underlying my approach is a simple but crucial assumption: it is possible to distinguish between the content of a religious tradition and the mode or modes of its expression. By drawing such a distinction I am able to entertain the idea that the concepts expressed in rituals may be the same, while the ritual "styles" in which they are expressed may be different. Seen from this perspective, the textualized and untextualized forms of ceremonialism may be understood, following Dumont and Pocock (1959b:45), as different ways of "saying the same things."

This does not mean, however, that differences of ritual style are unimportant. Simple linguistic analogies can sometimes be misleading, but my task is to translate certain kinds of communication. There are many forms of communication—ordinary speech, myth, and ritual, for example. The style one speaks in is not merely fortuitous: that a given person under a given set of circumstances uses standard Hindi rather than Chhattisgarhi conveys information about the speaker and his perceptions of his interlocutor and the prevailing circumstances. Similarly, that one "ritual dialect" is employed rather than another suggests a determining context. Some ritual styles have more prestige than others; some are regarded as appropriate for some people and not for others; some are appropriate in some sets of circumstances but not in others. It is vital to keep in mind that stylistic differences in ritual are no more accidental than stylistic variation in speech; this fact opens the way to understanding what I consider to be an important feature of Hinduism in Chhattisgarh: although the texts do not define an alternative form of religion, textualization nevertheless has important functional significance within the Chhattisgarhi religious system. The same thing may be said differently for different purposes; and meaning, in the largest sense, may be modulated by differences in style.

A religious system may be interpreted in more than one way. I shall treat Hinduism in Chhattisgarh as an expression of a view of reality, a view that deals with its social and nonsocial aspects, and with humanity's place in that reality. It is a point of view that provides for the possibility of dealing with the problems of experienced life, but in defining these problems in the way it does, it also provides for the uncertainty of human existence. It is an internally coherent and consistent viewpoint, and in this sense the religion of Chhattisgarh is a system. It is not, however, a theology. It is implicit in religious practice and thought, not explicit in rational discourse. It is a point of view that is formulated from certain basic ideas that shape religious behavior and are in turn validated by it. These ideas are not "ideology," for they lack the requisite explicitness of formulation. Nor are they concepts that are "unconscious" in the truest sense of this word, for they sometimes rise into considered discourse. They are, nevertheless, basic to Chhattisgarhi religion, and are the premises of religious thought and action. They formulate the conditions of existence itself: pure and impure, male and female, hot and cold. They also differentiate fundamental aspects of human and divine intention: benevolence and malevolence, renunciation and license. They are not, in the most literal sense, the "meaning" of ritual; they are, rather, the meanings that make meaning possible. To put it somewhat differently, these are the concepts in terms of which religious thought and action "make sense."

My analysis is based for the most part on ritual behavior, but I also draw upon mythology and the exegetical statements

of both informants and academic specialists as aids to understanding the meaning of ritual action. My basic plan is a movement from the concrete to the increasingly abstract. The next
chapter deals with the basic structure of ritual, and does so by
means of a highly detailed examination of specific ritual performances. Chapters 3, 4, and 5 are concerned with the range of
diversity of ritual expression as it emerges within the framework
of temporal ritual cycles. The last two chapters attempt to draw
together some of the main themes emerging from the discussions
of ritual by applying them in an analysis of the roles of religious
specialists and the structure of the pantheon.

2
The Foods of the Gods: Puja

Anthropologists frequently speak of the religious "beliefs" of the people they study. While this approach has a certain commonsense appeal, it is also fraught with difficulties. Rodney Needham (1972) has convincingly argued that words from other languages translated as "belief" in English have very different semantic characteristics, and that the English term's meaning itself is quite ambiguous. He suggests there is no demonstrable pan-human experience that corresponds to our notion of belief. This apart, it is certain that our idea of belief, at least in the most conventional sense, will not aid us in an examination of Hinduism in Chhattisgarh. There is practically nothing to be gained in questioning Chhattisgarhi informants about what they believe, for this is simply not the primary context in which religious matters are understood. In Chhattisgarh religion is a thing done, not a thing "believed," and as a result any effort to uncover the assumptions and principles underlying this religious system must seek them in ritual activity.

I shall treat ritual as a form of symbolic activity that conveys information. That is, I understand the activities that constitute ritual performances to have a discoverable meaning, and essentially my task is to apprehend it. This is by no means a new or novel approach. The assumption that rituals "say something" underlies one of the most important contemporary traditions in the anthropological study of religion and, in different ways, has constituted the point of departure for a rich and very diverse literature which includes the work of Edmund Leach, Victor Turner, Lévi-Strauss, and others. I am not primarily interested in the consequences of ritual for social integration. Nevertheless, it will become clear that the symbolic content of Chhattisgarhi ritual is linked in the most intimate way to social considerations. Chhattisgarhi ritual "makes statements." In part these are "forms of symbolic statement about the social order" (Leach 1964:14), and to the degree that this is so the religion of Chhattisgarh does indeed have social functions. However, Chhattisgarhi ritual also makes statements of more general import, statements that touch upon man's situation in the broadest sense. One of the most interesting features of Chhattisgarhi religion is that a degree of fusion is achieved between these two dimensions of ritual expression. Even so, the Chhattisgarhi materials suggest that the religious experience is not wholly reducible to the social.

In its totality Chhattisgarhi ceremonialism is an exceedingly complex range of phenomena, and any analysis of it must incorporate some procedure for systematically untangling this complexity. Fortunately the ethnography itself suggests a way to do this. Perhaps the most obvious fact about Chhattisgarhi ritual—one evident to the most casual observer—is that some of its features are highly variable while others are nearly constant. Clearly the first step must be to separate the variable aspects of ritual from those that remain constant, or nearly so. Variation, we must ask, on what themes?

I shall attempt to isolate these constants. In so doing I hope to show that Chhattisgarhi ritual, despite its manifest diversity, may be reduced analytically to a single "core ritual" which, in practice, is used in different ways, with varying forms of elaboration, for different purposes. More specifically, Chhattisgarhi ritual presents itself empirically as a mélange of conventional verbal formulae, stylized gestures, and physical manipulations of certain objects and materials. Closer scrutiny of the apparent confusion reveals that certain associated features appear regularly. These features constitute together the minimum requirement for what is called *puja* (worship, homage) in Hindi, and define what I consider to be the structural bedrock of Chhattisgarhi religious practice. We must look in the variation that lies over this structure for the specific meanings of particular rituals.

To separate the primary structure of Chhattisgarhi ritual from its variable aspects it will first be necessary to describe particular ritual sequences in some detail. By means of description and comparison it will be possible to disentangle elements basic to *puja* from contingent features whose presence or absence from a particular ritual sequence depends on the ritual's context and ostensible purpose. I have chosen four ritual sequences as a basis for this analysis. Since this chapter deals with the identification of uniformity underlying apparent diversity, I have picked these four because they seem to exhibit a maximum degree of variation in form and context. I observed two of the four in a village setting, although similar rituals may be observed in towns and cities as well. One, *pitar pak*, is essentially a family rite consisting of a very simple sequence of ritual manipulations involving a limited number of participants. The second, *matar*, is a villagewide festival. It is far more complex than *pitar pak*, and its participants number in the hundreds. I observed the final two examples in the city of Raipur, though similar rituals might be seen in villages as well. One is an informal *bhajan*-singing session. The other is a domestic *puja* called *saptashati path*, which is performed with a nearly maximal degree of textual elaboration. Despite the obvious differences between these very disparate ritual performances, they all exhibit basically the same structure.

Pitar Pak

Pitar pak, deriving from the standard Hindi *pitri paksh*, may be translated as "the fortnight of the fathers." The term refers to a period of the year when the eldest male member of a joint family must worship his agnatic ancestors, who are understood to be present in the home at this time. The ritual period falls during the first fortnight (*pak* or *paksh*) of the lunar month of *kunvar* (September–October). The requisite observances of *pitar pak* are supposed to take place on each day of the fortnight, but most families restrict elaborate formalities to the first and last days, or to the day of the fortnight that corresponds to the lunar date of the father's death. The following sequence of events was observed in Sitapur on the first day of the fortnight in the household of a family belonging to the Kurmi (farmer) caste. The head of the family emerged from the house at about 11:30 A.M. to go to the village tank for a bath. While a bath is usually a normal part of the daily routine, its importance is elevated on ceremonial occasions, because bathing purifies as well as cleans, and in this instance—as in all others—a state of purity is an essential prerequisite to ritual activity. With the bath itself, the ceremonial observance of *pitar pak* began. While at the tank the household head made an offering of water and a special kind of grass (*dub*) to his ancestors, pouring the water away from himself as he stood half submerged.

While this was underway, the women of his household— his wife and his sons' wives—were applying the finishing touches to an elaborate meal, which had been under preparation for some hours. As this was a special day, the cost and variety of the foods were greater than usual. Apart from the usual rice and lentils, the meal included fried breads, a sweet dish made from rice, and a type of small fried cake made from *urad* (one of the lentils), which is a traditional preparation during *pitar pak*.

When the head of the household returned from his bath the main part of the day's observance began. He entered the kitchen—a room of religious as well as culinary significance, which is always kept pure—carrying a plate of food together with a smaller dish filled with a brown liquid and a brass pot containing water, which he had brought with him from his bath. After he entered the kitchen one of his sons' wives appeared carrying a piece of burning cowdung cake, which she deposited on the floor at the base of an earthen stove. The household head squatted in front of the smoldering cowdung and, using his right hand, he sprinkled some water from his pot around it. He then placed a small amount of the brown liquid on the fire. He sprinkled water around the fire again, and then placed some of the food from his plate on the fire. Once more he sprinkled water around the fire, and then brought his two hands to his forehead, palms together, and bowed until his hands touched the floor, a gesture known as *pranam*. With this the ceremony was completed and the family proceeded to dinner on the veranda adjoining the kitchen.

I was told later that the elaborate manipulations in the kitchen had one main point: to offer food to the fire. This is a procedure known as *hom* (Sanskrit, *homa*), and the offerings were made to the fire, my informant said, "in the name of the ancestors." The brown liquid turned out to be a mixture of *ghi* (clarified butter) and *gur* (jaggery), and it was pointed out that this is one of the purest types of food offerings. Technically, I was told, the worshipper should have offered to the fire a small amount of every kind of food the family was taking in the meal afterward, but this is not absolutely necessary and would probably have extinguished the fire. The food consumed after the formalities is known as *prasad*.

Matar

Divali, the so-called "festival of lights," is one of the most important of the many calendrical festivals of north and central India, and is surely one of the most protracted as well. To Chhattisgarhi informants *divali* (or *dipavali*) refers not to a single rite, but to a complex of ceremonial events all of which are conceived to be related, and all of which cluster around the new-moon night of the lunar month of *kartik* (October–November). *Matar* is one of these rites.

The word *matar* denotes a vaguely conceived, apparently masculine, deity who is associated with one of the cowherder subcastes (the Kanaujia Ravats) of Chhattisgarh. As is the case with many of the minor Chhattisgarhi deities, the attributes of this god are so indistinct as to be virtually nonexistent. Informants can say little about him, and if he has any qualities at all they are coterminous with his role in the festival that bears his name. To my knowledge he is worshipped only once each year during this rite.

The festival, as I observed it in the village of Sitapur, began with extensive preparations in an open field located just outside the village. The area was first purified. This was done by applying a solution of cowdung in water. (Cowdung is considered a purifying substance, and purification in this fashion is a perfectly standard procedure.) Several poles, each about four feet long and forked at one end, were then inserted together in the purified ground with the forked ends up. These poles were said to represent the deity.

The next phase of the day's activities began in the village itself. A dancing party composed of men of two cowherder subcastes (the Kanaujia and Jaria Ravats) was formed, and late in the morning this party began dancing its way through the village. The party picked up a large crowd of spectators as it slowly wound its way through the lanes of the village and finally it made its way out to the field where the images of the deity had been placed. In the meantime, the cattle of the village had been assembled at this spot, and as the dancers and spectators arrived the cowherds attempted—not always successfully—to put ornamental collars around the necks of their own animals. While this was underway, clay lamps had been placed before the representations of the deity and had been ignited. Of the throng of cowherds in attendance before the god, several had become possessed and were lying on the ground, trembling dramatically. Finally, a large area was cleared around the deity. A herd of cattle was then driven at full gallop clockwise around the images, and when the dust from this had settled a herd of water buffalo was driven around the images in a similar fashion.

Following an afternoon in which the dancing party had visited each of the cowherder households individually, the final part of the day's ceremonies began around 6:00 P.M. Once again the dancing party began to move through the lanes of the village and picked up a crowd. Led by the dancers, everyone headed toward the field where the representations of the god were still standing. Earlier, a large quantity of milk had been placed before the deity in brass pots and was now awaiting the crowd. Having arrived at the field, the greater part of the male population of the village took seats in a series of large concentric circles around the god. Everyone, including the Untouchables of the village, was now given a quantity of the milk, which had been placed before the god. The milk was consumed on the spot as *prasad.* Those who interpreted these events for me made much of the fact that Untouchables were included in these festivities. I was told that on the day of *matar* "there is no untouchability." With the distribution of milk to all participants the festival of *matar* came to a close, although the dancing of the cowherds and the usual festival drinking and carousing went on well into the night.

Singing Bhajans

Bhajans are devotional songs, and the congregational singing of them exemplifies a religious style associated with the *bhakti* (devotional) tradition in Hinduism. In Chhattisgarh the songs may be sung in Hindi or in its Chhattisgarhi dialect. They may be written down or passed on orally. They may be set to traditional melodies, but increasingly they are sung to tunes borrowed from the films. The singing of *bhajans* is one of the most popular and conspicuous religious activities in rural and urban Chhattisgarh alike. These occasions have a variety of contexts, often occurring in conjunction with specific festivals or periodic rituals of other kinds. But often, too, *bhajans* are sung by groups of friends simply for the sake of the singing itself. These are usually informal groups of variable composition, which assemble periodically for the sole purpose of singing *bhajans*. Such groups are common, and in my experience they almost always cut across caste lines. The singing may be done without accompaniment, but it is also common for voices to be supplemented with a harmonium, drums, and cymbals.

The session I shall describe took place in the home of a clerk employed by Raipur's Public Works Department. As it happens, this man belonged to the goldsmith (Sonar) caste. Most of the other participants belonged to different castes, but all had similar educational and economic backgrounds. For the most part they were clerks or schoolteachers of Chhattisgarhi background; however, they spoke standard Hindi fluently and had some English.

The session was held in a storeroom in the host's home. Storerooms are used for religious purposes in many houses, and are often kept pure as a matter of course. This room was bare of furniture except for a wooden stool in one corner, upon which a vividly colored picture of Krishna as an infant had been placed upright.

The formalities began about 8:00 P.M. First the host sprinkled a few drops of water on the glass front of the framed picture of Krishna. He then sprinkled a small quantity of red powder on the picture. He explained later that in so doing he was honoring the god by symbolically applying a *tilak* (red spot) to the god's forehead. Then a garland was hung over the picture. Incense sticks were ignited and placed near the god, after which a *tilak* was applied to the forehead of each of the participants.

The actual singing of *bhajans* followed. On this occasion the time spent singing lasted only about two hours; sessions of this kind frequently last the entire night. When the singing was over, everyone but the harmonium player and the drummer stood up and faced the picture of Krishna. The host then ignited a piece of cotton soaked in oil, which had been placed on a brass plate. He held the plate in front of the picture and moved it slowly in a circular fashion while everyone sang. This sequence was identified by informants as *arti*, and was described as one way, among many, of honoring the god. Upon the completion of *arti* the plate was passed from person to person. Each man held his hands briefly over the flame and then brought them to his forehead as if he were transferring the vapors of the flame into his hair.

While the *bhajans* were being sung the host's wife had un-obtrusively placed a plate of sliced bananas before the picture of Krishna. This food was now distributed among all the partici-pants as *prasad*. Each man held his hands out, the back of his right hand resting on the palm of his left. As soon as the *prasad* was deposited in his hand, he brought his fingertips to his fore-head. The *prasad* was then eaten, and after a few minutes of conversation everyone went home.

Afterward the host told me that singing *bhajans* in this fashion is simply an elaborate form of *puja*, one way among many of worshipping the god. It is an expression of devotion (*bhakti*) to the god and, apart from the sheer pleasure of singing together, it imparts *punya* (merit) to the participants, which may lead to good fortune in this life or better fortune in the next.

Saptashati Path

The term *path* refers to the recitation of a sacred text. *Saptashati path* refers to the ceremonial recitation of the *Shri Durga Sapta-shati*, a Sanskrit text of Puranic derivation that consists of seven hundred stanzas on the goddess. At this point it is unnecessary to discuss the text in detail. It will suffice merely to note that the text praises the goddess, gives an account of the circumstances under which she came into the world, and describes the many victorious battles she fought against the *asuras* (demons) on behalf of the gods.

The *path* to be described here took place in the home of a Raipur businessman. He is a well-educated man and is prominent in the cultural life of the city. He considers himself a *bhakt* (devotee) of the goddess, and accordingly much of his religious life centers on ceremonial dedicated to her. And indeed in his case this is not surprising, because although his family has been in Chhattisgarh for generations, and although he speaks Chhattisgarhi fluently, his antecedents are Bengali, and his family culture reflects this fact. Because of a traditional orientation in this direction, Bengalis are more likely than not to center religious attitudes on the goddess, but it should be stressed that the goddess is an extremely important element in Chhattisgarhi religious patterns, and the *saptashati path* is held in many Chhattisgarhi homes, especially during the two periods of the year known as *navratra* (see below, ch. 5).

One might go to the trouble and expense of holding a special household ceremonial for any number of reasons. In the present case I was never told what the specific reason for the *path* was beyond the statement that the family was "facing certain difficulties." To overcome these difficulties the sponsor had made a vow to hold a *path*.

Reading—or more properly chanting—the *Shri Durga Saptashati* is an efficacious way of soliciting aid from the goddess. In so doing, one praises the goddess in the most extravagant terms, and one does so at considerable trouble and expense. Ideally, the sponsor should perform the *path* himself. This requirement is seldom honored. The text is in Sanskrit, and few have the necessary facility in that language to do a full-fledged *path*. We shall see, moreover, that the ritual manipulations that accompany the recitation of the text are very complicated and accordingly require a great deal of specialized knowledge of ritual form and idiom. Finally, a ceremony of this sort is time-consuming on a grand scale. The *path* to be described here requires nine full days of ceremonial labor for its completion, an expenditure of time that a man of affairs can ill afford.

In a ceremony of this sort, then, a number of factors converge in such a way as virtually to require that it be presided over by a specialist in ritual. This specialist is the Brahman priest, usually known as *pandit*. He must be, of course, a Brahman; he must know enough Sanskrit to recite the text properly, and he must be well versed in the elaborate physical manipulations that textualized ritual requires. In performing the *Saptashati path* the priest does a considerable task for his client. On each of the nine days of the ceremony the full text must be chanted. Before and after each stanza of the text, an additional stanza must be recited, bringing the total number of stanzas that must be chanted each day to 2,100. This takes the better part of the day, and the priest is not allowed to eat anything until the day's reading is over.

In the present instance the site chosen for the *path* was a spare room of the sponsor's house. This was a "pure" room in which the family's shrine was ordinarily situated. For the occasion of the *path* additional purifications were undertaken. The floor was washed with a solution of cowdung in water, a mixture with purifying powers. The floor was then decorated with designs executed with a paste of rice flour and water. A low platform was set up at one end of the room, and upon it were placed several framed pictures of the goddess Durga.

When the priest arrived on the first day of the ceremony he executed a series of bewilderingly complex ritual manipulations. Afterward it was explained to me what he had done. He began with a number of additional preparatory purifications. He first touched his mouth three times to water held in his right hand, thus purifying his mouth. Then he uttered an oath that he would perform the ceremony properly and to the best of his ability. The priest also purified all the materials to be used in the ceremony. First, the water to be used was purified; he accomplished this by uttering certain *mantras* and placing flowers, sandalwood paste, and sesame seeds in the water. The purified water could then be used to purify other materials to be used in the ritual. It was sprinkled over the flowers, fruits, and other offerings, and over the various utensils to be used as well. Finally, *bhut shuddhi*—the purification of the site of the ritual from evil spirits—was performed. Mustard seeds and rice were thrown about the room as certain *mantras* were being uttered.

These initial preparations having been made, it was time for one of the most important acts of the entire nine-day ritual sequence, the placing of the *kalash* (also known as *ghat*). This refers to a ritual device that acts as the material location of the deity during a ceremony. The goddess was in fact present in the room in the form of her pictorial images, just as she would be present in the form of a carved image were such included among the items on the altar. But in an elaborate ceremony such as this one the importance of pictures is secondary. Rather, the attentions directed toward the goddess centered on a rather insignificant looking object just at the base of the pictures. This was the *kalash*, which in this case consisted of a small brass pot containing water, curds, and *ghi*. Five mango leaves had been placed around the lip, and a coconut was set on top of the whole. The *kalash* is the most important item among all the physical paraphernalia of ritual. It represents, a priest explained, "the infinite in the finite," that is, a tangible form for the deity during a ritual. In the present instance the *kalash* constituted the principal object of worship in the ceremonies that followed.

Before beginning the *path* itself the priest worshipped his own personal deity. This was Vishnu, who was represented in the form of a small stone (*saligram*) kept on a diminutive brass altar. Sandalwood paste, flowers, incense, a lamp, and some food were offered to the deity. One additional step was necessary before the worship of the goddess. This was the worship of

Indra, of the guardian deities of the directions, and of the nine planetary deities.

With these preliminaries over, the priest was able to proceed to the worship of the goddess herself. The sequence was quite complex, but followed a pattern generally found in highly textualized ceremonials. The entire sequence, according to a priest, has one overall purpose: "to make the goddess feel like a welcome guest." Thus, the goddess must first be symbolically seated, a procedure known as *asan*. An *asan* (seat) in the form of a small, flattened piece of silver was placed near the *kalash*. The goddess must next be welcomed, a procedure called *swagatam*. The priest uttered certain *mantras* of welcome while holding his hands together before his face in the conventional gesture of greeting. Then followed *padya*, the washing of the goddess's feet. A small amount of water was poured into a small container near the *kalash*. In this fashion the goddess was treated as the most honored of guests. As the ceremony proceeded she was symbolically bathed, clothed, garlanded. She was given sandalwood paste, ornaments, and flowers. After she had been honored in this fashion her story, the *Shri Durga Saptashati*, was recited; this recitation constituted the core of each day's ceremony and took up most of the time.

Informants are clear, however, that apart from the recitation of the text itself the most important part of the ritual sequence is the offering of food to the goddess. Offering food is, of course, an integral part of hospitality, and food offerings are thus consistent with the overall purpose of the ritual. In the present case food offerings were presented to the goddess each day, and afterward she was presented with *pan* (areca nut, lime, and catechu folded in a betel leaf). "Just as we enjoy *pan* after eating, so do the gods," an informant remarked. At the conclusion of each day's ceremonies the food offerings were distributed to family members and friends as *prasad*.

In this fashion the first eight days of the ceremony passed. It was not until the afternoon of the ninth day that the true climax of the ceremony was reached. By about four o'clock on this final afternoon the priest had completed the recitation of the text. He was seated, as usual, in the center of the room and was surrounded by the materials and implements needed for the ceremony: brass and copper dishes, pots, incense sticks, a supply of sandalwood paste, copper spoons, a conch shell, a gong, etc. Incense was burning in the room, as were two oil lamps. Offerings to the goddess were placed here and there in the vicinity of the altar. These included coconuts, sweets, a red sari, some red shawls, and a large quantity of flowers, which by this time had piled up around the *kalash* so thickly as to conceal it almost entirely.

When all was ready, various foods were brought into the room. On previous days the goddess had been given relatively simple foods, mostly fruits and sweets, but on this day she was to be given a full dinner, with all of the elaborations associated with formal hospitality. Accordingly, all of the components of a truly festive meal were laid before the goddess: rice, *dal*, *puris*, vegetable curries, and other items. These were presented to the goddess and then allowed to remain in place during the remaining rites.

The next phase of the ceremony consisted of the sequence known as *arti*. In the present context the word *arti* denotes a special and rather dramatic way of offering certain things to the deity. There is a variant interpretation, however, in which *arti* is understood to constitute a method of clearing evil influences from the immediate vicinity of the deity. The essential gesture of *arti* is that of moving the object in question in a circular fashion (describing the written symbol of the sacred syllable *aum* when done properly) before the deity. While each object is being offered in this manner a conch shell is blown and a gong is sounded continuously. This is said to have the purpose of helping the participants concentrate on the deity by drowning out possible distractions. The items offered included an oil lamp of five flames, a small conch shell, clothing, a cluster of *bel* (wood apple) leaves, incense sticks, and a camphor lamp.

As soon as this sequence was finished preparations were begun for *homa* (or *havan*), the final and consummating part of the entire ceremony. A woman of the household entered the room with a container of sand, which she unceremoniously dumped into the middle of the floor. The priest then shaped the sand into a square platform about twelve inches on a side and two inches high. Other women appeared with baskets containing slender pieces of wood and leaves of the *bel* tree.[1] The wood consisted of a mixture of pieces of mango and *bel* wood. With the help of some of the women the priest carefully inspected the the *bel* leaves, throwing flawed ones aside. *Ghi* and red flowers were brought near, and the priest sprinkled sanctified water on these, on the *bel* leaves, and on the wood.

The priest then made a design on top of the sand platform and began to pile the pieces of wood there in such a way that a vertical air space was left at the center of the resulting structure. He placed some *ghi* and flowers on top of the pile, dipped a piece of wood in *ghi*, lit it, circled the pile of wood with the flame, and then ignited it all. More flowers were committed to the flames, and more *ghi* was ladled onto the pyre with a special copper spoon. When the fire was burning briskly the priest began dipping *bel* leaves in *ghi* and then placing them in the fire, all the while reading *mantras* from a book that was open in front of him. Each time he placed a leaf in the flames he would repeat "*svaha*" or "*om svaha*." Later I was told that *svaha* is the name of the wife of Agni, the fire god, and that she accepts the offerings on behalf of this deity. In this fashion a total of 108 *bel* leaves were consumed by the fire. When the final *bel* leaf had been offered up, the priest stood up and placed some flowers, a betel leaf, and a banana together on the fire. He then poured some curds and water on the fire, after which he retrieved some of the ashes on the back of his copper spoon. The priest smeared small

---

[1] The leaves of the *bel* tree (wood apple) are associated with Shiva because of a vague resemblance between the shape of the leaf and Shiva's trident, the *trishul*. The leaves play an important role in most ceremonial connected with Shiva or the goddess.

amounts of these ashes on the forehead, the center of the chest, and both shoulders of the man on whose behalf the *path* was being performed, after which ashes were similarly applied to members of his immediate family. This signified, I was told, a special blessing from the deity.

After the *homa* only a few final details remained. Participants placed coins for the Brahman priest in a dish containing a few grains of rice. All bowed to the goddess in deep *pranam*. The priest removed the mango leaves from the *kalash* and used them to sprinkle water from the pot over everyone in the room. Each person was careful to cover his or her feet, for none of this water, known as *shanti jal* (water of peace), should be allowed to touch them. Then flowers from the altar were distributed to those in the room. Everyone bowed in *pranam* to the priest, after which younger members of the family did similar obeisance to their elders. This marked the conclusion of the nine-day *path*, save for the distribution of food. The same food that had been offered to the goddess was distributed to everyone, the priest being served first and in a separate room.

General Features

The four ritual performances I have described display wide variation in ostensible purpose and context. Actually, as we shall see, the full range of variation in Chhattisgarhi ceremonial is far greater than the four examples alone might suggest. Ceremonies may be performed to persuade deities to grant specific favors for the worshipper, in conjunction with auspicious occasions or specific festivals, for individual salvation, or merely because "it's the custom" (*rivaz hai*). Rituals may center on interludes of possession, or be connected with the singing of songs or the recitation of texts. Some, like the *saptashati path*, are conducted entirely in accordance with textual ritual formulas, while others, such as *matar*, appear to have little if any relationship with the ritual prescriptions of sacred literature. Nevertheless, the striking fact is that despite this obvious diversity the four rituals described share certain features with each other and with most Chhattisgarhi ceremonial. These shared features are related directly to the ideas of purity and pollution, especially as these are applied in the manipulation of food.

Purity: Approaching Divinity

It should be clear from the four examples that the first condition of the ritual event is purity of context; indeed, this appears to be a universal rule of Hindu ceremonialism. Each of our four rituals took place in physical surroundings that were either kept pure as a matter of course (the kitchen being a prime example) or that had been purified for the occasion (the application of cowdung wash being a common technique). As a general rule, too, the principal actor or actors in ritual must themselves be in a purified condition before approaching or making offerings to the deity. This usually means that the worshippers will be freshly bathed and will be wearing garments appropriate to a condition of purity: a minimum of cotton, which is quite vulnerable to pollution; silk, if possible, which is more resistant to accidental pollution. While purity of context is essential for the ritual event, it is clear too that there is great variation in the degree to which actual purifying manipulations are carried out. In the case of the two village rites purification was rather perfunctory; in the *saptashati path* the preliminary purification was extremely intricate.

Purity must be understood in relation to the complementary notion of pollution. These two concepts are the poles of a conceptual opposition that is virtually omnipresent in Hindu life. This opposition has both social and religious implications, and indeed constitutes a point of fusion between these two cultural domains. In religious contexts it defines who or what may or may not be brought into contact with a deity. In the social-structural context it provides the conceptual basis for hierarchy (see esp. Dumont 1970) both as a pure ideology and in actual interactions among castes.

Systematic analysis of the purity–pollution concept has proven to be one of the most intractable problems of modern Indian studies. At first glance the underlying principles seem clear enough, but the apparent simplicity evaporates in the face of ethnographic detail. It is possible, however, to relate purity and pollution to certain physical indices which seem to serve as extreme anchoring points for all operational continua between pure and impure. Specifically, both purity and pollution are embodied in certain common substances, objects, and conditions, and these seem to be definitive of purity and pollution as they apply to concrete human situations. There are, for example, certain common substances that are considered very pure, and purifying in their application. These include the products of the living cow (milk, *ghi*, dung, etc.), and water from sources of special sanctity such as the Ganges. They also include materials commonly employed in rituals such as turmeric, cowdung ash, and sandalwood paste. Certain *mantras* are also regarded as purifying. Likewise, pollution has certain physical embodiments. All body effluvia are polluting, especially feces, urine, saliva, menstrual flow, and afterbirth. Products of dead cattle, especially beef and leather, are highly polluting. Decaying things are polluting (a common rationale for considering liquor to be mildly polluting: "It's a rotten thing"). Corpses, or anything having to do with death, are sources of extremely powerful pollution.

Speaking in general terms, there are essentially two ways to bring about a condition of purity. Certain substances or things seem to have the ability to ameliorate pollution directly. Cowdung appears to have this property, and is widely used as an agent of purification. Mixed with water and applied as a wash, it is employed as an agent of household purification and in many other ways besides. Ingestion of a mixture of the "five products of the cow" (milk, urine, dung, *ghi*, and curds) is said to be a particularly efficacious method of personal purification, though in fact I was never able to witness this procedure. Also, the application of specific *mantras* will effect purification.

However, the use of water is the most common method of purification, and here the principle involved seems to be somewhat different from that of direct amelioration. Water absorbs and transmits pollution very readily. Food cooked in water is regarded as quite vulnerable to pollution. Pots made from water-absorbent clay must be thrown out when a house is being purified after a birth or a death. While it is true that some water, such as that of the Ganges, has special inherent powers of purification, the evidence suggests that the efficacy of water as an agent of purification lies not in intrinsic purity, but rather in its capacity to absorb pollution and thus carry it away. Running water is preferred for bathing; in a river the pollution is carried downstream and there is minimal danger of its being redistributed over the body. When bathing is done from a container of water, the water is poured over the head and body in such a way that it flows downward from the least polluted part of the body, the head, to the most polluted parts of the body—the genital organs, anus, and feet—and thence away.

The physical imagery of purification, whether by direct reduction of pollution or by absorption and removal of pollution, suggests that pollution has a substantive character while purity does not. In other words, pollution is an existent; purity is its absence. To become pure is to rid oneself of pollution; it is not to "add purity." A person in a state of pollution is not purified by contact with someone in a state of purity. However, a person in a state of purity will become polluted by contact with a person who is polluted. Hence, to remain pure is to remain free from pollution; to become pure is to remove pollution.

Personal purity is a precarious condition. While most of the items and processes that fill the world are not polluting, it is, perhaps, one of the most notable aspects of Hindu life that the substances and processes that are most markedly polluting are the very ones that are most inherently present in the biological conditions of human life. Eating, elimination, sexual intercourse, giving birth, being born, and dying—all are sources of pollution. Thus, pollution is one of the true inevitables of the human condition. A living human being must eat and eliminate waste, and in so doing must come in contact with pollution. All human beings are born and will die; human life is thus framed by pollution. As a result, purity is an extraordinary condition, a contravention of most that is normal in human life.

To maintain a high degree of purity is to become involved in a complicated and incessant battle against life itself, which seems constantly to be intruding into the sanctity of the shrine or the time and place of ritual. Hence the many restrictions that surround such a place and such a time. Shoes must not be worn because leather is polluted, as is the dust of the streets. Women are barred during their menstrual periods and all are barred who have been in recent contact with death. The human actors in ritual must bathe before approaching the deity. The materials used in ritual, the sandalwood, the turmeric, the *ghi*, are pure by nature. The offerings and paraphernalia of ritual are purified by symbolic washing.

To all of this one further fact should be added. Purity and pollution, as they apply in concrete situations, are relational attributes. Purity, as a precondition for ritual activity, is not an absolute, but refers to the degree to which it is appropriate for a particular person, or a particular group of people, to come in contact with a particular deity or set of deities. A context of purity is always required when people approach gods. But some deities, most notably the gods of the higher castes and those housed in major temples, are far more exacting in this requirement than others. A person who belongs to a very low caste must bathe before participating in ritual; having purified himself he may approach his own deities. But under no circumstances, not even after the most elaborate purifications, may he come into direct contact with the deities of the higher castes, nor may he enter the inner enclosures of major temples. In this way divine and worldly hierarchy reflect and complement one another (see Harper 1964:151–52). The members of one caste may be said to be inherently less or more pure than the members of another, irrespective of the state of purity achieved by bathing or other means. This fundamental fact of worldly hierarchy appears to be associated in the most basic fashion with different degrees of access to a highly differentiated pantheon. This is a matter I shall discuss in greater detail in connection with the structure of the Chhattisgarhi pantheon.

At all events, the purification as a prelude to ritual is always required. As Dumont and Pocock (1959d:31) have suggested, purity may be best understood as a "condition" for beneficial contact with deities. The ritual event may be said to take place in a thoroughly artificial environment—one created and maintained by elaborate requirements of washing and treatment with purifying substances, and by equally elaborate restrictions of physical propinquity and contact. As such, it is a delicate state, which the very dust of the streets may defile.

Pranam: The Feet of the Gods

A gesture known as *pranam* was a conspicuous element in each of the rituals described above, and is in fact one of the most characteristic gestures of Hindu ceremonial. *Pranam* literally means "salutation," but salutation in a sense that is very special and that has an important set of contexts both in ritual and in other areas of Hindu life.

Pranam is a basic ritual gesture, which is appropriate before a deity in the absence of any other elaboration. Rural Chhattisgarh is filled with small temples and shrines, many of which face public roads. An observer may notice that when villagers pass in front of such shrines or temples they often make a gesture toward the god or gods inside. They do so by means of a slight forward inclination of the head with both hands brought together at the elevation of the face. Informants say that this is simply a way of "greeting" the god, or "giving respect" to the god.

In a more formal setting or in closer proximity to the deity the same gesture is elaborated. A group of men once accompanied me to the shrine of a village goddess. The shrine itself was a rather shabby little brick structure, which contained a few red-colored stones. Just in front of the temple door was a small pile of stones. Inconspicuous at first, these stones turned out to be representations of Thakur Dev, a village deity associated with the goddess in the shrine. Before venturing onto the ground in front of the temple, all present removed their sandals. Each man then saluted Thakur Dev before entering the shrine itself. Some men touched the ground at the base of the stones with the tips of both hands brought together, and then brought their fingertips to their foreheads. Others made a similar gesture using only their right hands. After paying "respect" to the god outside, the men entered the temple and saluted the goddess in a similar fashion.

Precisely the same gesture is a commonplace in ostensibly secular settings. In a rural hospital I once observed an old man in conversation with a doctor from whom he hoped to extract permission to defer payment for recent medical services. He punctuated each of his remarks by touching the feet of the doctor with his folded hands and then touching his forehead. During the election year of 1967 a visiting politician came to visit the house of the *mukhya* (headman) of the Satnamis of a village near Sitapur. The headman's wife emerged to greet the politician and immediately prostrated herself and touched her forehead to the politician's toes. Brahman priests, or any persons of very high status, are often greeted by having their feet touched, and younger people customarily touch the feet of their family elders when saluting them before or after a long absence.

When the difference in relative status between two individuals is not extreme, the standard gesture of greeting is clearly an attenuated version of the *pranam* gesture. Upon meeting an acquaintance one places the palms together before the face, saying "*namaste.*" In so doing, one informant explained, one salutes "that bit of god which is in every person." As the status difference between the two individuals becomes more marked, this gesture becomes increasingly similar to the touching of feet and forehead. In such circumstances the person of lower status may bow slightly and touch, or seem to touch, his folded hands to his forehead. If the status difference is more pronounced the person of lower status may do the full *pranam*, either touching, or making a gesture as if he were touching, the other person's feet, and then bringing his hands to his forehead.

The *pranam* gesture, then, is a way of indicating respect, which is ubiquitous in Hindu life. It is appropriate both before deities and before persons of higher status. The meaning of the gesture is obvious; it symbolizes distinction of status by physically indicating an equivalence between one party's feet and the other party's forehead. Its implications with respect to status are grounded in the purity–pollution opposition. The contrast between the two extremities of the human body, the head as noble and pure and the feet as base and polluted, is an idea that is apparently prevalent throughout the subcontinent, and one that has been described in detail elsewhere (see Carstairs 1961:77–79). When a person touches the feet of another and then his own forehead he is saying, in effect, that his purest and most noble part is the same or less than the basest and most polluted part of the other. He is accepting pollution from the other, an exemplification of what Harper (1964:181–83) has termed "respect pollution." The theme is one easily elaborated. The feet of the other may be washed, as often the god's feet are in *puja*. Sometimes the water in which the god's feet have been washed is drunk by the worshipper, a further elaboration of the same principle. The same theme is reflected in the final sequence of *arti*, when the effluvium of the flame is taken on the hand of the worshipper and applied to his face or head.

Prasad: The Food of the Gods

The physical setting of the ritual is purified; so too are the principal actors. The deity may now be greeted by *pranam* and the prescribed ritual sequence may go forward. Informants are quite clear about the purpose of all that follows. The deity, one is told, must be "honored." Honoring the deity may take any of a variety of forms. Garlands may be offered, a *tilak* may be applied, clothing may be given, *mantras* may be chanted, devotional songs may be sung, *arti* may be performed; or less conventional procedures, such as having a herd of cattle circumambulate the god, may be employed. But out of all this variation one requirement stands out as a constant: the deity must be fed. Food offerings were a central feature of each of the four rituals I have described, and such offerings are in fact characteristic of virtually all Chhattisgarhi ritual. Indeed, without a food offering of some kind the ritual would simply not be *puja* in the conventional sense of the term. The type of food given may vary widely; anything men eat the gods eat too, although the superior deities tend to prefer vegetarian fare. But always, in *puja*, some kind of food is given, and however the act may be elaborated under particular circumstances, the mode of giving seems always to be the same: food is given to the deity, it is taken back, and it is distributed to the worshippers as *prasad*. The food offering is as essential a part of the ritual sequence as the preliminary purifications, and, I shall argue, it is in some ways the central and indispensable act, the core around which all else is elaboration and overlay.

Food offerings in *puja* exemplify principles relating to food exchange that are operative in other areas of Chhattisgarhi life. In Chhattisgarh, as in India generally, the giving and taking of food is charged with meaning in a variety of contexts. In general, asymmetrical patterns of food exchange are used in the expression of relative rank in local caste hierarchies. The principles involved have been well described elsewhere (see Marriott 1968) so I shall not consider these matters in detail here. For now, it is sufficient to note that certain types of food prestations confer superior status on the giver and inferior status on the receiver. The degree of hierarchical distance implied in such a transaction depends in large part upon certain characteristics of the food that is exchanged. Cooked rice—a common, everyday sort of fare in Chhattisgarh—readily absorbs pollution from those who prepare and serve it, and accepting cooked rice from a person belonging to another caste would, in effect, be accepting symbolically a relatively high degree of pollution from the giver. Accordingly, the hierarchical distance implied by such a transaction would be relatively great. Foods cooked in oil or *ghi*—more expensive, festive fare—are more resistant to pollution by the preparer or server, and exchanges of this sort of food are considerably less relevant to differential status. The foodstuff that in exchange implies the greatest hierarchical distance of all consists of another person's leavings—this is known in Hindi as *jutha*.

Again, the hierarchical implication of the acceptance of *jutha*, as is the case with other forms of food, is rooted in the purity–pollution contrast. In the act of eating, food is contaminated by contact with the saliva of the eater. Thus, accepting *jutha* from another is an act of the most profound humility. In taking *jutha* from another person one is saying, in effect, "Relative to you I am so low that I need not fear pollution from you; I need not even fear pollution from your saliva." In the area of Chhattisgarh where most of my observations were made there were, to my knowledge, only two castes whose members would eat the *jutha* of others. These were the lowest castes of all—low, even, within the untouchable category—the Mehetars (sweepers) and Devars (swineherds and beggars).

The concept of *jutha* and the implications of its acceptance provides a context critically important for an understanding of the structure of Chhattisgarhi ritual. Food, as we have seen, is always offered to the deity. In turn, the deity in some way partakes of the offering. Sometimes the consumption of the food by the god is physically symbolized, as in *homa*, where the food is visibly consumed by the fire. "The flame is the tongue of the gods," a Pandit remarked in explanation. Sometimes the food is merely set before the god, often behind a concealing cloth. Here too it is assumed that the deity actually partakes of the food.

A Raipur lawyer assured me that if you take a quantity of food, weigh it carefully, put it before the god for a reasonable length of time, and then weigh it again, you will discover that a small portion of the mass of the offering has disappeared.

If, then, the deity "eats" the food that was placed on the altar, the food that is taken back for distribution is quite literally the leavings, or *jutha*, of the diety (a fact noted by Carstairs, 1961:162). And thus in eating this food the participants are according the most profound honor to the god. The underlying principle is the same as that of touching the feet of a superior, but here the implications of hierarchy are greatly augmented. Again, the idiom employed is what Harper has characterized as "respect pollution"; behavior resulting in pollution is done intentionally, "in order to show deference and respect; by doing that which under other circumstances would be defiling, an individual expresses his inferior position" (1964:181).

It is clear, therefore, that in its expression of hierarchy the asymmetrical exchange of foods that takes place in *puja* is in consonance with more general principles that order Hindu life. But beyond this, I think it is possible to show that the form that food exchange takes in *puja* is a necessary consequence of principles inherent in reciprocity as a pattern of human interaction.

In the presentation of food to the deity there is a sense in which the deity is being paid for past or future favors. The food itself may only be a part of this payment. Depending on the circumstances, offerings of clothing, money, precious metals, and so forth may also be made. But "paying" the deity in this fashion carries implications that could easily run counter to the overall purpose of the ritual. In ritual, as we have noted, the deities are supposed to be honored. Indeed, if the gods are to be gods at all, and thus worthy of worship, their superiority must be affirmed; were the divine not superior to the human, gods would scarcely be able to perform the services men typically ask of them. Here, then, lies the crux of an acute dilemma. Ritual should honor the god, yet at the same time it should pay the god; in fact, gifts are offered in ritual with this end in view. But taking food from the hand of another is demeaning, and to augment the presentation of food with more lavish gifts would seem to heighten the implication of dishonor. For, in the absence of some element of reciprocity within the framework of the ritual itself, the resulting symbolic configuration would be that of the unrepaid gift, and as Mauss (1967:63) points out, "The gift not yet repaid debases the man [here god] who accepted it." Thus, if the ritual is to have the net effect of affirming rather than negating the superior status of the god, reciprocity in some form must be incorporated within the ritual sequence. Hence, the necessity of *prasad*, the counterprestation.

The deity is initially given superior food. There is a general tendency to include expensive types of food in such offerings, and even when simple, inexpensive foods are provided, they are usually prepared under stringent conditions of purity. But the counterprestation, that from god to man, consists of food of the most inferior sort, symbolic scraps and leftovers, the polluted refuse of the god with all of its hierarchical implications. In *puja* the initial receiver, the god, becomes the giver, and the purity–pollution contrast is employed so that the god emerges from the transaction with the greatest honor. When *prasad* is received and eaten by the worshippers, the equilibrium that had been disturbed by the initial prestation is restored. The god has received payment *with* honor, and thereby the proper hierarchy has been maintained.

An asymmetrical transaction in foods, then, lies at the heart of *puja*, a transaction both expressive of and supportive of hierarchical distance between the divine and the human. But more is involved than this, for the transaction is characteristically not between individuals but rather between an individual deity and a group of people. In *puja*, as has been noted, food is not only taken back from the altar; it is distributed to a group of worshippers as well. This congregational focus was quite evident in the four rituals I have described; in fact, it appears to be a general

characteristic of Chhattisgarhi ceremonialism. The groups that
may be involved in ritual are varied—families, caste-mates, villages, neighborhoods, etc.—but a collectivity of some kind is
almost invariably to be found. It is appropriate, therefore, to
examine the social dimensions of *puja*.

I have already stressed the importance of food exchange in
Chhattisgarhi social organization. Its significance rests on the
hierarchical implications of unidirectional food prestations or of
reciprocal exchange in which one party observes more stringent
restrictions about what he will accept than the other. It should
be noted, too, that within this wider system of attitudes about
food transactions, simple commensality carries social implications as well. As a general rule, the sharing of food is associated
with relative equality and closeness of relationship. Thus, the
joint family eats from the same hearth. When, in the natural
course of events, the joint family splits, new hearths are built.
Local caste-mates may eat together and sometimes do so as a
group on festival occasions. If an individual breaks an important
rule of his caste, he is not allowed these commensal privileges;
and reacceptance is sometimes symbolized by a dinner in which
the local membership of the caste partakes, as a group, of food
from the offender's hand, after which he is once more a member
of the commensal circle.

From these implications of commensality, it is evident that
the distribution of *prasad* at the conclusion of ritual sequences
is an act that carries a potential sociological meaning. In the
context of commensal restrictions operating in Chhattisgarhi
society, the sharing of *prasad* in ritual can be construed as a symbolic statement of linkage between the participants—between
members of a family, between friends, between co-residents of
a village, or whatever. Let me stress, however, that in suggesting
this interpretation of *prasad* distribution in *puja* I am not advo-
cating a return to simplistic functional analyses of ritual resting
on a metaphysic of "sentiments of solidarity." Rather, I maintain
merely that careful analysis of Chhattisgarhi ritual reveals an

underlying structure, and that inherent to this structure are potential sociological implications evolving from principles (those of the purity–pollution contrast in its relation to food exchange and hierarchy) that operate on the widest possible scale in Chhattisgarhi society. These familiar principles are used in ritual, but with the difference that the setting they are employed in is in no way normal.

If we adopt this perspective it is of no little significance that *puja* provides a source from which all participants can take food and must take food. Almost everyone in our neighborhood in Raipur contributed something—time, money, or both—to the neighborhood celebration or *ganesh chaturthi*, a ten-day festival which occurs in the lunar month of *bhadon* (August–September). As it is not always convenient for everyone to be physically present at the *pujas*, which occur every night in conjunction with the festival, boys carrying *prasad* are sent around to each house. It was explained that even if one is not present at the ritual itself, *prasad* should be taken. "It's a neighborhood function," one informant explained, "and everyone in the neighborhood must take *prasad*."

It is clear, then, that while *prasad* is food, it is in no sense ordinary food. Normally, one may reject or accept food as inclination dictates within the framework of everyday restrictions. In the ritual context, however, the refusal of food carries a different meaning. For in refusing *prasad* one would not merely be rejecting the other participants, but one would be rejecting, in effect, the deity to whom the food had been offered. Thus, in ritual the principles of commensality operate in an extraordinary context. Commensality in ritual is not a simple matter of the group or the community *sui generis*, but rather of the definition of the group in relation to something else. In sharing the *jutha* of the deity, the group—whatever its composition—suppresses manifest differences within itself by reaching beyond the world of men, and mundane relationships between men, for a point of reference against which the group as a whole can be defined.

Whatever the normal cleavages within the group, for a moment it has become unified as one pole in hierarchical opposition to divinity.

Two possibilities seem to be inherent within the structure of *puja*. First, *puja* can provide a setting in which, paradoxically, the principles underlying hierarchy are employed in the partial or complete masking of hierarchy. In the normal course of events the purity-pollution contrast provides an idiom for the expression of hierarchical separation between men. In *puja*, however, the same principle is employed in the symbolic reduction of hierarchical diversity to unity, and this reduction can be of considerable scope as the inclusion of Untouchables in *matar* indicates. Worldly hierarchy is therefore momentarily eclipsed—reduced to relative insignificance by the overwhelming inclusiveness of the hierarchical opposition between the mundane and the divine.

But a second possibility exists as well. Although the basic pattern tends to mute hierarchy it is equally possible for the basic format of *puja* to be manipulated in such a way that hierarchy is reasserted. This can be done in a variety of ways, but the most common method is to formalize the manner in which *prasad* is distributed. Some participants might receive their share before others, and, if arrangements are at all elaborate, groups of participants might eat separately. It is possible, too, in a case of radical hierarchical separation—say between high castes and Untouchables—for some participants to be given the leavings of other participants, the *jutha* of the *jutha* of the gods. Except in the latter case, however, the logic of the rite is one in which worldly differences are "enclosed" within a wider opposition. Thus, though internal differences may be recognized, the group achieves definition as a unity in relation to the deity.

It should be noted finally that whether *puja* masks completely or reasserts worldly hierarchy, in the end it has the effect of sanctifying the principles upon which hierarchy rests. For, as I have stressed, hierarchy is conceptually framed by the purity–pollution contrast, and in *puja* this principle is vividly exemplified, and ultimately affirmed, in a setting that is at once dramatic, sacred, and public.

Ritual in Social Context

We have seen that the symbolic structure of *puja* is such that any particular instance of it is, in effect, a statement about social relationships. Moreover, *puja* is a form of expression that is applicable to virtually any social-structural circumstances, and it seems likely that almost every structural permutation of Chhattisgarhi society is at one point or another reflected in the exceedingly intricate system of interlocking ritual cycles that will be the subject of later chapters. In the remaining pages of this chapter, I shall simply sketch out a few examples to give the reader an idea of the range of possible social relationships that can be expressed in the symbolism of *puja*.

Perhaps the example that illustrates the structural implications of *puja* with particular clarity is provided by an elementary dyadic relationship, that of a form of institutionalized friendship known as *mitan*.[2] Two men (or two women), of the same or different castes, may become *mitan* as a way of declaring what is supposed to be an undying amity between them. There appears to be a good deal of variation in the actual ceremonies employed to seal this special state of friendship, but significantly the consumption of a special sort of *prasad* by both parties seems always to be the key element. In this respect the ceremony is simply a variant of *puja* in its most elementary form. *Mahaprasad* (great *prasad*) is preferred for this purpose—i.e., *prasad* taken, or said to be taken, from the altar of Jagannath at Puri in Orissa during the annual festival of *rath duj* and saved for these and for other special occasions.

The household unit finds frequent expression in religious ceremonies. In the description of *pitar pak* we noted an example

---

[2] For an excellent analysis of ceremonial friendship in Chhattisgarh see Jay 1973.

of such a ceremony, and there are many more. Most *pujas* performed for household deities fall into this category, and in many families such *pujas* are performed, however perfunctorily, every day. In addition, in later chapters we shall see that during the course of the year there are numerous special fasting days for women. These fasts are associated with various deities, and specific requirements differ. However, the basic format is quite uniform: there is a period of fasting followed by a *puja*. At the termination of the entire sequence *prasad* is distributed to household members and, if possible, to other relatives and friends.

Likewise, there are numerous occasions in which the village, as a unit, is given ritual expression. As we shall see later, many of the major festivals of the Chhattisgarhi sacred year are occasions on which villagewide ceremonies take place. *Matar* is only one example. Most of these festivals have a very similar format, despite obvious differences in ostensible purpose and content. The celebration almost invariably involves a procession of some kind, and the focal deities of the festival are often taken with the procession around the village. Usually the procession halts at individual houses whose inhabitants wish to make special offerings to the deity. At one or more points during the sequence *puja* is performed, and *prasad* is distributed to all at the termination of the ceremony.

An urban setting may alter the context in which *puja* occurs, but not its social-structural implications. In the city of Raipur individual neighborhoods often conduct ceremonies during festivals in much the same fashion as villages, though in the city such occasions are less frequent and active participation is taken less for granted. One urban ceremony that falls within this paradigm is *ganesh chaturthi*, a ten-day festival of Maharashtrian origin which has apparently been celebrated in Chhattisgarhi towns and cities for some time, although it is only now becoming well-known in rural areas. It centers on Ganesh, the elephant-headed son of Shiva and Parvati, and occurs in the early autumn when the rains have begun to slacken. Each neighborhood erects a temporary shrine in which a clay image of Ganesh is installed along with elaborate decorations. Here *puja* is performed daily, and *prasad* is distributed to families in the neighborhood. On the tenth night all of the images of Ganesh are taken in a single gigantic procession to a tank on the outskirts of the city, where they are disposed of by immersion. As one might expect, a palpable sense of neighborhood and neighborliness pervades the festival. The neighborhood as a whole is expected to contribute money for the shrine and the procession float, and the inhabitants are encouraged to witness the evening *pujas* or, at the very least, to accept *prasad*. The neighborhood emphasis of the festival is heightened by a citywide competition for the best-decorated shrine and the most elaborate float in the procession.

Finally, entire regions or subregions may be linked to particular ritual expressions. As we have seen, Chhattisgarh is a reginal entity with a long dynastic history and a cultural distinctiveness of its own. The sacred geography of the region provides one focus for Chhattisgarhi regional identification. Of all the sacred centers of Chhattisgarh, the most important is located at the town of Rajim, some 25 miles southwest of Raipur, where the largest *mela* (religious fair) of the region takes place annually. The fair begins on the last (full moon) day of the lunar month of *magh* (January–February) and continues through the lunar month of *phalgun* (February–March). Visitors are drawn from the entire Chhattisgarh region, and the Census Department estimates that as many as 100,000 people may attend in any given year (Dubey and Mohril 1965:44).

People come to the *mela* in order to bathe in the semisacred waters of the Mahanadi River[3] and to worship the deities in several old temples, which are concentrated in the Rajim area. There are six important Shiva temples in the vicinity, and visiting all of them is believed to constitute an especially meritorious

[3] The Mahanadi is the Ganges of Chhattisgarh, and Rajim is its Allahabad. Places where rivers join (*sangam*) are always sacred, and Rajim is the place where the Mahanadi and the Pairi flow together.

Mela crowds at the Rajivlochan temple, Rajim

pilgrimage. The most important sacred center of Rajim, however, is the Rajivlochan temple on the bank of the Mahanadi.
Rajiva lochan is an epithet of Vishnu, and the temple houses an
image of this deity. But if Vishnu is a pan-Indian deity, this
particular manifestation belongs to Chhattisgarh. The story of
the origin of the temple, a part of the folklore of the region, may
be paraphrased as follows:

Eight hundred years ago a Telin [a woman of the oil-presser
caste] named Rajiva lived in Rajim. One day this Telin happened to
put her empty oilpot on a stone she found by the side of the road. When
next she looked the pot was filled with oil. She went home and told the
story to her mother-in-law, who refused to believe her. So they both

went to the stone with an empty oilpot, and again when the pot was put on the stone it filled with oil. The stone was finally turned over and was discovered to be an image of Vishnu.

At the same time Jagatpal, the Raja at Ratanpur, had a dream in which a god told him about the image and said that a temple should be built to house it. When the Raja asked the Telin for the image she said that she would give it to him only if her name were connected in some way with the temple. The Raja agreed, and thus the temple is today known as the Rajivlochan temple.

The atmosphere of the Rajim *mela* is in some respects not unlike that of a county fair in the United States. Near the main encampment is a large bazaar where a great variety of merchandise is available for purchase: food of all kinds, household goods, cheap toys for children, fountain pens, pictures and effigies of deities, patent medicines, amulets, and the like. There is plenty of entertainment as well: acrobats, sideshows, hand-operated Ferris wheels and other amusements for children, and religious singing in the evenings. And so it is that the purely ritual aspects of the Rajim *mela* are very nearly submerged in a great profusion of other activities. Amidst all of the carnival clamor, however, each individual bathes, visits the temples, and partakes of the *prasad* of the deities. In the *mela*, then, under layer upon layer of elaboration, the familiar core sequence may be observed, but it is inconspicuous and seems almost lost in the surrounding clutter.

Constants and Variables

In this chapter I have tried to show that relatively simple structural principles operate beneath the diversity and manifest complexity of Chhattisgarhi ceremonialism. There appear to be two basic components in any ritual sequence. The first is the creation of a physical zone of purity within which the god or goddess may be approached. This zone is sometimes formed in a casual manner, but more often with considerable attention and exactitude.

The second component of the ritual sequence, which constitutes the core of *puja*, consists of a simple transaction in foods.

The transaction is a reciprocal one: the worshippers give food to the god, and the food is taken back and consumed by the worshippers. In the initial offering the god is given superior food, whereas the worshippers receive the symbolic leftovers, or *jutha*, of the god. The retrieval of the god's *jutha* enables the god to be "paid" for past or future favors without dishonor and, at the same time, establishes a hierarchical opposition between the god and the worshippers as a group. Chhattisgarhi ceremonialism has a strong congregational emphasis, and the ritual structure is such that normal cleavages within the group are momentarily obscured within the wider context of the hierarchical opposition that is established between the group as a whole and the deity. Underlying the whole is the purity–pollution contrast, which is exemplified in certain crucial aspects of social organization as well.

The line of argument I have pursued is not intended to be reductionistic, but rather to clear the ground for other kinds of analysis. If an understanding of the symbolism of Chhattisgarhi ceremonialism is to be achieved, it must be based on a comprehension of the most elementary levels of structure in Chhattisgarhi religious action. I have attempted to describe the basic framework within which ritual action takes place. This framework is itself susceptible to more than one level of interpretation. *Prasad*, for example, is a word rich in meaning. From one point of view it refers simply to the food that is taken back from the altar, but it also carries the meaning of "blessing." It is therefore possible for *puja*, as a ritual act, to be accommodated to a conceptual frame that admits a devotional relationship with a personal god. What is at one level a ritual expression of what Dumont (1960:46) has termed "the religion of the group" may at another level be linked to the doctrines of individual salvation associated with Hindu devotional traditions.

Equally important is that there is immense variability in the ritual content that may be developed within the basic structural framework I have described. The central focus of a ritual might be on the recitation of a text, on devotional singing, on animal sacrifice, on divine possession, or on any combination of these or other elements. The food offered might consist of sweets, a full vegetarian meal, or even meat. These and many other variables of the same order relate to crucial aspects of ritual symbolism, which cannot be dealt with within the analytical framework developed in this chapter. The symbolism embodied in this variation constitutes the focus for an entirely different level of analysis, and entails a very different approach to the data in subsequent chapters.

3
Rites of the Life Cycle

I shall now concern myself with variation in Chhattisgarhi ceremonialism. Rather than trying to strip away the elaboration that surrounds the structural core of *puja*, I shall now concentrate on this elaboration itself. It is in variation at this level that the meaning of a particular ritual expression is to be found. In turn, it is at this level that some of the most crucial organizing ideas in the Hinduism of Chhattisgarh are expressed and elaborated.

The related tasks of description and analysis are greatly aided by the fact that Chhattisgarhi ceremonialism presents itself within a series of temporal ritual cycles. While it is true that there are certain ceremonial events that, informants tell me, may occur at any time, observation reveals that even these tend to occur at points within the ritual cycles that are regarded as especially appropriate for defined types of ritual activity, and thus even "occasional" rites are contained within the more general pattern of temporal cycles. One such cycle is tied to the life-histories of individuals, and therefore may be said to refer to "relative" time. The others are organized in relation to celestial movements, and therefore refer to "absolute" time. Here, I shall deal with ceremonialism associated with the life cycle.

Ritual action acquires its full meaning in relation to certain presuppositions about the nature of the reality with which it is supposed to deal. In other words, ritual takes something for granted, and to make sense of ritual it is necessary to discover what these initial assumptions are. In Chhattisgarhi religion one of the most obvious of these assumptions is that there are powers or beings in the world; some are benevolently disposed toward man, others are not. Later we shall see that a simple division between benevolent and malevolent aspects of the pantheon is an oversimplification, because it ignores crucial distinctions of other kinds. But for the present it must be understood that in Chhattisgarhi religious thought it is assumed that there are profoundly malevolent forces that constantly impinge on human existence. Important aspects of Chhattisgarhi ceremonialism may be understood as efforts to counteract these forces by opposing them with protective and benevolent forces of equal or greater power.

However, the "map" of Chhattisgarhi religious thought and action is made much more complicated by the presence of another assumption of profound importance, an assumption that limits the ability of men to confront life's hazards and misfortunes with palliative ritual action. This is the idea of purity and pollution. In the preceding chapter we saw that this concept lies at the heart of the structure of ritual. We shall now see what some of the wider implications of this structure are. Purity carries the potential for beneficial contact with deities, and purity of person and place are the main prerequisites for ritual acts. Pollution, the converse of purity, carries the contrary implication of separation. Just as pollution imposes a barrier between man and man in the context of caste, so too it separates man from his deities. Pollution is a pervasive condition of life. It is rooted in the organic conditions of human existence, and is thus never fully escapable. This fact, in combination with the idea of potential malevolence at large in the world, yields what seems to be the central dilemma of Chhattisgarhi Hinduism: the necessity to deal with the divine world and the difficulty of doing so under conditions of pervasive pollution. This problem constitutes one of the most important foci of religious action, and the necessity of overcoming it constitutes a vital dynamic of Chhattisgarhi religion. Nowhere is this more evident than in the rites of the individual life cycle.

Chhattisgarhi Life Cycles

Pollution and danger are the main themes of the rites of the life cycle (*sanskars*). In Chhattisgarh, man and woman alike are understood to be born and to die in pollution. Birth and death are occasions that generate pollution so intense that the close kin of the newborn or the deceased themselves become polluted. Pollution separates man from man, and man from the gods. Religious and social interests are therefore threatened by these critical events. As a result, important aspects of the rites of birth and death are concerned with purification. Marriage presents a striking contrast. It is a time when the bride and the groom become divine in the sense that they are ritually treated as deities.

The other dominant theme in these rites is danger. Birth and marriage are times when the newborn child and the bride and groom are considered to be especially vulnerable to harmful beings and influences. This fact is reflected in various ritual precautions, which constitute an important part of the ceremonial of birth and marriage. They are also conspicuous throughout childhood, which itself is considered to be an extended period of vulnerability. There is also danger at the time of death, but here there is an odd reversal. The acute danger is not to the principal figure, the deceased; rather, he becomes potentially dangerous to others.

Birth

As is true of all of the rites of the life cycle, there is considerable variation in the particular details of ritual surrounding childbirth, even within a single region such as Chhattisgarh. Differences may be observed between localities, between castes, and even between different families of the same caste and locality. The greatest differences are to be found between the rites of the twice-born and non-twice-born castes. In general the rites of the twice-born are both greater in number and are subject to a far higher degree of textual elaboration than those of the lower castes. Nevertheless, there is a general area of overlap in which the basic ritual manipulations, and the themes they express, are very similar; it is this area that constitutes the basis for the description and analysis to follow.

For all Hindus of Chhattisgarh a concern with pollution is a pervasive theme in the events surrounding childbirth. We have seen already that substances expelled from the body are considered sources of pollution. Menstrual fluid is considered highly polluting, with the result that in most castes women are at the very least barred from the kitchen during their menstrual periods and in the higher castes are subjected to a period of rigorous seclusion. It is therefore scarcely surprising that the fluids and matter discharged with the infant are also considered heavily polluting. The pollution of childbirth is somewhat stronger and less tractable than other forms of personal pollution. It affects not only the mother and the newborn child, but also contaminates the household and may extend in mild form to nonresident agnatic kin as well. Pollution, however, is not the only problem arising at the time of birth. Pregnancy and childbirth are obviously times of physical vulnerability for mother and child, and this is all the more true in an area of high infant mortality such as Chhattisgarh.

Consistent with these realities, pregnancy and childbirth are conceived to be a period of great vulnerability to malign influences. Thus, danger is the second area of ritual concern during this period, and this fact is also reflected in the ritual acts surrounding childbirth.

During her pregnancy the mother-to-be should wear certain charms and amulets to protect her from agencies of harm, particularly from the evil eye (*nazar*, "the glance"). She may be encouraged to keep iron near her person, for iron is thought to have the capacity to ward off witchcraft (*jadu-tona*) and malevolent ghosts (*bhut-pret*). Eclipses are regarded as highly dangerous events, and if one occurs the pregnant woman is in extreme danger and must seclude herself within the house. Also, it is said that a pregnant woman should never go before a smallpox patient, for the sight of a pregnant woman is thought to anger the smallpox goddess, who is present in the patient in the form of the disease itself. Uncertainty and vulnerability precede the birth of the child and continue throughout the early years of life.

Pollution becomes a factor to be dealt with at the time of birth itself. With parturition comes pollution, and as a result it is the usual practice for an Untouchable woman to be hired as midwife. The mother is now in a state of heavy pollution and extreme vulnerability, and as a result she is usually confined to one room of the house. During this period she is thought to be extremely sensitive to cold, and frequently a stove is kept continuously burning in the room. Later we shall see that this concern with temperature has a very wide and important context in Chhattisgarhi religious thought. For several days (usually six) after the birth she does not bathe, although she may be rubbed with oil. The pollution of birth extends to the household as a whole and, I am told, sometimes to closely related agnates. They are mildly polluted and will remain so until purifying measures are taken. It should be noted, however, that the extension of birth pollution is relatively innocuous.

The pollution of death, as we shall see, is far more serious in its impact on the lives of the kin of the deceased.

For most Chhattisgarhi castes the most important day following the birth of a child is the sixth day; that day and the ceremonies associated with it are known as *chhati*. There is considerable variation according to caste and family custom, but certain elements are almost always present. The mother usually has her first bath since the birth of her child on this day and changes into new clothes. Her pollution thereby becomes less intense, though her final purification must await the completion of a sequence of several baths. On *chhati* day the mother is usually allowed solid food for the first time since the birth of the child. The purification of the household often occurs then, although there is some variation here. The important point is that some kind of purification is necessary. The house itself is cleaned, and frequently all the cotton fabrics contained in the house are sent to the washerman (Dhobi). The unglazed (and hence pollution-absorbing) clay pots of the house are thrown out to be replaced with new ones. The father, who has not shaved since the birth, is often shaved for the first time on this day, and sometimes this is also done to close agnates. Human hair has the capacity to absorb and hold pollution, and thus it should be removed. In some castes these acts of initial purification are delayed until the twelfth day after birth, but whatever the timing the underlying idea is the same: to rid the site of the birth, and those closely involved, of the residual pollution resulting from it.

Among most non-twice-born castes the name of the child is usually given on *chhati* day. Among the upper castes, whose ritual life tends more to be shaped by textual prescriptions, the name is bestowed in a special ceremony known as *namkaran*, which is usually conducted by a Brahman priest on the twelfth day after birth. Many people also ritualize the occasion of the child's first consumption of solid food. It should be pointed out that all of these rites are susceptible to textualization, but that although this is a traditional index of high caste status, it is no sure sign of rank, and there is no definite line between those who employ textual ritual styles and those who do not. Except in the case of the lowest castes, nowadays the Brahman's presence at life-cycle rites seems to be more a matter of the desire to have him and the ability to pay than of caste status. In any event, in cases where textualized ritual styles tend to prevail the exact time of birth is given to a Brahman priest, who prepares a horoscope for the child and on the basis of which he dictates the first letter of the child's name. The horoscope, if such is prepared, becomes a vital document when the child has grown to marriageable age, the matching of horoscopes (or at least the pretense thereof) being an important part of the matchmaking process among the higher castes, especially the twice-born.

The theme of vulnerability is a dominant concern at the time of birth and remains important throughout the early years, and, to a certain degree, throughout life. Infants and children are thought to be highly vulnerable to malicious beings, and indeed these are years of genuine vulnerability to illness, especially the gastrointestinal diseases. Very soon after birth the first ritual precautions are taken. These are various in nature, but many procedures center on the use of the color black. Informants were unable to explain clearly the reasons for the protective qualities of black, but it is generally held that black applied to a child's body will ward off harmful influences. Involved in this may be an idea of deliberately "flawing" the child so as not to attract the covetous attention of others. Lampblack (*kajal*) is applied around the child's eyes or in spots elsewhere on the body. A black string is frequently tied around the child's wrist or midriff. Amulets are often used as well. The most common type, known as *taviz*, is hung around the child's neck on a black string. It consists of a small sealed copper cylinder, which contains special herbs or a protective formula inscribed on paper.

Conceptions of the many hazards to which children are susceptible seem to be rooted in the idea of the axiomatic desirability of a healthy and beautiful child, and the correlative notion that healthy and beautiful children will arouse the jealousy of others. One informant expressed great surprise upon learning that our daughter (born in Raipur) had been weighed after she was born. This, my informant stated, was a dangerous thing to do, for anything that might draw attention to the well-being of a child will attract the attention and envy of others. This, in turn, may lead to witchcraft directed against the child. The notion that beautiful and healthy children may attract the attention of witches is consistent with the fact that childbearing represents in an important sense the consummation of the life of a Chhattisgarhi woman. To be a mother is to be a complete woman, and only with the birth of children is a woman's position in her husband's family fully secure. It is not surprising, therefore, that one of the most acute of the many dangers to which children are subject derives directly from the cruelest frustration of this supreme affirmation of a woman's identity and place in the scheme of things: death in childbirth. A woman who dies in childbirth is said to become one of the most viciously malevolent of the various minor spirits who haunt the countryside. The ghost of such a woman (or the composite ghost of such women) is known as *Churalin*, and is conceived to be a demoness who seeks the blood of attractive and unprotected children. The idea of feminine malice is an extremely important idea in Chhattisgarhi religious thought, especially in conceptions of witchcraft, and we shall encounter it again in later chapters.

Despite the purifications that occur after parturition, a residum of birth-pollution continues to adhere to the child. Hair, as I have already noted, absorbs pollution, and at times of birth and death close agnates shave as a way of ridding themselves of birth and death pollution. In the same fashion it is common for the hair of children to be shaved off at some

Mundan: A child's first haircut at the Rajim mela.

point during the early years to remove the final vestiges of
birth pollution. This rite, known as *mundan*, is optional, but
it is very common. The time at which it is done varies with
caste and family custom. It is sometimes done during the
first year of life, sometimes later. The rite is usually performed
on some festival occasion, one of the most popular times being
the full moon day of the lunar month of *magh* (January–
February). It is often done at the site of one of the many religious
fairs that occur on this date. When performed at a temple the
rite appears to have votive overtones. The child is shaved
completely by a barber. The hairs are either rolled up in a

ball of the dough of unrefined wheat flour (*ata*) and placed in a river, or they are saved until it is convenient to do so.

Later Changes of Status

For those of less than twice-born status, the years before marriage are not divided by elaborate rituals marking changes of status. Such individuals are, in effect, fully formed as persons in the ritual sense from early childhood. However, this is not the case for boys belonging to the twice-born castes.[1] The designation "twice-born" (*dvija*) may be taken for precisely what it says; male members of these castes are born twice, once at the time of physical birth, and once ritually when they are invested with the *janeu* (sacred thread) in a ceremony known as *upanayana* (initiation). The sacred thread, which is worn looped over the left shoulder and right hip, symbolizes a pride and a burden. Those who are entitled to wear the sacred thread are granted a clear superiority over the general run of men, but this superiority exacts a price, namely the tedium and inconveniences of adhering to the rules of purity which are incumbent on those of twice-born status who have undergone initiation. Those who take the sacred thread are, at least in theory, obligated to shape their lives in accordance with these rules.

The ritual preconditions of twice-born life are quite complex and have been described in considerable detail elsewhere (see, for example, Harper 1964 and Carstairs 1961). For present purposes it is enough to note that life for the twice-born is filled with traps and hurdles that would be of little concern to those of lower status. For those who take the matter seriously (and some do not), wearing the sacred thread carries the obligation to avoid contact with polluting substances, things, and people and to effect self-purification whenever such contact cannot be avoided. There is variation in the stringency with

[1] For a more detailed discussion of the life cycle ceremonies of the twice-born see Stevenson 1920.

which these rules apply. The rigor appears to be least in the case of the Kshatriyas, for whom vegetarianism is not an obligation. But generally rules of personal purity are an important aspect of twice-born status, and their observance gives twice-born life a dimension of structure and regulation not seen among lower castes. Much of this is regarded as an unjustifiable inconvenience by younger informants, and it has become increasingly common for the thread-tying ceremony to be forgone until just before marriage. It must be said too that the sacred thread has become a somewhat debased emblem, at least by traditional standards. Members of lower castes have taken to wearing the sacred thread, and at present the sacred thread by itself is no sure sign of twice-born status.

Nevertheless, the investiture of the sacred thread, the "second birth," remains an important sacrament for the twice-born in Chhattisgarh. The age at which the ceremony takes place varies, the only requirement being that it must take place before marriage. The rite should be overseen by a Brahman priest, and contains essentially two elements. One is the investiture of the sacred thread itself, the outward symbol of the boy's new status. Once in place the sacred thread must be assiduously protected from impurity. For example, it must be looped over the wearer's right ear during urination or defecation. The second element of the ceremony is the symbolic beginning of the boy's education in sacred scripture which, in classical ideology, could only begin with the investiture of the sacred thread. The officiating priest becomes the boy's *guru* (religious teacher in the traditional sense) and instructs him in the *gayatri mantra*. I am told that it is taught "in a different form" to Brahmans, Kshatriyas, and Vaishyas. Having been invested with the sacred thread and heard the *mantra*, the boy is now complete as a twice-born man. According to the theory underlying the ritual, he now enters a phase of celibate studentship (*brahmacharya*), which will end with his marriage.

The second birth of the twice-born is somewhat weakly reflected in a rite in which persons (men and women) of less than twice-born status are initiated by a *guru*. The initiate is taught a supposedly secret *mantra* by his or her mentor, who may be a Brahman priest but is more commonly a Bairagi. The Bairagis are a caste of quasi-mendicants and minor religious functionaries. Their main role seems to be that of cooks in intercaste dining situations. The initiation apparently usually takes place during the initiate's teen-age years. The initiate is often given a necklace made from beads of the *tulsi* plant (the *tulsi mala*) in what is possibly an imitation of the investiture of the sacred thread. There are no Bairagis resident in Sitapur, but two Bairagi brothers live in the nearby village of Tulsi, and these serve as *gurus* for the people of Sitapur. Ideally, specific families of *gurus* will be linked with specific families of initiates for generations. After initiation the *guru* is said to be "like a father" to the initiate, and the initiate must shave in the event of his *guru*'s death. Informants were unable to specify any special privileges resulting from initiation by a *guru*. It seems clear that this initiation is less important than the investiture of the sacred thread among the twice-born, and in many instances it is omitted altogether.

The question of when girls achieve ritual adulthood is somewhat complex. Marriage frequently occurs before puberty, although in such cases cohabitation is delayed until the girl is physically grown. To my knowledge there is no puberty rite, as such, for girls. When asked about this a Pandit once told me that celebrating the puberty of a girl would be illogical because "in old times she would no longer belong to her father's house"—she would already have been married. Suffice it to say that the real watersheds in a girl's life occur at the times of her first menses and at her marriage in whichever order they occur.

With her first menstrual period a girl becomes subject to certain ritual proscriptions from which she is freed only by pregnancy and, ultimately, menopause. Women are regarded as highly polluted during their menses. They should not enter temples at this time, should not approach their household deities, and in most castes are required to stay away from the kitchen. Caste and family custom may dictate additional forms of seclusion. Women bathe at the conclusion of their menstrual periods and with this become functioning members of their households and society once more. The fact that women are subject to ritual seclusion during their menstrual periods, and the consequent implications of feminine pollution, are consistent with the more or less general tendency for the woman's role to be regarded as distinctly subordinate. Women may eat the leavings from the plates of their husbands, and indeed are required to worship their husbands as deities on certain cere-monial occasions (below, ch. 5).

Marriage

It would be highly misleading to state that there is a particular marriage rite in Chhattisgarh. In fact in most cases there is an elaborate sequence of rituals leading to the married state, and the nature of this sequence varies greatly with caste and family circumstances. Accordingly, I shall not attempt here to provide a comprehensive description of the marriage cycle, which in any event could itself provide the substance of a monograph. What follows, rather, is a summary description of some of the major features of the purely ritual aspect of marriage as it is seen in Chhattisgarh. I have omitted a discus-sion of the complex and in some cases variable conventions of gift-giving. I have also generalized across caste lines, but have indicated the main areas of variation.

The principal rules governing the selection of marriage part-ners in Northern and Central India (clan and village exogamy; *jati* endogamy; a general tendency to strive for genealogical and spatial distance in establishing new affinal ties) are well-known and need not detain us here. Likewise, the typical selection process has been well-described elsewhere (see Mayer 1960:202–13). Among lower Chhattisgarhi castes it is the bride, not the groom, who is sought, and accordingly it is the groom's father who typically initiates the search and proposes the match. The reverse obtains among higher castes. After the proposal there is a period of mutual examination between the two families. In higher castes this includes matching of horoscopes. The final settlement of the marriage usually hinges on a satisfactory financial arrangement between the two fathers. Among the upper castes this is a matter of dowry; among the lower castes a matter of brideprice. Although the observer is sometimes told that the brideprice system is on its way out, in fact it seems to be practically the norm in rural Chhattisgarh. The sums involved can be quite substantial, often in the hundreds of rupees, and clearly play an important role in easing the financial burden of the bride's father, who bears the main expense of the marriage ceremony itself.

The time of the marriage[2] is usually fixed by the family of the bride. This may or may not be done in consultation with a priest; if it is, the time is based on astrological calculations. Before the actual marriage ceremony takes place there are certain preliminary ceremonies in the homes of the bride (*dulhin*) and the groom (*dulha*). There are great differences among families and castes, however, both with regard to the nature of these preliminary ceremonies and the degree of elaboration with which they are undertaken.

Before almost all marriages a pavilion known as *mandap* or *mandva* is erected in the house of the bride. In most marriages a similar structure is installed at the groom's house as well. These pavilions constitute the physical locales of the preliminary

---

[2] This description applies to primary marriages (*vivah*). In Chhattisgarh there is also a secondary form of marriage known as *churi pahanana* ("putting on the bangle"). This highly abbreviated ceremony is used for the remarriage of widows and divorced women. While unknown among the higher castes, divorce is quite common among the middle and lower ranking castes of the region.

ceremonies. The marriage ceremony itself will take place in the bride's pavilion. The focal object within each pavilion is a wooden stake known as *mangrohan*. According to one informant, this stake is "the god of the wedding." Also, at some point during these preliminaries, offerings are made to the goddess in a local shrine or temple.

During this initial period it is the custom among most castes for the women of both houses to undertake a ritual gathering of earth to be used in the ceremonies connected with the marriage. Details vary, but usually the women of the household move in procession to a spot outside the village, usually near a temple or a pipal tree, where they offer *puja* to *dharti mata* (mother earth) and collect a small amount of soil. The soil is placed in the loose end of the sari of the mother of the bride or groom and is taken back to the house, while a larger amount is brought in a separate container. The soil is used for the construction of the marriage altar and a special stove, which is employed for the preparation of food to be consumed during the festivities. I am told that small amounts of it may also be mixed with the oil and turmeric with which the bride and groom will be anointed.

Usually the bride and groom undergo a series of anointings with a mixture of oil and turmeric before the marriage, a sequence known as *tel charhana*. Details differ, but the ceremony in some form or another seems to be universal. In some cases it is quite perfunctory, but it is often done in a sequence of three or, less commonly, five days. The anointing is done by the female relatives of the bride and groom. Beforehand they anoint the image of the village goddess, then the bride or groom. Sometimes a *kalash* is also anointed.

Two ideas appear to mingle in this operation. Informants state that the purpose of the oil and turmeric application is to beautify, to make the skin lighter or "more shining." But it must be noted too that the anointing constitutes a treatment that would be appropriate for the image of a deity, and the preliminary anointing of the goddess and the *kalash* suggests even more strongly that this ritual sequence falls within the paradigm of acts of worship, and that the bride and groom are being treated as goddess and god. In fact, from this point forward, the bride and the groom are treated quite literally as deities, as objects of worship in their own right. In the ritual sense the marriage represents the high point in both of their lives (however ephemeral the marriage might actually turn out to be) and this is expressed in their treatment as living manifestations of divinity.

However, although they are god and goddess within the context of the marriage, they are at this time particularly vulnerable to malevolent beings and the machinations of witches. As is the case with children, this notion would appear to be linked with ideas of beauty and desirability and an attendant notion of jealousy. This is a time of great fulfillment for the marriage partners and, at least theoretically, they are at the height of their physical beauty. Therefore, they must be protected. During the period of the preliminary ceremonies they should be confined to the household except for calls of nature. It is particularly important that their bodies not be exposed to the gaze of unknown persons, especially unknown women, who might be witches. A tall pole to which two bundles of grass have been tied is erected in front of each house. They serve as an emblem of the matrimonial activities taking place within, and also function "like a *taviz*" to protect the house from witchcraft and other potential dangers.

The anointing with oil and turmeric usually takes place in the houses of the bride and the groom. In most cases, however, the actual marriage rites take place in the bride's home. In rural areas the bride would necessarily be from another village, and even in urban areas, where the groom would not need to travel far, the symbolic treatment of him is based on the assumption that he will travel to a distant place. The sequence of events leading up to his departure varies considerably between families and castes, but certain elements are almost always present. At some point before the departure, an elaborate dinner will be held for relatives and friends. At some point there is usually a *puja* of the groom's ancestors. *Puja* of Gauri-Ganesh (the god Ganesh and his mother, Parvati) is also performed, a necessity before beginning an important enterprise. Just before his departure the groom receives a special bath. He is then dressed in fine clothes. The women of his family apply *tilaks* to his forehead and touch his feet, at which point the wedding party (*barat*) can leave.

The composition of the groom's wedding party is variable. It should include the groom's father (who may be replaced by an elder brother or other agnate if the father is not living) and close male relatives, ideally including a paternal uncle, a maternal uncle, and, if possible, a sister's husband. The sister's husband plays a role of special importance in the events to follow, as he is regarded as the groom's special confidant, guardian, and mentor. In some instances women accompany the wedding party. A barber is sometimes included as general factotum, and, in the case of the higher castes and the well-to-do, a Brahman priest. The party leaves the groom's village with great fanfare, often accompanied by a village-style band.

Marriage lore portrays the groom as a handsome prince who steals the bride away from her natal family. In accordance with this fantasy, an effort is sometimes made to mount the groom on horseback for at least a token part of the journey. The bulk of the trip, however, is by whatever means of transportation is most convenient: train, bus, or bullock cart. The groom is thought to be quite vulnerable to agencies of harm during the trip and steps should be taken to protect him. He should be wary of the attention of unknown persons. Iron has the capacity to ward off dangers of this kind, so it is kept on his person, usually in the form of a knife. In one wedding in which I participated a small boy was hired to stay near the groom to absorb any evil influences that might have been cast in his direction.

The departure and movement of the groom's party is usually timed to ensure its arrival at the bride's village in the evening. In urban areas the precise nature of these arrangements is determined by the particular circumstances that obtain in each case. In all cases, however, an elaborate reception is arranged for the groom's party. In villages the groom's people (*baratis*) are met by the bride's people (*gharatis*) at the outskirts of the village. A village-style band is usually present at the reception, and sometimes a party of dancers. In the city, western-style bands are more common. The two groups greet each other formally, embracing and reciprocally applying *tilaks* to each others' foreheads. Then members of the groom's party are conducted into the village to their place of lodging. Here the bride's people wash the feet of the groom and his party, and refreshments are provided.

At some point during the period following the reception, the groom customarily enters the bride's house to pay respects to her family. Also, during this initial sequence it is customary for an exhibition of "joking" (*majak*) behavior to take place. Usually the bride's younger sisters tease the groom. They attempt to feed him certain inedible items (perhaps uncooked leaves or cakes of cowdung), which he refuses to take. They insist that he eat, but he continues to refuse, finally getting off the hook by offering money to the girls. A good deal of off-color joking accompanies this horseplay.

The rite that seals the marriage is known as *phera* or *bhavar* and consists of several circumambulations of the marriage pavilion by the couple. Informants state that without this rite there is no marriage; with it, the marriage is complete, even though additional rituals may follow. It is often carried out on the day following the groom's reception. In some cases, however, there is a lapse of a day or two during which additional ceremonies take place. Before the *phera* the bride is given a special bath. She is then presented with ornaments, brought by the groom's party, which she will wear during the final ceremony. She puts on these ornaments and her other wedding finery. In the meantime the groom has been called from his place of lodging. He too is wearing his wedding clothes and special headgear that conceals his face. When he arrives at the wedding pavilion the bride's mother and other female relatives greet him formally. Usually they perform *artis* before him. If a Brahman priest is present he formally purifies the groom by sprinkling him with water. In some cases the groom performs *puja* of Dulha Dev (the "Bridegroom God"). The bride, whose face is also veiled, is then joined by the groom and the final phases of the ceremony can now go forward.

The nature of the ritual surrounding *phera* itself varies greatly among castes and even among families within a given caste. The rites may be relatively simple, performed and supervised by the principals themselves, or they may be highly elaborated and conducted and supervised by a Brahman priest. Most marriages in rural Chhattisgarh are of the simple variety, performed without the assistance of a Brahman. For the twice-born, however, a Brahman is considered a necessity. It is my impression that it is considerably more common for Brahmans to preside over the weddings of the non-twice-born in urban areas than in rural areas. Informants cite cost as the main reason for not engaging a Brahman, though in the case of the untouchable castes Brahmans would certainly not officiate.

When done in the simpler fashion the circumambulations occur with very little additional ceremonial elaboration. Before the ceremony a white square (*chauk*), perhaps a yard on a side, has been drawn on the floor under the marriage pavilion. Inside the square is a *kalash* with a flame burning in a lamp on top, and other ritual devices. The clothes of the bride and groom are tied together, and after this is done the pair then slowly walks around the square. Seven circuits seems to be the rule, though I am told this can vary. A flat grinding stone (*sil*) is usually placed nearby with seven little heaps of rice mixed with turmeric on top. After each circuit of the square the groom touches the bride's leg, at which point she sweeps away one of the piles with her foot. They both take very small steps and they both keep their faces

Phera: Bride and groom circumambulate the marriage pavilion.

modestly (and protectively) downward. With the final circuit the marriage is essentially complete, though certain formalities remain.

If a Brahman is presiding the ceremony will be conducted in more precise accord with textual formulas, and is therefore a good deal more complex and lengthy. Under the priest's direction the father of the bride makes a formal declaration of intention (*sankalp*) to marry his daughter. A formal *puja* of Ganesh is performed, along with *pujas* of the nine planets, the ten guardians of the directions, and the sixty-four *matrikas* (mothers, goddesses). The parents of the girl present the bride to the groom in a formal sequence known as *kanyadan* (the gift of the virgin). A *homa* will be performed. After the seven circuits there will be additional *pujas*.

In both simple and formal marriages the bride and groom sit together after the circuits. Previously the bride has been to the groom's right; now she is seated at his left hand. The mother and father of the bride approach the couple, wash their feet, and apply *tilaks* of rice and turmeric to their foreheads. Other relatives and guests may do the same. These acts are, of course, within the paradigm of worship; bride and groom are being treated in the most overt fashion as deities. If there is a Brahman priest in attendance he is given his payment (*dakshina*); he then gives final blessing to the couple, and the ceremony is finished.

In most castes a *puja* of the family gods follows the marriage ceremony. Among some castes the participants in the wedding engage in a form of horseplay with turmeric, and sometimes colored water, which closely resembles the play associated with the festival of *holi* (ch. 5). In addition, there is usually an elaborate feast following the marriage rites, the scale of which is determined by the wealth, standing, and caste-status of the bride's father. In Sitapur it would be expected that a well-to-do Kurmi would invite the entire village, excluding only the untouchable castes, in addition to his own relatives. In an urban setting the guests would typically be more varied, including schoolmates, workmates, colleagues, and various friends of the principals. The groom is supposed to be the first to partake of the food, and generally the bride is expected to eat from his plate.

The newly married pair usually leave for the groom's house on the day following the wedding, but it is regarded as incautious to make this journey on Tuesday, Saturday, or new moon day (*amavashya*). The bride may be accompanied by her brothers or other agnates. When they arrive the couple performs a *puja* of the family gods of the groom, and *tilaks* are applied to their foreheads. If the bride and groom are old enough, the marriage is consummated immediately. Otherwise—and this is commonly the case in rural areas—the initial visit to the groom's home is for ceremonial purposes only, and is of relatively short duration. The bride is then returned to her natal household until she is old enough for cohabitation. The time at which the bride is finally taken from her home to live with her husband is marked by a ceremony known as *gauna*. The time of its occurrence depends, of course, on the age of the bride at marriage. Even after she finally moves to her husband's home the bride's ties with her natal family are not regarded as completely broken. She usually makes frequent visits to her father's home during the early years of marriage, and she is expected to do so during the festival of *tija* (ch. 5). At least in popular imagination she continues to maintain an affectionate relationship with her brothers who, in turn, are obligated to protect her and are seen as her last refuge in the event of trouble with her husband or his family. Nevertheless, the ties between a girl and her family of birth are greatly attenuated by marriage. As elsewhere in India, it is a truism of Chhattisgarhi life that, in contrast to sons, the daughters of a house ultimately must belong to others.

Death

Birth and marriage are times of danger, times when the central figures are thought to be highly vulnerable to malevolent powers. As a result, they are occasions when the central figures—the newborn child and the bride and groom—must be protected. Death is also a time of danger, but death, by contrast, is a time when the central figure, the deceased, becomes a source of danger to others. It is this fact which gives the mortuary rites of Chhattisgarh their distinctive characteristics.

Broadly speaking, a death presents the living with two crucial problems—intense pollution and a potentially malevolent ghost. The pollution of death is of far greater intensity than that of birth. It is, indeed, a more intense pollution, with more far-reaching effects, than that of any other event in Hindu life. Because of its strength the close kin of the deceased find themselves in what can only be described as a situation of ritual crisis. They are polluted by the death of their kinsman, and are as a result cut off from normal social intercourse with those outside the family. At the same time they are cut off from normal dealings with the gods. They should not approach the gods, and in many families the family gods are removed from the house as soon as possible after the death and are not returned until the mortuary rites are completed. The pollution of death, in sum, results in a radical change in the status of the family with respect to society and the divine world. The rites of the dead consist in large measure of an attempt to deal with this pollution, and, ultimately, to normalize the status of the family.

However, the pollution occasioned by death is not the only thing with which the survivors must contend. As we shall see, death places a heavy obligation on the kin of the deceased to cut his spirit free from this world and to see it safely and comfortably on to the next. Not to do so is to run the risk of incurring the wrath of the potentially malevolent ghost of the deceased. This obligation augments the problem of pollution. The spirit of the deceased must be aided by a series of offerings. These offerings, and the accompanying rites, necessitate prolonged contact with the spirit of the deceased, and a prolonged state of pollution is the result. In this way the twin themes of pollution and danger from the unsatisfied ghost are tightly interwoven in the rites of death.

Popular conceptions of the fate of the spirit (*jiv*) after death are generally quite vague in Chhattisgarh. Upon inquiry one is usually told that a person is rewarded or punished in another existence in accordance with his or her *karm*, or deeds in the present life. The standard against which conduct is ultimately measured is *dharm*, norms of proper behavior, a concept that embraces all aspects of social and ritual obligation and proscription. Notions of what form rewards or punishments take are generally ill-formed, and are sometimes contradictory. Some say that evil deeds (*pap*) are punished in hell (*narak*). Others say that the dead are punished by rebirth in one of the more loathsome of the 8.4 million possible reincarnations. To be reincarnated as a leech or as a worm in the stomach of a dog are cited as possible punishments. But there is wide agreement that the consequences of evil deeds can be arrested or circumvented, primarily by ritual means. The accumulation of merit (*punya*) in this life will be rewarded in another—either by rebirth in an advantageous situation in this world or by rebirth in heaven (*swarg*), where one may exist until the accumulated merit has drained away. Good deeds produce merit, but of all good deeds the most potent are ritual acts: keeping fasts, regular worship of deities, and, above all, acts of charity—especially giving to Brahmans or wandering mendicants.

Notions of the reward or punishment of deeds in this life according to their moral or ritual character exist, then, in Chhattisgarhi religious thought. However, these matters are of only marginal concern in the rites of death. Rather, at the time of death the most important consideration is a form of ghostly existence (the *pret-yoni*), which lies just beyond death's door for every individual. For suicides this state is regarded as permanent; for others, it is normally a passing phase. The essential idea is that death does not immediately propel the spirit from the world, but rather consigns it to a threshhold existence, half in and half out of the world, a state of existence in which the spirit is a burden to itself and, because of its envy, a menace to the living. The spirit in this form is a "ghost" (*pret*), and it must remain in this form until it is transformed by ritual means into an ancestral spirit (*pitri*). This marginal state of the deceased is the crux of the matter in the rites of death, not the prospect of ultimate reward or punishment, and much of the ritual may be seen as an effort to loosen the ties that still hold the ghost of the deceased to this world both in the interest of the soul's well-being and the safety of the living.

The manner in which funerary rites are conducted is, as in the case of other rites of the life-cycle, subject to great variation in Chhattisgarh. Different castes have different customs. Financial considerations also play a role in determining the elaborateness of the ceremonies. The major distinction is between those who burn and those who bury their dead. In general lower castes tend toward burial while upper castes almost always favor cremation. Burning is expensive, which likely inhibits some from burning their dead. Children are usually buried, even among castes where cremation is required for adults. Despite the great variation, however, the themes that underlie the rites of death are essentially the same in all castes.

The most elaborate funerary sequence involves cremation. It is regarded as vital that the corpse be burned as quickly as possible after death—easily understandable in view of the nature of the Indian climate. The governing rule is that the corpse should be burned before sundown on the day of death, though exceptions sometimes occur. The corpse is washed and wrapped in cloth, white for men and red for women. It is placed on a stretcher to be carried to the burning grounds (*marghat*). It is carried there by men, usually kin but sometimes friends, who move as quickly as they can. As they move they shout: "Rama's name is truth; such is the fate of all men." The place of burning is usually near a river, where the ashes may be submerged after the incineration of the body. A Brahman priest might or might not officiate at the cremation. The corpse is placed within a pyre of wood with its feet pointing south, in the direction of the realm of Yama, the god of death. *Ghi* is sprinkled on the pyre and it is then ignited by the chief mourner—ideally the eldest son of the deceased, otherwise a brother or other relative. The men then go to the river (or tank as the case may be) for a bath before returning home. This is the first of a sequence of ablutions required during the period of mourning.

The period of mourning begins at the moment of death. From this day until the tenth day after death (among most castes) the close agnates of the deceased are in a state of deep pollution. Food touched by their hands would not be accepted by others, nor would it be offered. They subsist on the simplest types of food and do not shave during the ensuing period of mourning. In many cases the family deities are removed from the household as quickly as possible. The house itself is deeply polluted, and is not a fit habitation for the gods. Thus, from the moment of death the members of the family of the deceased are cut off from their fellow men and from the gods.

The mourners usually return to the burning ground to collect the remains on the third day. A number of things might be done at this point depending on caste custom and family preference. The bones and ash might be "cooled" (*thanda karna*) by disposing of them in the river at this time. Alternatively the ash might be disposed of at this point and the bones saved for disposal by immersion at some later time. In all cases, however, the bones are ultimately disposed of by immersion in water, either in a nearby stream, in the Mahanadi (preferably at Rajim), or, if the family of the deceased has the means, in the Ganges at Allahabad. This should be done as quickly as possible.

Once submerged in water the bones and ash are understood to have been "cooled," and the use of this idiom of temperature links at least one element of the funeral rites to an idea of far broader application in Chhattisgarhi religion. "Cooling" by immersion in water is an extremely important manipulation in Chhattisgarhi ritual, occurring as a terminal act in a great variety of very different rites. As we shall see in later chapters, it is an important element in rites involving possession. In these rites the deities are understood to have entered the bodies of certain of their worshippers. In so doing they have, in effect, crossed the barrier that separates the world of direct experience from the world of the gods, and are tangibly present at the site of the ritual. The stereotyped manifestations of possession usually become most pronounced during a procession in which the images of the deities and other ritual paraphernalia are taken to a body of water. The images and other materials are at last "cooled" in the water, and as this is done the deities become quiescent and withdraw from the bodies of the devotees, just as the images have been physically withdrawn from the site of the worship and submerged in the water. The same idea of withdrawal is suggested in the "cooling" of the bones of the dead in mortuary rites. As the bones are immersed the last physical vestiges of the dead vanish, and, with this, the final link with the world of the living is broken. The spirit has now, it is hoped, crossed the barrier that separates the living from the dead, and that separates man from the gods (which, in effect, the dead will be when they become *pitris*), and has gone on to meet whatever fate awaits it.

If the deceased is a married man his widow breaks her bangles, removes her ornaments, and the *sindur* mark in the part of her hair (a sign of the married state)—acts that signify her widowhood. Usually the men and women of the house come out from the house each day during the mourning period for a bath in a nearby tank or river, each group walking single file. There is a good deal of variation in details, but in many castes it is the custom for special offerings known as *pinda dan* (the gift of *pindas*) to be presented to the spirit of the deceased. This is invariably done by the twice-born, and appears to be common among other castes. These offerings consist of specially prepared balls (the *pindas*) made from rice or coarse wheat flour (*ata*). The *pindas* should be offered daily from the third day after the cremation to the tenth day. The ceremony should be performed by the chief mourner, preferably in a spot beneath a pipal tree. After being offered, the *pindas* are either fed to a cow or the crows, or are disposed of by immersion. *Pinda dan* bears a superficial similarity to the food offerings of *puja*, but in fact these are not food offerings in the same sense at all. Rather, the *pinda* is directly identified with the deceased. One informant explained that the purpose of the *pinda* is not really to feed the spirit of the departed in the strictest sense, but rather to provide the spirit with a material vehicle by means of which it can escape the ties that bind it to this world. Each of the *pindas*, my informant went on to say, represents a portion of the spirit's new "body." In this new envelope the spirit can journey on to the realm of Yama, and from there to wherever it is destined finally to go. Were the *pindas* not offered, the spirit would remain a troublesome ghost.

On the final day of mourning, which is usually (though not always) the tenth day for deceased men, close agnates of the deceased are shaved. The chief mourner must have his head shaved. Others need only a trim or a token touch of the razor, particularly if they are older than the deceased. Relatives other than close agnates are not required to have this done, but those who attend the rites will at least accept a touch of the razor as a courtesy. The cutting of hair signifies the removal of pollution. The house of the deceased must be cleaned and purified, and the family's clothing and other cloth articles should be sent to the washerman. Unglazed clay pots should be thrown away and new ones purchased. It is not necessary for nonresident agnates of the deceased to purify their houses but, at least in some castes, they should send their clothing to the washerman and throw away their clay pots. With these acts the removal of death pollution is virtually complete, although additional purifications may take place. After final purification the household deities may be brought back into the house.

In some instances the final day of mourning is marked by a ritual in which offerings are given to a special funerary priest known as the Mahabrahman (Great Brahman). The Mahabrahman is despised as an inferior sort of priest by the ordinary Brahman priests, but informants insist that during the funerary rites he is the "greatest priest." I have not witnessed this rite, but from informants' accounts it is clear that it is a procedure that elaborates the theme of "giving substance," which I have already discussed in connection with the giving of *pindas*. He is presented with a quantity of *khir* (boiled rice and milk), which is sometimes spread in the shape of a human figure on a brass platter. This is then eaten by the Mahabrahman, who starts at the feet and ends up at the head. As he eats the *khir* he cries out from time to time that he cannot continue, that the *khir* has changed to blood. At each interruption the family of the deceased must give him some money to induce him to continue. The entire performance is suggestive of deep pollution, which accounts for the low status of the Mahabrahman in all contexts but that of the funeral. It is said that in eating the *khir* the Mahabrahman is removing the last traces of the deceased from this world and is providing him with substance for a body in the next—the same notion that underlies the offering of *pinda*. In addition, the Mahabrahman is sometimes given material gifts—money, clothing, furniture, and the like—which are said to be for the use of the departed spirit.

Purification of house and family having been effected, and the spirit of the deceased having joined the ancestral spirits, the final phases of the rites of death deal with normalization of relationships within the family and between the family and the rest of the world. If the deceased is a male the chief mourner will be invested with a turban in a rite known as *pagbandhi*. This signifies that he assumes the position of the deceased as head of the family. The funerary sequence culminates in a feast, often given on the thirteenth day, which symbolizes the normalization of the family's relationship with the larger social order. Only in the absence of the pollution can hospitality be extended and accepted. The scale of the funeral feast varies widely according to the caste, financial resources, and prominence of the deceased and his family. Ordinarily the feast is attended by relatives, local caste-mates, friends, and neighbors, but a feast for an important or wealthy man is likely to be much larger. It is also considered especially meritorious to feed Brahmans (the ideal number is thirteen) on the thirteenth day. Since these concluding sequences involve the distribution of food they constitute an affirmation by the recipients of the return of the family of the deceased to a condition of normality and, with this, a return to their normal place in society. The deceased, however, is not forgotten. Among higher castes there are additional offerings, which must be made during the year following the death, and among all castes the deceased, along with the other ancestors in the patriline, is worshipped by the head of the family during the fortnight of *pitar pak* each year. At the conclusion of the fortnight of ancestor worship the head of the family must shave, a repetition of earlier acts of purification.

Conclusion

The life cycle of the individual is characterized by a swing between episodes of pollution. Childbirth results in a state of pollution that is contagious within the household and that adheres to the child. The early ceremonial of the life cycle may be seen, in part, as an amelioration in successive states of the residual pollution of birth. For most people the process ends early in childhood. However, for males of the twice-born castes the process is not culminated until the investiture of the sacred thread. Having received the sacred thread, the twice-born male has attained his full status as a member of his caste, and is subject to all of the restrictions with respect to pollution that this status entails.

It may be said that in a ritual sense the life cycle of the individual, male or female, reaches its highest point with marriage. The preliminary phases of life have passed, and the individual's social personality is, with marriage, fully formed. The ceremonies of marriage provide a ritual setting in which the bride and the groom are raised to a truly exalted status. During this single brief interlude the bride and the groom are treated as if they were living images of deities; they become, in effect, god and goddess.

In death, as in birth, pollution is released, but the pollution of death far surpasses birth pollution in intensity. Both occasions seem to have one thing in common—that the individual undergoes a truly radical change of status, from one mode of existence to another. In birth the human spirit is joined to substance; in death it withdraws from it. Seemingly the union and separation of substance and spirit both entail pollution. This represents a curious reversal of a far more general pattern in which the union of divinity and substance occurs in a setting of heightened purity, that of *puja*. It is the context of *puja* within which men normally deal with divinity, and in this setting divinity intrudes momentarily into the experienced world to receive the attentions and offerings of the worshippers, or even to possess them. At the conclusion of the ritual the deity departs, and with this the paraphernalia of worship are "cooled." Likewise, during the course of funerary rites the spirit of the deceased withdraws from the sensible world. The remains are then "cooled," in significant contrast to the efforts that are often made to keep the mother and newborn child warm at the time of birth. The homology between the patterns of cooling in ordinary *pujas* and funerary rites suggests an identification between divinity and the animating spirit of man. They are the same to the degree that both are manifest as heat when they penetrate the world of experience and assume substantial form: the heat of the altar and the warmth of life. This is an identification of some importance, and will be discussed again later. However, there remains one important difference: when the human spirit enters the world in birth, and leaves it in death, pollution is produced; the gods, by contrast, join and leave substance in an artificial setting that is made especially pure.

The difference is more apparent than real. As we have seen, the idiom of "respect pollution" is central to *puja*; the worshipper accepts pollution from the deity as an expression of hierarchical distance between the deity and himself. What is a form of pollution in relation to the deity retains the implication of pollution only within the relationship between the deity and the worshipper; from the standpoint of the worshipper's relations with his fellow human beings, acceptance of the *jutha* of the deity is not demeaning.[3] The implication

---

[3] It should be added that under certain circumstances acceptance of *prasad* is indeed demeaning. A Brahman, for example, cannot accept the *prasad* of the deities of the lower castes.

of *puja*, in sum, is that the purity of the gods is so great, in relation to the orders of this world, that what is pollution in relation to the deity is innocuous or even pure in relation to what is pure and what is not in humanity. Likewise, there is a sense in which certain ritual sequences may be seen as the acceptance of a form of "respect" pollution, which is analogous to death pollution. In *javara*, a ritual devoted to the goddess (described in detail below), the focus of worship consists of wheat seedlings. The goddess is present in these for the duration of the ritual; she departs when they are "cooled" by immersion at the end. Once cooled, the seedlings are distributed to the participants, who place a few strands over each others' ears as a sign of amity. The parallel seems clear: with the cooling of the seedlings divine spirit has left substance, and there is accordingly a valid sense in which the participants accept and exchange the "corpse" of the goddess, again an exemplification of "respect pollution." Because it is the "corpse" of a deity, however, this pollution is innocuous to men. Not so in the case of a human corpse. The deceased was human, not divine, and the survivors are not protected from the implications of the resulting pollution by the vast hierarchical gulf that separates men from the gods. Thus, the pollution of death becomes a central problem with which the funerary sequences must deal. The same principle would apply in the contrast between the purity that surrounds the "birth" of a deity (in the form of a *kalash*, or whatever) at the beginning of a ritual event and the pollution occasioned by the birth of a human being. In this fashion the rites of the life cycle are linked to a conceptual order of broad import in Chhattisgarhi religious culture.

Pollution, however, is not the only area of convergence between the rites of the life cycle and more general considerations. As we have seen, the other crucial theme in these rites is that of vulnerability—especially vulnerability to malevolent powers and beings. In birth and marriage the central figures, the newborn (and mother) and the about-to-be-married, are in a state of danger, and ritual precautions and protections are necessary. In death the deceased becomes acutely dangerous to others, and the funerary rites may, in part, be interpreted as efforts to cut altogether the links that hold the spirit of the deceased to the world in which he lived so that he will not become a malevolent ghost.

Envy seems to be involved in these dangers. In the case of the dead, it is the envy of the spirit of the deceased, half in and half out of the world, for the living. In the case of childbirth and marriage the roots and qualities of jealousy have a different character. Here the unifying strand seems to be the sense of fulfillment that surrounds these occasions, especially from a feminine point of view. The child is ardently desired, treasured by the family, and represents the very centerpiece of the mother's identification as a complete woman. In marriage the beauty and desirability of the bride and groom are at their peak, and their good fortune is made conspicuous by the festivities of marriage. As a result they should be concealed as much as possible from the jealous eyes of outsiders. Marriage is fulfilling for both parties, marking the entrance into a crucial phase of life. But this is especially so for women, for only in marriage can the ideals of motherhood, to which feminine identification is so firmly fixed, be actualized. Children and marriage, in sum, represent occasions lying close to the heart of conceptions of legitimate channels for the realization of feminine ideals. The sorrow of the unmarried or childless woman is too familiar a theme of Indian life to require elaboration here. In subsequent chapters we shall see that these aspects of the notion of danger in childhood and marriage are consistent with a link between the idea of the feminine and malevolence, which is quite widespread in Chhattisgarhi religious culture. It is present in the seasonal ritual cycle, in the structure of the pantheon, and in popular conceptions of the very witchcraft from which children must be so assiduously protected.

4
Days and Weeks

I shall now focus on patterns of ceremonial activity organized within temporal frameworks that are universal in application and that coordinate ceremonial activity throughout Chhattisgarhi society. The day, the week, the month, and the year are all involved, and I shall move in progression from smaller to larger units.

The Daily Cycle

While Chhattisgarhi ceremonial cycles provide an array of possibilities for ritual action, the extent to which these possibilities are realized is highly variable, depending in part upon the inclinations of individuals, and in part on caste and family custom. This variability is nowhere more evident than in the matter of daily ritual observance. For some the day is richly overlaid with ceremony; for others there is little if any formal ritual. For almost everyone, however, there is at least some ritualization of daily life, especially in the area of body cleanliness and the preparation and consumption of food.

A pious man should rise before sunrise. He should meditate on the qualities of his chosen personal deity (*ishta devta*) and should bathe and perform *pujas* before taking his morning meal. *Pujas* and meditations should play an important role in the remainder of his day. Obviously, however, for most people the requirements of workaday life do not permit the realization of this ideal pattern; indeed, most people are not pious enough in temperament to subordinate their lives to religious considerations to this degree. Few individuals engage regularly and seriously in these devotional patterns apart from certain priests, mendicants, and those relatively rare individuals, mostly elderly, who seek salvation in the classical sense. For most people the ritualization of daily life is found on an entirely different plane, being in large measure tied to the routines of bathing and eating.

Bathing is not just a matter of personal physical cleanliness. It is also a ritual act with a significance that must be understood in relation to the idea of pollution. We have seen that purity is an ephemeral state, a condition constantly threatened by the intrusion of aspects of life that would destroy it. The most basic biological processes of life are polluting, and thus purity is always exposed to pollution. Accordingly, Hindu life requires continual adjustment to the realities of pollution; bathing is a key part of this adjustment. One should always bathe before approaching a deity or engaging in ritual activity. But bathing should also be an integral part of the daily pattern of life; one should at the very least bathe in the morning before beginning the day's activities. Without a purifying bath the individual is barred from the presence of the gods and, significantly, from the kitchen of the household—itself a kind of shrine in its own right. This does not mean that everyone bathes fully every day. It is, however, an important ideal and one observed with considerable rigor, especially among the highest castes.

It is best to bathe in the running water of a river, but most people in Chhattisgarh are unable to do so. In Raipur there are many tanks used for bathing by the less affluent elements of the population, and the cement platforms built around wells are often employed as bathing platforms. In Sitapur the village tank is used for bathing. Bathrooms, usually facing the main interior courtyards, are found in larger houses. Bathrooms and latrines are separate rooms; one cannot become pure in a chamber which is the most polluted area of the house. When total immersion is not possible, bathing is accomplished by pouring water over the body, never by immersing the body in a restricted container of water such as a tub. When the Western practice of bathing in a tub was described to informants the reaction was one of distaste. Water absorbs pollution, and flowing water may carry it away. But water may also transmit pollution and, in the confined space of a tub, water would transmit the intense pollution of areas like the anus to the rest of the body.

Ritualization of daily life also occurs in connection with food, primarily the concern of women. Cooking, serving, and eating food are activities with ritual implications. In the majority of households the preparation of food takes place in what is essentially a zone of purity of the same sort that surrounds a deity in *puja*. Food is particularly vulnerable to pollution during preparation, and to allow the food to become polluted would be to transmit pollution to those who consume it. In general the strictness with which the kitchen is protected is greatest in high-caste households, but in every household the kitchen is regarded as a place of special purity. Men and women alike should bathe before entering the kitchen if they have been in contact with a source of pollution. In most castes women are barred from the kitchen during their menstrual periods. In some families women wear silk when doing kitchen work because silk is more resistant than cotton to accidental pollution. The kitchen and the hearth are in a true sense the citadel of the household, the area most assiduously protected from intrusions from the outside world. Even in highly westernized households, where shoes may be worn in most of the house, footwear must be removed before one enters the kitchen.

If the kitchen is a zone of purity analogous to that which is a precondition for *puja*, then we might expect by extension that the preparing and serving of food is, in fact, an act of worship. This is indeed so in two senses. In many families the serving of each meal constitutes quite literally a form of *puja* to a deity. Before the food is eaten it is encircled with drops of water while a *mantra* is repeated. In this way the food is first offered to a deity, and then the meal itself becomes *prasad*. But there is another sense, not different in principle, in which the meal constitutes an offering to a deity. This is from the point of view of the female server. "The husband," informants say, "is the god of the wife." There is much truth in this common maxim. There are festival occasions such as *dassehra* (below, ch. 5) when wives are required to worship their husbands in precisely the same fashion as one might worship the image of a deity. The same principle is reflected in the serving of meals. The head of the household is fed first. Afterward his wife takes her own meal, a pattern suggestive of taking *prasad*.

The kitchen lies at the heart of the sacred geography of the household. The family shrine, if such exists, is also important. It is sometimes located in the kitchen area for the simple reason that this is a place of guaranteed purity. It is sometimes situated in an adjacent storage area or in a room set aside completely for this purpose. But wherever the family shrine is located, the same rules that protect the purity of the kitchen apply to it. Various deities are represented in household shrines. In village houses the family deities are frequently local or caste-specific deities, represented by stones or other objects to which *sindur* has been applied. In the houses of city-dwellers and the twice-born one is more likely to find elaborate shrines housing carved images of deities with a textual provenance. Commercially sold prints of deities are found in almost all houses in village and city alike. The frequency and seriousness with which family deities are worshipped varies widely. Except on festival occasions their worship is generally left to women.

There is one additional object subject to daily veneration in virtually every Hindu household in the region—the *tulsi* (basil) plant, which is usually grown on a special platform in the family courtyard. It is generally tended and worshipped by women. This plant is strongly associated with Vishnu. It is always found in temples housing Vishnu or any of his *avatars*. It is, to my knowledge, never found in temples of Shiva. It is said to be extremely pure, and its leaves may be offered to the deities (but not to Shiva) in *puja*. It has the property of warding off malevolent beings, and it is said that a house surrounded by *tulsi* plants is immune to intrusion by ghosts. It is thought to have medicinal properties as well, and its leaves are used in the compounding of numerous folk remedies. But above all the plant is a goddess. As a goddess, the plant has a special association with Saligram. Saligram is Vishnu in the form of a small stone, and is a common household deity. I heard the following story about Tulsi, the goddess, from a priest from a village near Sitapur:

Tulsi, whose original name was Brinda (Vrinda), was married to a man named Jalandhar. She was extremely devoted to her husband. Jalandhar was himself a devotee of Shankar (Shiva). Brinda's devotion to her husband was so intense that she undertook severe *tapasya* (austerities) on his behalf, and she obtained a promise from the gods that Jalandhar would be immortal.

Jalandhar then became extremely proud and haughty, and thinking that he was immune to any harm, he began to war against the 330 million gods. One day he happened to see Parvati (Shiva's consort) and, completely overcome by her beauty, he began to pursue her. When Shankar observed this he was shocked at the behavior of his disciple.[1] Shankar tried to fight Jalandhar, but he discovered that there was nothing he could do to harm him. In frustration, he finally went to Vishnu for help. In the meantime Brinda had observed these events, and she herself went to Vishnu and asked him to aid her husband in his quarrel with Shankar. Brinda's request had the force of command because of her *tapasya*. Vishnu thus found himself in a dilemma; he was committed to helping both Shankar and Jalandhar.

---

[1] In Hindu tradition, coveting the wife of one's *guru* ranks with Brahman-killing as one of the great sins.

Vishnu finally hit upon a clever plan. He fashioned a duplicate of Jalandhar and sent it to Brinda as her husband's corpse. When she saw the body she cried out, "Oh, my husband." Immediately all that she had accomplished for her husband by her *tapasya* was undone, because she had acknowledged the false rather than the real Jalandhar as her husband. Vishnu then told her the truth of the matter: that this was not the body of her husband. He added that by this time her husband would be dead anyway.

Brinda was extremely angry upon hearing this, and she told Vishnu that she would curse him and turn him into a stone. Because of her *tapasya* she had the power to do this, but Vishnu had equal power and he threatened to turn Brinda into a root. In the end Vishnu became a stone, which is known as Saligram, and Brinda was turned into a root. The root grew into the plant which is known as *tulsi*.

This tale, which provides a mythological context for two of the most common objects of religious veneration, introduces us to an idea that has an extremely important role in Chhattisgarhi religion. This is the idea that renunciation (*tapasya*) is a source of power, and that the power obtained by renunciation can be used to challenge the gods themselves. The tale also emphasizes sacrifice as an essential attribute of the wifely role. This is a theme we shall see again.

Apart from the ritualizations of daily life centering on bathing, the hearth, the serving of food, the family shrine, and the *tulsi* plant, there are many other religious observances that might or might not be a matter of daily practice depending on individual circumstances. For the few with highly developed religious sensibilities meditative exercise and elaborate devotional ritual might be a matter of daily routine. Many people make daily visits to temples or shrines to obtain *darshan* (view, audience) of the deities housed therein. Unless some special circumstance prevails (such as an eclipse) temples are open to the public during the morning and evening hours when the priests make offerings and perform *arti*. After *arti*, *prasad* is distributed. Observances of this sort, however, are highly variable, and do not constitute a part of the normal daily pattern for most people.

The Sacred Week

The seven-day week is a basic division of both secular and sacred time in Chhattisgarh. The secular, or civil, week is the same as its western equivalent: Monday through Friday and to some extent Saturday are regarded as workdays. Sunday is a government holiday, as is the second Saturday of each month. Some shops are closed on Sundays, but most remain open. The civil week is relatively less important in rural areas than in towns and cities. However, in rural and urban areas alike the seven-day week has extremely important ceremonial functions. This "sacred week" is homologous to its secular counterpart and consists of seven named days. Each day has particular planetary and religious associations, which govern the sorts of ceremonial (and to some degree secular) activities appropriate on that day.

Itvar: Sunday

Sunday is conventionally regarded as the first day of the seven-day sacred week. Beyond this, its ceremonial importance is limited. Sunday is astrologically associated with the sun, and is accordingly a day especially appropriate for its worship, although the sun is in fact rarely worshipped in any formal way. Informants maintain that the sun is a "good" celestial body because the sun is the giver of all good things. Sunday is therefore a relatively auspicious day for human enterprises.

Chandravar: Monday

Monday is associated with the moon (*chandra*), and since the moon is an auspicious body the day itself is an auspicious one. Monday is also associated with Shiva, and it is this latter association that determines the ceremonial character of the day. Those who regard themselves as devotees of Shiva should honor him on this day if on no other occasion. If Monday should coincide with the new moon (*amavashya*) it is particularly important to worship Shiva, this occasion being known as *somvati*.

One of the most characteristic of the many religious activities of Chhattisgarhi women is periodic fasting. As we shall see, there are many types of fast, and many occasions upon which fasting is appropriate. One of the most important of these observances is the *solah somvar vrat*, the "sixteen Mondays' vow," a votive sequence consisting of sixteen successive Mondays of fasting. While in theory anyone may undertake this sequence of fasts, in fact it is conventionally undertaken by married women and is regarded as a method by which women can further the welfare of their husbands. *Puja* is performed for Shiva at the conclusion of each of the fasting days, and if possible the story of the origin of this particular fast is repeated. I paraphrase this story as follows:[2]

One day Shiva and Parvati came into the world. During their wanderings they came to a temple. There Parvati suggested that they pass the time by playing a game of dice. While they were playing, a worshipper, a Brahman, came to the temple. Parvati asked the Brahman who he thought would win, and the Brahman named Shiva. In the end Parvati won, and in her pique at the Brahman she cursed him with leprosy.

A few days later some goddesses came to the temple and saw the pitiable state of the Brahman. They told him that Shiva alone could help him, and they described to him the supreme vow, the sixteen Mondays' vow. He must fast, they said, for sixteen successive Mondays. On each fasting day he must put on clean clothes, and make three cakes from *ata* (coarse wheat flour). He must procure clarified butter, incense, molasses, *bel* leaves, and all of the other materials necessary for *puja*. At the end of each fasting day he must offer one of the *ata* cakes to Shiva and break up and distribute the remaining two as *prasad*. In this way he would be able to please Shiva and obtain whatever boon he wished.

The Brahman did as he was directed and was cured of leprosy. He then began to lead a supremely happy life. One day Parvati returned to

[2] From the *Solah Somvar Vrat Katha* (The Story of the Sixteen Mondays' Vow), a pamphlet containing instructions for the observance of the fast and the story behind it. The pamphlet exemplifies a form of popular religious literature that is ubiquitous in Chhattisgarh and that provides an important link between popular religious observance and Puranic lore.

the very temple where she had cursed the Brahman. There she saw the Brahman and noticed that his leprosy was cured. She asked how this came to be, and the Brahman told her of the sixteen Mondays' vow. Then Parvati herself used the vow to cure her son, Kartekiya, of disobedience. Word of the efficacy of the remarkable vow passed from Parvati to her son, and then to a friend, and then to many others. Each person was able to obtain his or her desire by means of the vow, and ultimately its fame spread throughout the world.

The story is typical of the tales that accompany fasts and other religious observances. It describes some of the specific steps necessary for the occasion, and provides a context for it in Puranic mythology. The story is of interest here because it hints at some rather important characteristics of two major figures in the pantheon: Shiva and his consort Parvati. In the story Shiva is portrayed as a benevolent deity. His wife, by contrast, seems to have a malicious side which can be excited by a real or imagined slight. Yet in the end the power of Shiva, which we are told can be tapped by the fast, overcomes misfortune caused by the goddess. As we shall see later, this theme in the story is consistent with a pattern of much wider application in Chhattisgarhi religion in which the potentially malevolent power of the goddess is checked or contained by the benevolent power of the god. This is an important feature of the relationship between masculine and feminine aspects of divinity in the pantheon.

Mangalvar: Tuesday

Tuesday is astrologically associated with Mars. Mars is a planet whose astrological associations are generally bad: "The red color of Mars, and his consequent traditional association with the idea of war and bloodshed, are sufficient to have established him as a planet of ill-omen" (Underhill 1921:33). Tuesday is therefore inauspicious, a poor day to begin a journey or enterprise. The primary ceremonial association of Tuesday is with certain forms of the goddess, just as Monday is linked with Shiva. We shall discuss the various manifestations of the goddess in more detail in a later chapter. For the present it is enough to say that female divinity has both benevolent and malevolent aspects, and it is the sinister or malevolent aspect of the goddess that is stressed when she appears in certain forms such as Kali, Mahamaya, Shitla, etc. These are the forms of the goddess that are of principal importance on Tuesday, and this seems consistent with the more general inauspiciousness of the day. Special *artis* are held in the temples of the goddess on Tuesdays, and those who consider themselves her devotees, or who have some special favor to ask of her, should fast on Tuesdays and make offerings to her.

Tuesday is also a day regarded as particularly appropriate for the worship of Hanuman. Hanuman is depicted in the *Ramayana* as Rama's principal servant, companion, and ally in battle. In Chhattisgarh he is a major deity. He is primarily a protective god, and his worship on Tuesday seems consistent with the fact that Tuesday is inauspicious—that is, a day on which protection is needed. This seems a reasonable supposition in view of the fact that Saturday, the least auspicious day of the week, is also an important day for the worship of Hanuman. I shall have more to say on this subject in connection with Saturday and its planetary and ceremonial associations.

Budhvar: Wednesday

Wednesday's planet is Mercury, an auspicious planet. In Chhattisgarh Wednesday does not seem to have any special ceremonial associations of importance. It is, however, regarded as a good day upon which to begin a journey or enterprise.

Guruvar: Thursday

Thursday falls under the influence of Jupiter, a benevolent planet, and as a result Thursday is also generally auspicious. Chhattisgarhi informants do not associate Thursday with the worship of any particular deity, but the *Saptavar Vrat Katha* (a popular text dealing with ceremonies associated with the days of the week) maintains that this is a day especially appropriate for the worship of Shiva. If this pattern was ever present in Chhattisgarh, it is not evident now.

Shukravar: Friday

Friday's planetary association is with Venus, an auspicious planet, and it is therefore generally an auspicious day. According to the *Saptavar Vrat Katha* Friday is a day especially appropriate for the worship of a benevolent goddess known as Santoshi Mata, the daughter of Ganesh. In practice, however, Friday has no particular ceremonial associations.

Shannivar: Saturday

Saturday is unquestionably the most important day of the Chhattisgarhi sacred week. To begin with, it is by far the most inauspicious day of the week, a result of its association with the planet Saturn (Shanni). Saturn is the most malevolent of the planetary deities. He is depicted as a warrior, and in astrological theory he is associated with darkness, disease, and stubbornness of character. His favorite offerings include black *til* (sesamum), black cloth, objects of iron, oil, and *urad*, all of which have associations in other contexts with death and the darker aspects of life. It is appropriate to worship Saturn on Saturday, either by making some private gesture or by making a formal offering at one of his temples. To my knowledge there is only one such temple in Raipur, and none at all in the vicinity of Sitapur. In Raipur women representing themselves as priestesses of a Saturn temple go from house to house on Saturdays, soliciting offerings of oil and money.

Informants could tell me relatively little about the characteristics of Saturn as a deity save that he is extremely dangerous and that when angry he will inflict seven and one-half years of bad luck. The *Saptavar Vrat Katha*, however, contains a lengthy account dealing with Saturn, which I paraphrase as follows:

One day the nine planets had a dispute over who was the greatest of them all, and being unable to decide the matter among themselves they went to Indra for a judgment. Indra was afraid of the anger of those who would lose, so he referred them to Raja Vikramaditya on earth. The Raja ordered his servants to prepare nine thrones, each of a different metal. On the day of judgment Saturn was seated on a throne of iron. Iron is among the basest of the metals, and Saturn was infuriated. He reminded the Raja of the seven and one-half years of bad luck which were within his power to inflict. He also reminded the Raja of Rama's exile of fourteen years, which resulted from Saturn's anger. He then left in a rage.

Later Saturn returned to the Raja's city, Ujjain, in the guise of a horse-seller. The Raja unwisely purchased a horse, and when he mounted it the horse took flight in the air and carried the Raja far away from Ujjain to a very remote place. There the Raja wandered in great thirst and hunger. He finally made his way to a city. A wealthy man took pity on him and brought him to his house for a meal. While the Raja was eating he saw a marvelous thing; there was an expensive necklace hanging on the wall next to a picture of a peacock, and as the Raja watched the peacock ate the necklace. The Raja was then accused of the theft of the necklace and was brought before the king of that city for judgment. He was punished by having his hands and feet cut off, and was cast from the city. He finally made his way to the house of a poor but sympathetic oil-seller, who allowed him to earn his keep by driving the bullocks of the oil press. In this fashion, seven and one-half years went by.

One day the princess of that kingdom heard the singing of the mutilated Raja and decided at once that she must marry the possessor of that voice. Her father objected, but she was adamant and in the end they were married, her father finally conceding that "fate is irresistible." Then one night Saturn appeared to the Raja in a dream and declared that he would grant him a boon. The Raja implored Saturn not to subject others to the troubles he had endured. Saturn agreed to this, but asked what the Raja might want for himself. The Raja asked to be restored to his original form, which was done. News of what had happened spread rapidly throughout the city. The rich man who had accused the Raja came to make his peace. The Raja forgave the man, saying such things are the "play of fate." The rich man invited the Raja to come to his house for dinner once again, and while they were eating the peacock vomited forth the necklace.

When the Raja returned to the palace his bride's parents apologized for everything that had happened. Raja Vikramaditya forgave them readily, stressing that everything that had happened was the result of fate and nobody's fault. He then asked permission to leave the city and return to his home. He was given rich gifts at the time of his departure, and received a joyous welcome from his subjects when he arrived at the gates of Ujjain. The Raja began worshipping Saturn regularly and made a practice of giving flour to ants (a meritorious act). In this way, by the grace of Saturn, he lived a happy and prosperous life.

The happy ending is entirely conventional in stories of this type. The heart of the tale concerns the misfortunes that may intrude into anyone's life, even that of a great monarch. One phrase is pivotal: "the play of fate" (*bhagy ka khel*). Saturn, as portrayed in the story, seems to stand for the inexplicable misfortunes that are so characteristic of human life. As surely as the planets move in their heaven, there are forces that will undo the purposes of mankind, and these forces can never be fully anticipated. No matter who you are, fate can deal a heavy blow. Yet it is important to note that the point of view expressed in the story is by no means wholly pessimistic. The blows of fate may be countered, and the story suggests that one way of doing so is to appease Saturn directly. If misfortune cannot be always anticipated, palliative ritual action is nonetheless always possible.

In general, the forces that underlie human misfortune may be dealt with by opposing them with protective forces. This leads us to the association between Saturday and the deity Hanuman. Hanuman is one of the most important deities of Chhattisgarh, and in many ways is the protective deity *par excellence*. His shrines and temples are everywhere. Virtually every village has a small shrine devoted to Hanuman, and the same is true of most neighborhoods in towns and cities. He is also represented in the temples of other deities. His cult is easily one of the most conspicuous aspects of popular Hinduism in the region.

Hanuman is sometimes regarded as an *avatar* of Shiva. His parents were Vayu, the Wind God, and a nymph named Anjana. Anjana was the wife of a great chieftain and was renowned for her beauty. She was observed one day by the Wind God. He blew up her garment, was charmed by what he saw, and embraced her. He then told her that she would be delivered of a son who would have the power of moving through the air like himself. When Hanuman was born Indra became frightened of his potential power and threw a thunderbolt at him which knocked him to the ground and broke his jaw. When the Wind God saw this he became angry and ceased to blow. This frightened the other gods, and in order to mollify the Wind God, Brahma gave Hanuman the gift of invulnerability to weapons of war. Indra gave him the additional boon that he would die only by his own consent.

Later in his life Hanuman offended a certain great sage and was punished by a curse, which caused him to forget his powers until he met Rama, the seventh *avatar* of Vishnu and the hero of the *Ramayana*. The epic tells how Hanuman, then the leader of the monkeys, met Rama for the first time and regained full knowledge of his great strength and powers. Hanuman then went on to become Rama's devoted servant and ally in his war against the demon Ravana.

Chhattisgarhi informants are fully familiar with the details of Hanuman's career because of his central role in the *Ramayana*. The Tulsidas version of the epic is beyond any question the most important religious book in Chhattisgarh. It is read by the literate as a form of religious exercise. The repetition of the epic is pleasing to Rama and a source of religious merit. One of the most common forms of devotional activity is the collective singing of portions of the epic, an activity for which literacy is not required. In many villages and residential communities special associations are formed precisely for this purpose. Typically groups of men gather in the evening, often on the veranda of a temple, singing in response to the verses of the text as they are recited by a Pandit. In the immediate vicinity of Sitapur there is usually at least one session of this kind each week, and frequently more than one.

In their interpretations of Hanuman's role in the *Ramayana* informants tend to stress one characteristic of Hanuman above all others: his intense devotion to Rama. Hanuman is regarded as the very type of the devotee (*bhakt*) of Rama, and in this regard he is frequently pointed to as an object for human emulation.

Ramayana-singing

Various episodes in the *Ramayana* are commonly cited as illustrations of ideal devotion. After the destruction of Ravana, Rama and his consort Sita returned to Ayodhya (Rama's capital) to be crowned king and queen. At the coronation Sita gave Hanuman a necklace of pearls. Hanuman began breaking each pearl with his teeth, explaining that he wanted to see if the pearls contained Rama—otherwise they would be of no value to him. On another occasion Hanuman ripped open his chest, showing that images of Rama and Sita lay where his heart should be. The latter episode is represented in a popular print.

Hanuman is a celibate deity, and informants relate this characteristic to his devotion to Rama. Since his life is devoted utterly to the service of Rama, sexual connections would be harmful distractions. So celebrated is Hanuman's celibacy that he has come to be a symbol of *brahmacharya*, sexual renunciation, and young men who have difficulty maintaining celibacy are advised to worship him. There is a feeling that women should not be allowed to come close to Hanuman's effigies, though this is not a strict rule. Hanuman has a son, but his birth did not result from a normal sexual union. The story goes that after his great exploit of setting fire to Ravana's capital, Hanuman had worked himself into a great sweat. He bathed in the sea, and a drop of his perspiration found its way into the mouth of a fish. In due course the fish gave birth to the great hero Makardhvaj.

While seemingly incongruous, it is nevertheless true that Hanuman, the symbol of sexual renunciation, is a strikingly masculine deity. He is immensely strong, and in his popular representations he is usually portrayed as a kind of monkey-faced Hercules with bulging muscles and a gigantic club. He is, among other things, the patron deity of wrestlers, and his prowess as a warrior is celebrated in the *Ramayana*. In fact, Hanuman's celibacy is far from inconsistent with these attributes. More will be said concerning the implications of sexual renunciation in chapter 7, and I shall not explore the matter in detail here. It may be noted, however, that in the Hindu tradition sexual activity is usually regarded as debilitating to men. Morris Carstairs cites a rustic aphorism that expresses succinctly a prevailing attitude about masculine sexuality: "it takes forty days, and forty drops of blood, to make one drop of semen" (1961:83). The converse of this principle is, of course, that sexual renunciation will lead to the acquisition of power, and in the texts the point is again and again made that great force is concentrated when the seed is "drawn up" (see O'Flaherty 1969a:311ff). Hanuman's celibacy is therefore perfectly consonant with his attributes as described in the *Ramayana* and, indeed, with his power and efficacy as a protective deity.

Hanuman: A popular print
Rama and Lakshman sit on Hanuman's shoulders.

There is an important sense, however, in which Hanuman is
not an autonomous deity; his power is great, but ultimately this
power devolves from his connection with Rama, a god of even
greater power. His celibacy, after all, is an aspect of his devotion
to Rama. Informants seem to conceive of Hanuman as a sort of
intermediary between Rama and mankind. One might suppose
that people would address themselves to the more powerful deity,
but informants state that Rama is far too great a deity for ordinary people to approach directly, so instead they go to his principal servant. An analogy is frequently drawn between Rama and
Hanuman and an important official and his office flunky. Ordinary people are afraid to go directly to the official for fear that

they would be ignored or humiliated. Instead the usual procedure is first to approach the servant with a gift of some kind in hopes that he will expedite matters—very much the way things operate in a good many offices.

Hanuman may thus be described as a kind of instrument by means of which individuals may manipulate supernatural forces for their own ends. Because of his special connection with Rama, he constitutes a medium of access to this powerful and benevolent deity. His relationship with Rama is one of utterly selfless devotion, which extends to sexual renunciation in the service of his master. The same sexual renunciation would appear to enhance his role as intermediary. In effect, he himself assumes the burden of renunciation on his worshippers' behalf, and this enables him to tap the benevolent power symbolized by Rama and use it for their benefit. The benevolence of a great deity like Rama is simply too remote from the world of experience to be of immediate usefulness in the everyday affairs of men. In the figure of Hanuman this abstract power is made concrete in the form of a deity of good will, strength, and availability.

Hanuman may be worshipped at any time and for any purpose, but Tuesday and Saturday are reserved as especially appropriate days. The worship of Hanuman would appear to counteract malignant forces abroad on these days. On Tuesday and Saturday special *artis* are performed in Hanuman temples, and individuals who consider themselves devotees of Hanuman, or who want some special request filled should fast on these days.

Conclusion

A number of important elements in Chhattisgarhi religion appear in the ritual cycles of the day and the week. One is the idea of purity and pollution. The ritualization of daily life is largely a reflection of concern with pollution as expressed in patterns of bathing, food preparation, and eating. In turn, this is an illustration of the pervasiveness of pollution and the ephemerality of purity—facts of overarching importance in Chhattisgarhi religion.

The idea of renunciation as method for acquiring and controlling power appears in the story of Tulsi and in the lore surrounding the figure of Hanuman. This is an idea that will be seen in other contexts in later chapters.

Finally, in the ritual cycles of the day and the week we are introduced to a principle of basic importance in the organization of Chhattisgarhi religion—the differentiation of the pantheon. The pantheon consists of an array of beings with different qualities and attributes, who accordingly affect human experience in different ways. Some are primarily malevolent, others are primarily benevolent. Some are "high," others are "low." Rama, remote from the affairs of the human world, is clearly superior to his servant Hanuman, who although ultimately less powerful has few scruples about involving himself in the affairs of his human worshippers. This hierarchical dimension is crucial to the structure of the pantheon. Moreover, we have noted that the pantheon is differentiated along sexual lines and we have seen hints in the story of the sixteen Mondays' vow that there is a connection between feminine divinity and potential malevolence. This is a theme I shall elaborate in later chapters.

5
Months and Years

Ceremonies associated with the salient events of the life histories of individuals, with the daily routine, or with the days of the week belong to relatively simple ritual cycles. Ceremonies belonging to the much more complex monthly and annual cycles are embedded in a calendrical framework that itself requires explanation. Accordingly, a brief description of the Hindu lunar–solar calendar follows.

The Lunar Month

In Chhattisgarh, as elsewhere in North and Central India, the lunar month (*chandra mas*) consists of one complete cycle of lunar phases from full moon to full moon.[1] Each month ends on the full moon day (*purnima* or *punni*) and the next month begins on the day following. The new moon (*amavashya*) divides the lunar month into two fortnights (*paksh* or *pak*),

---

[1] Ruth and Stanley Freed (1964) have described the Indian lunar–solar calendrical systems in great detail. For further information I refer the reader to the Freeds' definitive article.

a dark fortnight (*badi* or *krishna*) in which the moon is waning, and a light fortnight (*sudi* or *shukla*) in which the moon is waxing. Each lunar month consists of thirty lunar days, which average about 23 hours and 37 minutes in length (Freed and Freed 1964:71). The names of the days of the lunar month are derived from the Hindi names of the numbers from one to fourteen. Thus, the fifth day of either fortnight is designated *panchmi* from *panch*, "five." The fifteenth day of the dark fortnight is, of course, *amavashya*, and the fifteenth day of the light fortnight is *purnima*.

There are twelve lunar months in the lunar year. Each lunar month consists of 29.5 solar days (Freed and Freed 1964:68), which complicates considerably the coordination of the lunar and solar years. Coordination is accomplished by occasionally adding a lunar month to a given year, and, less frequently, by dropping a month. The lunar year is considered to begin officially with the first day of the light half of the lunar month of *chaitra*. Here follows, then, a list in order of the lunar months and the approximate solar equivalents:

chaitra	March–April
baisakh	April–May
jyeshth	May–June
asharh	June–July
shravan or *savan*	July–August
bhadrapad or *bhadon*	August–September
ashivan or *kunvar*	September–October
kartik	October–November
margashirsh	November–December
paush	December–January
magh	January–February
phalgun	February–March

We shall be examining ceremonies and festivals that fall on various named dates, which are calculated within this system. A lunar date is known as a *tithi*. A given *tithi* is indicated by naming the month, the fortnight of the month, and then the number of the day within the fortnight. Thus, a festival known as *nag panchmi* (cobra fifth), which occurs on the fifth day (*panchmi*) of the light (*sudi*) fortnight of *shravan*, is designated *shravan sudi* 5. Under ordinary circumstances, single solar days are dated for ceremonial purposes as lunar days, even though the actual lunar and solar days do not coincide exactly. Apparently the rule is that a solar day is understood to be the equivalent of that lunar day which was underway at sunrise (Freed and Freed 1964:74). Lunar days that do not overlap with any sunrise are dropped, and if any ceremony is to be held on such a lunar day, it is held on the solar day within which the lunar date occurred. If a lunar day is in progress during two sunrises, then the two solar dates are considered to be the same lunar date (Freed and Freed 1964:74–75).

All of this may seem relatively straightforward, but the results of independent calculations of ceremonial dates can vary. During my stay in Chhattisgarh I purchased several lunar-solar calendars, and found occasional disagreement on the correlation of lunar and solar dates. The final authority on these matters is the *panchang*, or almanac, which is used by Pandits in the determination of dating and celestial movements as they apply to matters of ceremony and astrological calculation. Since these almanacs are prepared by different authorities they sometimes disagree, with the result that ceremonies in different localities sometimes occur on different solar days.

Monthly Ceremonial Regularities

Like the days of the sacred week, many of the *tithis* of the lunar month have regular and constant ritual associations. Unquestionably the most important of the days of the lunar month are *purnima* and *amavashya*, full moon and new moon. A number of annual festivals fall on both *purnima* and *amavashya*, but these dates are of special significance even in the absence of specific festivals. Both are considered fasting days by the orthodox. *Purnima* is an extremely auspicious date, but the status of *amavashya* is somewhat ambiguous. Numerous festivals occur on *amavashya*, including *divali* (below) with all its overtones of beauty and wealth. But on the other hand *amavashya*, along with other more clearly unlucky days, is regarded as an inauspicious day for bride and groom to begin their postnuptial journey to the groom's home.

The fourths of both light and dark fortnights are considered important *tithis*. They are generally regarded as appropriate days for the worship of Ganesh, the elephant-headed son of Shiva and Parvati. Ganesh's major annual festival, *ganesh chaturthi*, occurs on *bhadon sudi* 4. Dark fourths are generally regarded as inauspicious, and are known as *samkashta chaturthi* (difficulty fourths). It is thus not inappropriate that Ganesh, sometimes known as "the remover of obstacles," is worshipped on these dates. Except for the festival of *ganesh chaturthi* most people in Chhattisgarh do not perform *pujas* for Ganesh on the fourths, though the link between Ganesh and these dates is well known.

There is a general association between eighths and female deities. In many calendars light eighths are designated *durga ashtami*, occasions upon which Durga, an important goddess, should be worshipped. Shitla, the goddess of smallpox, is worshipped on the dark eighth of chaitra.

The elevenths (*ekadashis*) of each month have considerable ceremonial importance, especially to orthodox Vaishnavas. The elevenths are associated with Vishnu and are considered fasting days. Observance of the *ekadashi* fasts is confined mainly to the twice-born castes, especially women, though there are exceptions. Each of the twenty-four *ekadashis* of the year is named, and each has a particular story attached to it. These stories are compiled in the *Ekadashi Vrat Katha* (*Stories of the Ekadashi Vows*), a popular text available throughout Chhattisgarh, and presumably throughout the other Hindi-speaking areas of North and Central India as well. The most important of the *ekadashis* are *devuthni ekadashi* (*kartik sudi* 11) and *devshayani ekadashi* (*asharh sudi* 11), of which more below.

The Annual Festival Cycle

The passage of the lunar year is marked by a great number of festivals and other ritual occasions. It might well be said that the observance of ceremonial occasions tied to the annual calendrical cycle constitutes the greater portion of the ceremonial life of most people. In Chhattisgarh there are some forty-odd occasions of this kind. Some are of significance only to individual castes or other restricted sections of society. Others exist more in theory than in fact; they are known, but are not celebrated on a wide scale. I shall not attempt to describe them all. Rather, I shall concentrate on what seem to be the most widely observed and generally important of the annual rites.

The pattern of ceremonies that unfolds during the course of the lunar year is by no means an arbitrary one. The Chhattisgarhi sacred year passes in conjunction with the annual cycle of seasonal change, which influences profoundly the activities of the inhabitants of the region. I shall demonstrate how intimately the ceremonial calendar is bound to the cycle of the seasons. In North and Central India the seasonal year may be divided into essentially three parts. One is the hot season (*garmi*), which begins roughly in March and ends with the onset of rains in June. The second is the rainy season (*barsat*), which begins in June (or at least should begin then) and comes to a gradual end by October. The third season is not so well defined physically as the first two, and for this reason I have chosen to call it "autumn-winter-spring." Its heart is the winter season (*sardi*) of the months of December and January, but the cold weather has no clear boundaries, blending gradually into warmer weather in February, and being in no clear way bounded from the autumnal transition of late October and November. The agricultural cycle is determined by these natural oscillations of climate, as is the epidemiology of the region. The yearly ceremonial cycle seems to respond to both sets of factors.

The Hot Season: The Time of the Goddess

The ceremonial year begins in hot weather. The official beginning of the lunar year occurs on *chaitra sudi* 1, and *chaitra* is the first of the hot season months. As the winter months come to an end the average temperature slowly rises. By *chaitra* it is very hot indeed, and at the hot season's peak in May the temperature reaches an average maximum of 107° F and an average minimum of 82°, with occasional spells as high as 117–18° (Nelson 1909:37). Rainfall is practically nonexistent during these months. To the great relief of everyone the hot season comes to an end with the arrival of the monsoon rains in mid June.

From the standpoint of ceremonial activity, the hot season months have two important features. First, the hot season is preeminently the marriage season, a fact probably related to the absence of crucial agricultural work during this part of the year. Second, and equally important, the hot season is dominated by one aspect of Chhattisgarhi religion, the worship of goddesses. The various goddesses may be regarded as different manifestations of a single composite figure, that of Devi, "the goddess." The goddess-worship of the hot season is oriented toward certain sinister forms of female divinity in which a link between physical heat and what might be termed "ritual heat" (see Beck 1969) finds particularly vivid expression. Later we shall see that this aspect of the personality of the goddess is a vital element in the structure of the pantheon. There are five major hot season rituals. Of these, two (*shitla ashtami* and *javara*) are directly linked to the goddess in these sinister forms. Another (*akti*) is weakly linked to the goddess, but has other associations as well. One (*ram navmi*) is concerned with the benevolent god Rama, and occurs, as I shall show, in a meaningful juxtaposition with one of the rites of the goddess. The final major rite of the hot season (*savitri puja*) is concerned with an entirely different aspect of the goddess and with an entirely different conception of the feminine, and provides a fitting termination for the hot season's ceremonial cycle.

Shitla: The Cool One

In Chhattisgarh, smallpox is especially prevalent during the hot season. Moreover, the disease is regarded as essentially a religious phenomenon, and popular conceptions of it are strongly tied to ideas of ritual heat and heating. The disease is associated with the goddess in her "parochial" or "local" forms (see chs. 6, 7). In these forms she is known—among many other names—as Shitla, Mata (the mother), the "seven sisters," or the "twenty-one sisters." The expression seven sisters is characterized by informants as a reference to seven different varieties of smallpox, each distinguished by a particular type of skin eruption. In Sitapur she is known as Mahamay, a contraction of Mahamaya, which is a textual name. Whatever her name, she is linked with smallpox, and she is greatly feared, particularly in the hot season when she moves about the country-side entering the villages, houses, and bodies of those with whom she is annoyed.

Shitla literally *is* smallpox in the sense that a case of smallpox is regarded as an instance of possession by this goddess. The symptoms of smallpox, the raging fever and rashes, are regarded as indications of the goddess's displeasure. The therapy of the disease is essentially ritual, consisting in general of measures designed to cool the goddess's anger and effect her withdrawal from the body of the patient. These procedures are known generally as *mata seva* (the service of the mother). The goddess is honored with *puja*. Songs may be sung for her.

The patient's feet may be washed in milk or water, an act of homage to the goddess who occupies the patient's body. Leaves of the *nim* (margosa) tree are dipped in water and applied to the patient's body in an effort to cool the goddess and thereby lower the patient's fever.

Victims of smallpox are believed to possess oracular powers, a logical assumption in view of the fact that the patient is possessed by the goddess. Informants tell of instances in which smallpox patients have been able to predict the coming of visitors who have not yet left their own houses. The goddess, through the mouth of the patient, may make various requests that in the interests of the patient's recovery must be honored. She may, for example, request the sacrifice of a goat, and at the very least a drop of blood obtained by nicking a goat's ear should be applied to her image in a local shrine. Care must be taken that the goddess see nothing that might increase her anger. People who appear before the patient should divest themselves of ornaments, because the sight of them would make the goddess jealous. Pregnant women are also barred from the vicinity of the patient, for they too are believed to incite the goddess's anger.

At the heart of the Chhattisgarhi conception of the goddess as smallpox is the idea of heat. Fever is one of the most conspicuous symptoms of the disease and is associated with the goddess's anger. The therapeutic measures employed in smallpox cases are designed to be "cooling" in their effects. The goddess's anger is reduced with offerings, and the heat of her presence is dealt with directly by means of cooling applications of water. The same principle is suggested by the prohibition of fire near the patient. It is regarded as harmful to allow lamps to burn in the house with a smallpox victim. Oil should not be heated in the vicinity of the patient, as this too would aggravate the disease.

The name Shitla means literally "the cool one." This designation seems euphemistic; in fact, as she is normally encountered by human beings, the goddess is manifestly hot, and she must be cooled if the unpleasant consequences of her anger are to be avoided. This theme is developed in a folktale (from Dubey and Mohril 1965:92–94), which relates the story of seven virgin sisters who were abandoned by their poverty-striken father. The sisters wandered about and accomplished various miracles with *nim* shoots, which they carried with them. Finally they arrived, hot and thirsty, at the scene of a smallpox epidemic. A kindly woman offered them water, and as they were refreshed and cooled with the water the disease subsided. The same idea underlies the treatment of smallpox; the goddess, dwelling in the patient's body, is cooled, and as she is cooled the disease is abated.

We have already seen the theme of heating and cooling in other ritual contexts, and we shall see it again. At this point, however, we may note that in Chhattisgarhi culture it is assumed that objects, substances, and processes may have intrinsic thermal characteristics. The resulting taxonomy of "hot" and "cold" is one of broad application, but is particularly evident where foods are concerned. Certain foods—especially meat, liquor, and oily foods—are regarded as intrinsically "hot," and it is said that illness will result if they are consumed in excess, or if they are eaten under inappropriate circumstances. (Hot food, for example, should not be eaten in very hot weather.) Likewise, certain foods are regarded as "cold," and they too will produce illness if eaten in excess. Lemons and onions are thought to be especially cold, and it is said that carrying these items on one's person in hot weather will prevent sunstroke. The *nim* tree is also thought to be intrinsically cold, and informants maintain that the shade of the *nim* tree is more cooling than that of any other. I shall simply note in passing that both the *nim* leaf and the lemon play an important role in ritual connected with the goddess. We have already seen that the *nim* leaf is employed in the cooling applications of water in smallpox therapy.

Shitla is worshipped whenever there is a case of smallpox. She also has a festival of her own which, appropriately, is part of the hot season ritual cycle. This occasion is known as *shitla ashtami* (Shitla eighth) and falls on the dark eighth of the month of *chaitra*, the first hot season month. *Shitla ashtami* is not observed in every household, possibly because of increased knowledge of vaccination. It is, however, still observed in many households in village and city alike. One of the most important aspects of the rite is the extinguishing of all fires in the house, and abstinence on the part of the family from all cooked foods. Here again we see the theme of hot and cold; when Shitla enters the house it must be a cool place. Otherwise, the ceremonial aspects of the occasion are standard. A *kalash* is prepared, food offerings are made, and *prasad* is taken in the usual manner.

Javara

Chaitra sudi 1, as we have already noted, is the official beginning of the new lunar year. However, the significance of this date as the beginning of the year is entirely eclipsed by the fact that it is the opening day of one of the most important ritual periods of the hot months. This period is known as *navratra*, meaning "nine nights," and it occurs twice during the lunar year: once during the first nine days of the bright fortnight of *chaitra*, and once during the first nine days of the bright fortnight of *kunvar*. The two occasions thus divide the year into two parts at points that correspond roughly to the vernal and autumnal equinoxes. While *navratra* refers to the name of a ritual period, the actual rites held during *navratra* are known as *javara*. *Javara* is one of the most important of the calendrical ceremonies of Chhattisgarh because it is the principal ritual of the goddess. It is performed during both *navratra* periods, and the rite is essentially the same each time.

Javara, unlike *shitla ashtami*, is not devoted to the goddess under a specific name. In Raipur the rites are held in the temples of Mahamaya, Durga, Shitla, Kankali, and others. In villages the ceremonies are held at shrines of the goddess whatever her local designation might be. The specific names are not very important. Rather, the significant fact is that the goddesses honored by the rites of *javara* all reflect a particular aspect of feminine divinity. These are all goddesses who are directly or potentially associated with malevolence, disease, and death—an association I shall discuss in greater detail in chapter 7. In addition, these are goddesses who accept blood sacrifice. The distinction between female divinity in this form and in a more benevolent one is a crucial aspect of the structure of the pantheon, and one we shall encounter again.

Javara: A goat is sacrificed to the goddess at the Kankali temple in Raipur

Because *javara* is a rite of the goddess it is held in the major temples of the goddess as a matter of course during the *navratra* periods. Indeed, in such temples the *navratra* periods represent the high points of the ceremonial year. The same rites are held on a lesser scale in shrines of village goddesses, though because of the high costs involved the village celebration is sometimes forgone. *Javara* is also held in private homes. It is usually sponsored by individuals for some specific purpose, often in fulfillment of a vow to perform the ritual if some sort of request made of the goddess has been granted.

The central act of the rites of *javara* is the planting of wheat on a specially prepared altar made of manure. Its upper surface is shaped into a minute representation of the Chhattisgarhi countryside. Miniature divisions are separated by tiny ridges about one inch high, the resulting pattern bearing a striking similarity to the walled rice fields of Chhattisgarh. The wheat is planted in these small "fields." The planting takes place on the first day of *navratra*, and the seeds are then allowed to germinate and grow for nine days. A *kalash* is prepared (sometimes more than one) and kept near the altar. The *kalash* has a lamp on top which must be kept burning throughout the nine-day period. The seedlings themselves are supposed to be the goddess in substantial form. One informant, a Brahman priest, explained this by saying that seeds (*bij*) contain *shakti*, or energy, which is a common name for the goddess who personifies energy or force. The rate at which the seedlings grow is said to be an augury of the general welfare in the months to come. In all of this there seems to be a suggested identification between the goddess and the crops in the fields, the growth of which bears a direct relationship with human prosperity.

In the evenings people gather near the place where the seedlings are growing to sing *javara* songs. In the city of Raipur singing contests are held in the Shitla Temple to which various groups or neighborhoods in the city send competing parties of singers and musicians. The *javara* songs are dedicated to the goddess:

> Oh Kali, killer of the demon, you carry many weapons in your hands;
> Your eyes are red and you wear the bloody necklace of skulls.
> Sixty-four yoginis, the horrible ones, dance to the sounds of a war-band.
> Oh Mother, sit on your throne and tell us how the terrible sounds will come,
> As the clouds make noise at the time of the rainy season.
> After hearing your voice Bakasur [a demon] and all [the demons] will run away.

And:

> Oh Mother, you sit on the throne in benign form.
> All the gods of heaven sing your praise because their troubles have vanished.
> Oh Mother, you are comforted by all, as the rich are fanned and cooled by their admirers.
> Sixty-four yoginis dance around you.
> Oh Shitla Mother, sit on the highest peak of the mountain where the eagle sits.
> Narad [a sage] plays the veena, and others have tied bells to their feet as they dance in your honor.
> Bhagvan Narayan [Vishnu] is also singing songs of your victory with folded hands.
> Therefore, Oh Mother, I appeal to you and sing your songs, and request that you fulfill my desires.
> Oh Mother, I remember you and praise you.

The ceremony reaches its climax on the morning of the ninth day of *navratra*. I shall describe this climax as I observed it at the end of *javara* rites held in the house of a Kurmi (farmer) in a village near Sitapur. In the morning a large number of people congregated in the courtyard of the house. Several men were seated in one corner singing *javara* songs to the accompaniment of cymbals and two large drums. After approximately an hour of singing the seedlings, which had been

removed from the altar, were brought in clay pots to the courtyard and set in a decorated square which had been drawn
with rice grains in the center of the floor. Some of the men
then began a kind of dance. They trembled and jerked as they
moved around the courtyard. Each dancer held a long slender
rod which was shaped into a *trishul* (trident) at one end and
was sharpened to a keen point at the other. A lemon was impaled
on the sharpened end of each of these rods. The dancing continued with gathering fervor. Finally one of the dancers went
into a seizure. He froze in one spot and began howling and
barking. This was evidence of possession by the goddess.

A goat was then led into the courtyard and over to a
man who stood in a corner holding a large knife. An assistant
straddled the animal with his legs, holding it firmly between
his knees. A cloth was held up to conceal the scene from most
of the spectators and the goat was quickly decapitated. Another
goat was led to a point directly before the square where the
seedlings had been deposited. This animal, too, was decapitated
behind a cloth. One of the dancers then threw himself prone
and began licking at the blood slick on the floor. Another
produced a whip resembling a cat-o'-nine-tails, which he
brandished at the spectators in a threatening fashion. Another
dancer appeared with a chain festooned with barbs. This he
kneaded in his right hand until blood appeared. These phenomena, again, are indications of possession.

Three women now approached the square containing the
seedlings in single file, the first in line trembling in the same
fashion as the possessed dancers. A pot containing seedlings
was placed on each woman's head. Then they filed slowly out
of the courtyard and into the lane that ran in front of the house.
As the first woman emerged from the doorway the man sponsoring the ceremony knelt at her feet. There he cut a lemon
in half and executed a *pranam*. A procession then formed.
First came the possessed dancers, then the singers and musicians
and a man who walked backward carrying a pot of smoldering

*Javara seedlings carried from their shrine in a village household
A devotee (lower right) touches the feet of the leading woman.*

incense, then the women carrying the seedlings, and finally
a woman who carried a basket of *nim* leaves.

The procession moved circuitously through the village,
pausing briefly at each major intersection of the village lanes.
At each stop a lemon was cut at the feet of the leading woman.
As the procession moved along, the metal rods carried by the
possessed dancers were put to use. One of the dancers pushed
his rod through the fleshy part of his upper arm. Another
used his rod to pierce his tongue, and then from time to time

Javara: A possessed devotee

swung the rod through a 90-degree arc, twisting his tongue grotesquely out from his mouth. In each case a lemon was stuck on the sharpened end of the rod while it remained in the flesh of the dancer.

Finally the procession left the village and moved toward one of the three village tanks. There the musicians and singers, along with most of the spectators, retired to a shady spot beneath a large tree. The pot of burning incense was placed before a small shrine of the goddess. The seedlings were then taken from their pots and carefully washed in the water of the tank. At the same time other incidental materials of the ritual were submerged in the deeper water of the tank, where they were allowed to remain.

After the immersion of the seedlings and other items, the mood of the ceremony became dramatically different. The singing and drumming ceased, and the manifestations of possession fell away. At the time the procession had arrived at the tank some coconuts had been broken at the feet of the women carrying the seedlings, and these were now distributed in small fragments to the participants and spectators as *prasad*. Most ate their portions on the spot. The freshly washed seedlings were given in small amounts to the men who then placed them behind each others' ears as a mark of friendship. With this, the assembled people began to disperse. Later the sponsor shared the meat from the sacrificed goats with his family and friends.

The events described are typical of the terminal phase of *javara* wherever it is performed, though of course details may differ. The people who are possessed on these occasions are said to be devotees (*bhakts*) of the goddess, and the possession is interpreted as a sign of her favor. We have noted that possession by the goddess in smallpox is directly associated with heat. The same is true of ritual possession. It comes over the devotees, informants say, "like a fever" (*bukhar*). The frenetic setting of possession is itself suggestive of heat, as is the self-inflicted violence that often accompanies possession. However, possession when it occurs in ritual settings is controlled, and in this vital respect it differs from the possession of smallpox. The leaves of the *nim* tree, we have seen, are proverbially cold, and their cooling influence is employed in the therapy of smallpox. *Nim* leaves are present as part of the setting of the concluding phases of *javara*, and are carried with the seedlings in the final procession. Lemons, we have noted, are cold to the degree that their proximity is thought to ward off sunstroke. Lemons play a particularly conspicuous role during the climax of the rite. Each time the procession pauses, lemons are cut at the feet of the women who carry the seedlings, a cooling offering for a now fervid goddess. Lemons are placed on the sharp ends of the rods which pierce the devotees' flesh, suggesting ultimate containment of the bizarre manifestations of possession.

When the procession finally arrives at the tank the seedlings are taken from their pots and washed in water. As we have already noted elsewhere, this procedure is known as *thanda karna*, "to cool." As the seedlings are washed, the frenzy of possession dies. The goddess, now "cool," becomes quiescent and withdraws from the devotees' bodies. The wheat seedlings, now "cooled," are distributed among the men who exchange them in friendship. The emphasis of the ceremony is no longer on heat and possession, but on coolness, sharing, and amity. Thus, it is in the cool aftermath that the social implications of the rite emerge most strongly, and it is at this point that the sharing of *prasad* begins.

Ramnavmi

It is significant that *chaitra sudi* 9, the last day of the hot season *navratra*, is not merely the final day of *javara*, but is the date of another festival as well: *ramnavmi*, or "Rama's ninth." Likewise, the autumn *navratra* (occurring in *kunvar*) also ends in a festival associated with Rama: *dassehra*. The termination of the bloody and rather frenzied rites of *navratra* with ceremonies dedicated to the vegetarian and benevolent Rama suggests the domination of one sort of divinity (that represented by the sinister goddesses) by another (that represented by Rama and other deities resembling him). This is a point of some importance, and one to which we shall return in discussing the structure of the pantheon.

Ramnavmi is celebrated as the birthday of Rama. Chhattisgarhi informants are certainly aware of this festival, though it is not widely observed in rural areas. In Sitapur it is not celebrated. Where there is a temple dedicated to Rama it is an important event. In Raipur elaborate *pujas* are performed in the Dudhadhari Math (Raipur's principal Rama temple) on *ramnavmi,* and *prasad* is distributed to all comers.

Akshaya Tritiya or Akti

There are no important calendrical observances from *ramnavmi* until *baisakh sudi* 3.[2] This date is celebrated as *akshaya tritiya,* or *akti* as it is termed in Chhattisgarhi. The occasion has more than one level of associations. To begin with, it is said to be the birthdate of Parashuram, or "Rama with the Axe," the sixth of the ten *avatars* of Vishnu. In Puranic legend Parashuram is alleged to have killed all of the Kshatriyas of the earth twenty-one times over. He did so because the Kshatriyas were on the point of wresting the rule of the world from the righteous Brahmans (Danielou 1964:170–71). It is also said that the *treta yug,* the second great age of the world during which Rama lived, began on this date.

These, however, are primarily textual associations, which have little bearing on the festival of *akti* as it is observed in Chhattisgarh. Rather, at the level of popular religion the festival has basically two aspects: the ritualized gift of water, and agricultural rites and the beginning of the agricultural year.

On *akti* a pot of water should be given to a Brahman, to a temple, or to one's daughter or sister. The water is supposed to be a gift to the goddess, and the pattern seems to reflect the theme of cooling in relation to divinity in this feminine manifestation. Many people also make offerings of *channa,* a cold food, to the goddess. It is a day, as well, upon which cool things should be served at mealtime. On *akti* it is regarded as meritorious for merchants to put out a water stand in front of their shops.

In villages *akti* has the additional significance of being an occasion that marks the beginning of the agricultural year. On

---

[2] *Hanuman jayanti* (Hanuman's birthday) falls on *chaitra purnima.* There are special observances in Hanuman temples, but this is not a major festival in Chhattisgarh despite Hanuman's popularity in the region.

akti it is customary for farmers to make an offering of rice to Thakur Dev, the protective deity of villages. After this, some manure, *ghi*, water, seed, and a *kudali* (a small picklike implement) are taken to the fields. The *ghi* is burned (a crude *homa*) and the soil of the field is symbolically broken with the *kudali*. Some seed and manure is then placed in the field. This marks the beginning of the plowing season, and although plowing usually does not begin on this day it may be started on any succeeding day. Also, on *akti* agricultural contracts are fixed for the coming year.

Savitri Puja

Savitri Puja occurs on *jyeshth amavashya*, and is one of the most important fasts of the year for women in village and city alike. Though technically it lasts for three days, from *jyeshth badi* 13 to *amavashya*, it appears for the most part to be observed on *amavashya* only. The occasion is celebrated by married women, and its purpose is said to be to bring about a long married life (that is, to protect the life of the husband) and the birth of many sons. The fast is associated with the story of Savitri, a tale as widely known as any religious story. Various versions are current, but the following, related by an informant, seems to contain the essence of all of them:

In ancient times a king of Madradesh had a son by the name of Satyvan. Narad, the great sage, foretold that this boy would have a very short life, and at the same time predicted that the father's kingdom would come to an end. In time, as Narad had predicted, the kingdom was destroyed, and the king and his family became paupers. But despite extreme poverty, Satyvan's wife, Savitri, never uttered a word of complaint, and served her husband and his parents with devotion.

One day Satyvan went to the forest for firewood. He was suddenly struck by a tremendous pain and he died under the branches of a *vat* (banyan) tree. Yama, the lord of death, came to take Satyvan's soul. When Savitri observed this she decided to obey love and duty to the end by following her husband into the realm of the dead. As she followed

Yama and her husband she overcame one obstacle after another. Yama was greatly pleased by this evidence of devotion of a woman to her husband, and as a reward he gave life back to Satyvan, who awoke under the banyan tree with no memory of what had happened. Yama also gave Satyvan's father back his kingdom. Savitri led a blessed life from this time on, and had many sons.

Preparations for *savitri puja* are made by fashioning clay images of Savitri, Satyvan, and Yama, or by drawing their pictures on the wall. Married women fast during the day, and food offerings are made to the images or pictures and, if possible, to a banyan tree. It is considered particularly meritorious for married women to circumambulate a banyan tree on *savitri puja*, ideally 108 times.

Savitri is treated in the ritual as a goddess, but interestingly we are dealing in this instance with a goddess whose characteristics are quite different from the goddesses of the other hot season rituals. Shitla, we noted, is represented in a folktale as seven unmarried sisters. We shall see in a later chapter that in fact all of the sinister goddesses are represented in contexts that tend to deny, mask, or minimize their marital connections. Savitri's married state is stressed, and far from being sinister she emerges as a paragon of virtue. Earthly women are expected to fast on *savitri puja* in imitation of Savitri's selflessness, and from this self-sacrifice will emerge the greatest of worldly benefits from a woman's point of view—a long life for her husband and many sons.

The story of Savitri is an extremely important one. Savitri is regarded as a model of virtuous womanhood, and her devotion to Satyvan is frequently cited as an example for women to follow. In the figure of Savitri, marriage, self-sacrifice, and benevolence are linked in a way that contrasts strikingly with other female deities. The association of marriage with virtues of this order is a crucially important one, and we shall take up this subject again. For the present, it provides a vivid counterpoint to some of the major themes of the other rites of the hot season.

The Rainy Season: The Sleep of the Gods

In Chhattisgarh the rainy season usually begins in mid-June. The initial downpours are striking in their physical effects. The temperature drops steeply to an average maximum of about 86° (Nelson 1909:37), and the red lateritic dust of the Chhattisgarhi countryside becomes mud. Soon the dominant color of the countryside changes from red to green and the work of the yearly agricultural cycle begins in earnest.

In the lunar calendar there is no single date that officially represents the advent of the rainy season. There are, however, two ritual occasions that might be considered markers of the beginning of the rainy season: *rath duj* and *devshayani ekadashi*. *Rath duj* (chariot second), otherwise known as *rath yatra* (the chariot trip) falls on *asharh sudi* 2. This is the famous festival of Krishna as Jagannath, "Lord of the World." On this occasion wherever there is a Jagannath temple—and there is one in almost every major population center in this part of India—the images of Jagannath, his brother Balabhadra Balarama, and his sister Subhadra are taken from their sanctuaries and are drawn in public procession in large chariot cars, or *raths*. The images are taken to temporary shrines until *asharh sudi* 10, when they are drawn back to their temples. The processions are said to celebrate the journey of Krishna and his brother from Gokul to Mathura in order to kill their wicked uncle Kamsa. *Rath duj* is associated with the great temple complex at Puri in Orissa, and almost all my Chhattisgarhi informants were aware that the most important celebration of *rath duj* takes place there. A pilgrimage to Puri during *rath duj* is extremely meritorious.

Rath duj is not one of the most important festivals of Chhattisgarh, although it is celebrated on an impressive scale in towns and cities. It does, however, have a seasonal significance. It is one of the first ritual events of the rainy season, and informants say that if there is no rain by the time of *rath duj*, then this portends scanty rains and a poor crop to come.

Rath duj: Jagannath is drawn through the streets of Raipur
Devotees crowd around the car to receive prasad.

Asharh sudi 11 is a major *ekadashi* known as *devshayani ekadashi* or *vishnu shayani ekadashi*. On this date Vishnu (or "the gods," depending on the telling) is said to go to sleep. He then slumbers through the rainy season, not to awaken until *devuthni ekadashi* (*kartik sudi* 11) four months later. Vishnu is an extremely powerful and very benevolent deity, and his withdrawal into sleep suggests something ominous about the rainy season. Indeed, this suggestion is confirmed by the fact that activities connected with weddings are not supposed to be undertaken during the period between *devshayani ekadashi* and *devuthni ekadashi*. With this we are brought to certain general features of the rainy season.

If an underlying theme in the hot season ritual cycle is the control of potentially dangerous heat, many of the ceremonial aspects of the rainy season seem to relate to forces that are equally malignant, but far less uniform in character. My informants stopped short of describing the rainy season as an *ashubh* (inauspicious) time of year, but it is clear that this is a season full of actual dangers, and a time when human beings must exercise extreme caution. At the most mundane level, when the rains are in full force scorpions and poisonous snakes are driven from their natural burrows and are likely to be found in the most unexpected places. Mud (*kacca*) houses are particularly vulnerable. This is a serious hazard, and during the rains one must quite literally tread carefully. But more important than snakes and scorpions are the diseases of men and cattle, which seem to be especially prevalent during the rains. Gastrointestinal diseases are the major problems and these are among the most important causes of infant mortality in India. These diseases are spread principally by fecal matter, which finds its way into water supplies. Populations are especially vulnerable during the rainy season because wastes are washed into tanks and wells by the enormous quantity of surface runoff resulting from heavy monsoon showers. In villages the fields are used as latrine areas, and in the poorer wards of the city any vacant area may serve the same purpose. Given these conditions, the only sources of pure water are tube wells, and even this water may become contaminated if it is piped underground, as some seepage into water mains is inevitable. Thus, the rainy season is a time when illness is widespread, and this colors much of the rainy season ritual cycle.

Though the rains begin in *asharh*, in a normal year *shravan* is the first full month of rain. During *shravan* and the succeeding month, *bhadon*, monsoon showers come in some form almost every day; accordingly, these two months may be regarded as the heart of the rainy season. At the beginning of this period certain protections against disease-causing influences are commonly undertaken. In villages, and in the older wards of the city of Raipur, the boundaries of houses are often sealed against malign influences by means of lines drawn with cowdung water around the circumferences of the houses and crude drawings executed on outside walls. Ritual boundaries are also sometimes thrown up around entire villages. Thakur Dev is said to stand at the boundaries of villages, protecting those within from intrusion by sinister forces, but sometimes this is insufficient. During the month of *shravan* in 1967 a village about four miles from Sitapur was particularly troubled by illness. Special measures were therefore undertaken. There are three major lanes leading into this village, and just to the side of each of these lanes (the point where they are intersected by the boundaries of the village) a plow had been buried with its point facing outward from the village. Next to each of the inverted plows was a red and white flag, indicating the presence of deities. The people of the village seemed disinclined to discuss the plows. Later I was able to find out more from my informants in Sitapur. The village had been afflicted by a disease of cattle, which had been attributed to witchcraft. When this happens to a village it is said that the "village is destroyed" (*ganv bigar gaya*), and the people of other villages are reluctant to go there. The inhabitants of the village concerned are normally somewhat sensitive on this topic. Three years previously, an informant from Sitapur told me, Sitapur itself was struck by an epidemic of cattle disease. The plows were set up in the same manner, and the Baiga put his *mantra* (ch. 6) into them. The disease stopped, and they were never troubled again.

Rites of Protection

There are three calendrical ceremonies of the rainy season that may be interpreted as rites of "protection," though they have other aspects as well. These are *hariali* (or *hareli*), *nag panchmi*, and *raksha bandhan. Hariali*, falling on *shravan amavashya*, has two major aspects. First, on the morning of *hariali* each farmer worships his agricultural implements, a rite known as *nangar ki puja* (the *puja* of the plow). Second, it is an occasion for the ritual protection of cattle from the diseases common at this time of year. Early in the morning the village herds are taken to an open field by the Ravats. Their owners accompany them carrying a special kind of cake made from coarse flour. These cakes, together with small packets of salt, are then fed to the cattle, and what is left over is given to the Ravats. Later the Ravats will prepare medicine for cattle by mixing these leavings with special herbs and roots.[3]

Nag panchmi, meaning "cobra fifth," is directly linked with protection from snakebite. Its date, *shravan badi 5*, falls, as we have seen, at a time of year when snakes are particularly dangerous. Usually the occasion is observed by offering milk and coconut to a highly stylized picture of a cobra, which has been drawn on a wall. People sometimes leave dishes of milk in the fields for the snakes. *Nag panchmi* and *hariali* share one important feature. On the nights of each of these festivals witches (*tonhis*) are said to be extremely active. They are said to gather late at night at cemeteries and burning grounds, where they dance. They are nude, and their unbound hair swirls around their heads while fire drips from their mouths. Practically everybody claims to know someone who has seen this dance from a distance.

Raksha bandhan, meaning literally "tying on protection," falls on *shravan purnima*. On *raksha bandhan* (or *rakhi*) some people call Brahman priests into the home to tie paper and tinsel amulets to various items around the house. Individuals may tie amulets to each others' wrists, and it is customary for girls and women to tie them to the wrists of their brothers. A fictive brother-sister relationship may be established by the tying of

---

[3] Another festival associated with cattle is *pola* (or *pora*) which occurs on *bhadon amavashya*. On *pola* day bullocks are worshipped, and are decorated with tinsel ornaments. In families who own no real bullocks, clay models are worshipped instead. Clay models of bullocks are also given as toys to children.

rakhi. These amulets are supposed to be protective in nature, hence the name of the festival.

The Fasts

Fasts for women occur throughout the year, but at no time of the year are they more conspicuous than during the rainy season. There are three major fasts at this time, and each hinges on the theme of protection, especially the protection of children or husbands. These three fasts are: *bahula chauth* (*bhadon badi* 4), *harchhat* or *khamarchhat* (*bhadon badi* 6), and *tija* (*bhadon sudi* 3). The most important of the three is *tija*.

Tija (or *tij*) may be undertaken by married women for the long life and prosperity of their husbands or by unmarried women in order to get a "good husband." It is one of the most important annual occasions for women, and is celebrated in both rural and urban areas. The following story of *tija*—one of many versions—was related to me by an informant:

In ancient times there was a Maharaja named Dakshaprajapati, who ruled in Himachal Pradesh. A daughter was born to him, to whom the name Parvati was given. The astrologers said that her fate in life would be a good one, but that she would have to perform severe *tapasya* (renunciation or austerity) in order to gain a husband.

After some years had passed, the Maharishi Narad (a famous sage) arrived at the Maharaja's palace and informed his host that Parvati would become the wife of Mahadev (Shiva). This, he said, would come about as the result of her renunciation. When she was old enough for marriage, Parvati went to the jungle and there began her *tapasya.* Seeing the severity of her renunciation, Indra became worried, thinking that she might become more powerful than the gods. So he sent Kamdev (the god of sexual desire) to divert her.[4] This was unsuccessful. Indra then sent the Saptarishis to tell her that because of her *tapasya* she might choose a husband from among Vishnu, Brahma, and Shiva. She told them that from the beginning she had wanted Shiva. Shiva himself then sent the Saptarishis to Maharaja Dakshaprajapati

---

[4] This episode parallels the well-known temptation of Shiva by Kama. See O'Flaherty 1969b:19ff.

to inform him of the impending wedding, and in the end the wedding was celebrated with great magnificence.

Shiva gave his promise of marriage to Parvati on *bhadon sudi* 3. For this reason women should fast on this date, and in the evening do *puja* of Shiva and Parvati and wish for the good fortune of their husbands.

This story of the marriage of Shiva and Parvati is an extremely well-known Puranic episode. The theme of renunciation, especially sexual renunciation, plays an important role in the story. We have noted already the connection in Hindu thought between renunciation and the acquisition of special powers. Hanuman's renunciation seems to play a special role in relation to his great strength. In Parvati's story the same theme is evident, though here in a feminine context. Parvati, by means of her *tapasya*, reached the point of becoming more powerful than the gods themselves. Indra attempted to undo Parvati's *tapasya* by sending Kamdev, the god of sexual love. But his intervention was ineffective, and in the end the threat to the supremacy of the gods was averted by the marriage of Parvati to Shiva.

This episode carries implications of great import in Chhattisgarhi religion. I shall leave detailed considerations of these points for later, but it will be useful to note again that two contrasting manifestations of feminine divinity seem to be embedded in the ritual cycles. In the rites of the hot season we were introduced to the conception of a sinister, potentially malevolent, meat-eating goddess who appears as Mahamaya, Kali, Shitla, etc. Now we learn that Parvati once grew so powerful by means of renunciation that she constituted a threat to the supremacy of the gods, a threat that disappeared with her marriage to Shiva. Parvati, in fact, is primarily a benevolent goddess, and she never receives blood sacrifice. The story seems to suggest that Parvati has a potentially destructive side, and that this aspect of her character is somehow contained by marriage. It is, after all, with her marriage to Shiva that the threat to the gods disappeared.

In any event, the fasting of women in *tija* is identified with the *tapasya* of Parvati, and any powers this exercise in renunciation may generate are for the benefit of their husbands. At the beginning of the fast a small shrine for Shiva is set up in the house. A square is drawn in white on the floor, and a wooden platform is placed in its center. A brass plate is put on the platform, and on this a *shiv-ling* (the phallic form in which Shiva is usually worshipped) is fashioned from sand. A *kalash* is placed on the floor before the platform. Fruits and flowers are offered to the god, and fasting is undertaken for twenty-four hours. The fast is broken with the taking of *prasad*, and later the materials of worship are disposed of by immersion in water.

Married women usually go to their natal homes to celebrate *tija* during their first year of residence with their husbands' families. On subsequent *tijas* the return trip is optional. Brothers must present gifts (usually a sari) to their married sisters on this occasion. Husbands also usually present saris to their wives.

The other principal fasts, *khamarchhat* and *bahula chauth*, are similar in format, although the associated myths are different. Both fasts are undertaken for the protection of children. *Bahula chauth* is associated with the story of a cow who sacrificed herself to a tiger to save her child, and *khamarchhat* seems to be associated with the goddess Chhati (so named from the ritual of the sixth day after birth), a relatively featureless goddess associated with the protection of children.

During the month of *bhadon* there are two additional annual rites which have a very different character from that of the fasts. These are *janam ashtami* (*bhadon badi* 8) and *ganesh chaturthi* (*bhadon sudi* 4). *Janam ashtami* is Krishna's birthday, and in Krishna temples his birth is reenacted. The infant Krishna is rocked in a cradle to the accompaniment of song. *Ganesh chaturthi* is a festival of Maharashtrian origin. It is a major event in Raipur and in large towns. In villages it is only now becoming well-known, and is not yet celebrated in Sitapur. It is the principal festival of Ganesh, one of the two sons of Shiva. Shiva's other son, Skanda, does not play a significant role in Chhattisgarhi religion. It is of interest that Ganesh was not born of a normal sexual union. Just as Parvati gains immense powers through *tapasya*, so too Shiva, the "great ascetic," gained his powers in renunciation. In Chhattisgarh two stories about the birth of Ganesh may be heard, one in which Ganesh was formed from the slime of Shiva's body, and another in which he was formed by Parvati from the dirt of her own body. Later in his life, Ganesh fell under the malignant glance of Shanni, and in this way he lost his head. (There are other versions of this story.) His father, Shiva, replaced his head with the head of the first animal he came across, which happened to be an elephant.

In Raipur on *bhadon sudi* 4 temporary shrines are erected, in which clay images of Ganesh are installed. Here *puja* is performed every morning and evening for ten days. Other events—*bhajan*-singing, cultural programs and the like—may also take place in the evenings. On the tenth night, the images from all the shrines in the city are taken in a single gigantic procession to a tank on the outskirts of the city, where they are "cooled" by immersion. The images are carried in elaborately decorated floats. The decorations reflect religious and patriotic themes. The procession is accompanied by a cacophony of film music from loudspeakers, and many young men dance in the streets. Ganesh is a lighthearted, pleasure-loving deity, and cheerful music and dancing are consistent with his character. In the end, the images are lowered into the water with appropriate *mantras*, and a few flowers may be thrown over the spot where the images were submerged.

The Fortnight of the Fathers

The dark, or *badi*, fortnight of the lunar month of *kunvar* is known as *pitar pak* (or *pitri paksh*), "the fortnight of the fathers." As we have already seen, this is a time when the agnatic ancestors are understood to be present in the households of their descendants. At this time an astrological event is said to occur, which opens a direct pathway between the *pitrilok*, the abode of the ancestors, and this world. The form in which *pitar pak* is observed varies rather widely, particularly between high and low castes, but some sort of food offering to the ancestors of three ascending generations in the patriline seems to be universal. At a minimum these offerings might consist of bread thrown on the roof for crows (who personify the dead). Alternatively, there may be elaborate offerings supervised by a Pandit. In all cases, the actual offerings must be given by the eldest male of the family. There are hints of pervasive pollution during *pitar pak*. Men who are taking the occasion seriously do not shave until the fortnight is concluded, and the twice-born must change their *janeus* at its conclusion.

Five days during the fortnight are of particular importance. The first day is known as *pitri baith ki*, when the fathers "sit," and some sort of observance is common on this day. The ninth day, known as *matri navmi*, "mothers' ninth," is reserved for ancestresses. The last day is known as *pitri kheda*, the "departure" of the fathers, and this too is a day of importance. In addition, two days of the fortnight are set apart for offerings to one's own mother or father if either is deceased. In either case, offerings are made on that *tithi* of the fortnight which corresponds to the *tithi* on which the death occurred.

The Autumn–Winter–Spring Cycle

It is not possible to designate any particular occasion that marks the end of the rainy season and the beginning of the transition into winter. Climatologically there is no obvious boundary. The rains simply become less frequent and evenings become cooler, ushering in a transitional period. There are three ritual occasions which, if not actually boundary dates, are at least signals of the change of season. One is *devuthni ekadashi* (*kartik sudi* 11), when Vishnu arises from his long slumber of the rainy months. Another is *sharad* (autumnal) *purnima*, which occurs on the full moon day of *kunvar*. In this festival milk and *khir* are exposed to the rays of the full moon and then eaten. They are said to have been transformed into *amrit* (ambrosia) by the action of the moon's rays. However, *dassehra* (*kunvar sudi* 10) is probably the most important of the initial events in the autumn-winter-spring cycle. These months have a relatively large number of what might be called "territorial" festivals—ritual events that can be interpreted as ceremonial expressions of territorial units of varying size and clarity of definition. Some are village festivals. Others are events, such as religious fairs, with much larger constituencies. Since *dassehra* is celebrated with a *ramlila* in many localities, it is the first of these, although it has other important aspects as well.

Dassehra

Rama has two major festivals during the lunar year, one in *chaitra* (*ramnavmi*), and one in *kunvar* (*dassehra*). As we have noted, *ramnavmi* may be seen as a kind of punctuation mark at the end of the hot season *navratra*, occurring on the final day of the nine-day sequence. Similarly, *dassehra* comes just after the autumn *navratra*. The autumn *navratra* period begins on *kunvar sudi* 1 and terminates on *sudi* 9. The same *javara* rites as those of the hot season *navratra* are celebrated during this period. The only difference lies in the relative importance of the *javara* rites during the two periods. Although the autumn *javara* is an important ritual event, it is partly eclipsed by *dassehra*, which is a far more important occasion than *ramnavmi*.

Dassehra, also known as *vijay dashmi* (victory tenth), celebrates the defeat and slaying of the demon Ravana, and a re-enactment of this episode from the *Ramayana* (a drama known as *ramlila*) is a major feature of the festival in many localities. In Raipur this occurs at an area just outside the city which is set aside specifically for the annual performance. Here there is a gigantic statue of Ravana, recognizable by his fearsome appearance and ten heads. On the afternoon of *dassehra* day this area begins to fill with throngs of people from the city and from the

The image of Ravana surrounded by dassehra crowds at Raipur

surrounding countryside. The drama begins at about 5:30.
Ravana, impersonated by an actor, sits at one end of a long raised
platform surrounded by his demonic soldiers. Rama, his brother
Lakshman, and his servant Hanuman are seated at the other
end. Ravana rises from his throne and swaggers downstage.
Hanuman rises to meet him and they engage in a highly stylized
battle. Hanuman finally retires, and Lakshman advances to do
battle. Again the outcome is inconclusive. Finally Ramchandra
(Rama) himself rises from his throne and advances down the
stage. Everyone knows that the end is now near. One of Rama's
attendants hands him a fire-arrow (the *agni ban* of the *Ramayana*).

One fire-arrow is shot at Ravana, then a second and a third. As the third fire-arrow is released, Ravana's standard begins to burn and Ravana falls to the floor. Hanuman now clubs the body mercilessly. Ravana's death occurs just at sunset, and is met with cheering from the crowd and fireworks. Afterward the actors impersonating Rama, Lakshman, and Hanuman are taken in a triumphant procession to Raipur's most important Rama temple, the Dudhadhari Math, accompanied by a crowd who will worship Rama at the temple, and who will receive *prasad*. Along the routes away from the site of the celebrations peddlers are selling leaves known as *sonpatti* (leaves of gold). These are exchanged between friends on *dassehra*. The leaves are said to be sacred because they resemble the footprints of a cow.

In most homes in both village and city the household gods are worshipped on *dassehra* day, and it is customary for artisans to worship their tools as well. Also, in many households wives worship their husbands. The husband is, for the moment, taking the part of Rama, returning in triumph from a great victory. A square in white is drawn on the floor and a wooden platform placed in the center. The husband stands on the platform while his wife washes his feet, places a garland around his neck, and applies a *tilak* of red powder, curds, and rice to his forehead. She then performs *arti* before him, and presents him with an offering of coconut, *pan*, and the like. She bows in *pranam* before him, after which he is fed his evening meal.

Divali

The term *divali* is a contraction of *dipavali*, which in turn derives from the words *dip* (lamp) and *avali* (row), and refers to the lighting of lamps, which is one of the most characteristic features of the festival. *Divali*, which is at least as much a state of mind as a concrete event, is the most festive time of the year. As *divali* approaches houses and business establishments are completely cleaned and repaired. Fresh whitewash is evident everywhere. Chalk designs known as *rangolis* are executed by girls in the streets in front of their houses. Vendors of sweets and fireworks line the city streets. Film music blares from loudspeakers set up in the business sections of towns and cities. Four distinct events occur during this period, all of which cluster around the new moon night of *kartik*. One is *lakshmi puja*, essentially a domestic rite. The other three—*gaura*, *gobardhan puja*, and *matar*—are both caste and village festivals.

Laksmi puja, occurring on *kartik amavashya*, is an occasion for the worship of Lakshmi, Vishnu's consort and the goddess of wealth. This is the central event of *divali*. With the coming of darkness lamps are lighted and placed around the outside of houses. Informants say that the purpose of the lamps is to help Lakshmi find her way into the house. Inside the house a special temporary altar is prepared for Lakshmi. Her principal manifestation in this world is wealth in all its forms. Symbols of wealth—coins, ornaments, and perhaps a few cowrie shells—are therefore, placed on her altar. *Puja* is performed with offerings of sweets and milk. The sweets are then passed around the family as *prasad*. Consistent with the emphasis on wealth, the next morning many people gamble. *Lakshmi puja* is an occasion of particular importance to merchants. On *amavashya* night Lakshmi is worshipped in the form of account books in business establishments, and the beginning of the new business year is calculated from the time of this *puja*.

Gaura is a festival of the Gonds, although everyone may participate. It is celebrated in villages and in the older sections of Raipur where Gonds are present. The observance of this festival actually begins some days before *divali*, but it reaches its climax on the day following *lakshmi puja*. *Gaura* is one of Shiva's many names (just as *Gauri* is one of Parvati's names), and the festival celebrates the marriage of Shiva and Parvati.

When I observed the festival in Sitapur the Gond women of the village went in procession with a drummer to the fields on *amavashya* day. There they gathered clay from which the images of Shiva and Parvati would be made for the rites to come.

The sua nach

Informants likened this procession to a similar sequence in which soil is obtained for use in human marriages (ch. 3). When the procession returned the clay was deposited in a clean place, where the images were to be made. The Gond women spent the remainder of the day performing the *sua nach* (the parrot dance), a traditional Gond dance. Parties of women moved from house to house with a basket containing an image of a parrot, a small lamp, and some uncooked rice. At each house this was set on the ground and the women danced around it. They accepted contributions for the dancing and said that one of the reasons they perform the dance is to help defray the costs of the *gaura* celebration.

The clay images of Shiva and Parvati were brought out in the small hours of the morning following *lakshmi puja*. Each image was a few inches high and was set on a wooden platform about one foot square. The image of Shiva was covered with gold leaf and the image of Parvati with silver. Each image was placed on a man's head and in this fashion taken around the village. The procession was headed by a party of musicians and dancers and was likened by informants to Shiva's own tumultuous wedding party. The musicians and dancers, Ganda by caste, were hired as a group by the village to provide music and entertainment for the duration of the *divali* festivities. Similar groups

Nachkar: A Ganda man with a party of musicians during divali

may be seen everywhere in the region during this period. The dancers are young men dressed in saris and blouses for the occasion. With padding to simulate breasts and a liberal application of cosmetics they often look very feminine indeed.

The procession wound its way through the streets, stopping for a time at intersections, until it finally arrived at a platform that had been prepared for the marriage of the god and goddess. Here a marriage pavilion had been erected, and the images were carried around it in seven circuits in simulation of a wedding. This, in effect, married the god and goddess, and they were then placed side by side while the Gond women sang. The theme of the singing was marriage:

> It is told from sister to sister,
> Without the mother nothing can be done.
> Your husband [Shiva] without you is but a brother and a brother.
> And during this time of marriage we sisters are assembling.
> You and I will be a couple and enjoy.

The singing continued through the remaining hours of darkness. When light began to appear a *homa* was performed on the platform, and once again the god and goddess were carried in procession. Possession occurred during it, and in this respect it was not unlike the final procession of the rites of *javara*. Two women became possessed, as did a number of men. As the parade halted at each intersection, some of the men demonstrated their possessed state by submitting to strokes from a kind of fiber whip known as the *sant*. Informants stated that possession will come naturally to those who "yield," "assent" (*mante hain*) and who have sufficient devotion for the god and goddess. If a devotee of the deity hears the drumming and singing, then he will feel the possession coming upon him "like a fever." When the scourge is applied he will feel relief.

The images were finally taken to the tank, where they were "cooled" by immersion. At the same time coconuts were broken for *prasad*, and the fragments were distributed to everyone present. While the "cooling" of the images was taking place, the

Gaura: Shiva and Parvati are taken in procession to the village tank

possession of the devotees died. Informants stated that at this point they are telling the deities, "now be peaceful" (*ab shant ho jao*). The gold and silver leaf was taken from the images as they were immersed, and was distributed among all the men who were present. The men applied little bits of it to each others' foreheads. This is regarded as a gesture of friendship, and parallels the reciprocal presentation of seedlings at the conclusion of the *javara* rites.

The day following *gaura* is *kartik sudi* 1. For merchants this is an extremely important day—in fact the first day of the commercial year—and each merchant attempts to negotiate at least

Gaura: A possessed man submits to the whip

a token transaction on this day with every other merchant with whom he maintains a standing commercial relationship. For most people, however, the most significant aspect of this date is the festival of *gobardhan puja. Gobardhan*, sometimes taken to mean "cowdung wealth" (*gobar*, "cowdung"; *dhan*, "wealth"), derives from the name of a famous hill in Mathura District. When Krishna was a youthful cowherd (Gopal) he once lifted the Hill Gobardhan and used it to protect his fellow herdsmen from a violent rainstorm. This is said to have been the first indication of Krishna's divinity, and the festival of *gobardhan puja* celebrates the event. In each home a representation of the hill is made out of wet cowdung. The model is about one foot on a side with tiny representations of the cattle and cowherds of the associated story placed here and there upon it. This is worshipped with the family cattle, if such exist.

In Chhattisgarhi villages the celebration of *gobardhan puja* in individual households often occurs together with a villagewide celebration, the latter being in the hands of the Jaria Ravats, the subcaste of Ravats believed to be indigenous to the region. When I observed the rite in Sitapur, a party of Ravats (both Jaria and Kanaujia) was formed in the afternoon, and went from house to house with the Ganda musicians, performing a dance known as the *gahira nach*, which may be seen everywhere in the region during the *divali* period. A distinctive feature of the *gahira nach* is the brandishing of *lathis*, the heavy bamboo sticks the Ravats employ in their occupation as cowherds.

The drumming and dancing are interrupted every few minutes so that one of the dancers can shout out a *doha* (couplet). On the last line of the *doha* the dancing begins again. The *dohas* are on religious themes, often drawn from the *Ramayana*:

> You demons have taken the form of a begging mendicant and have come for alms.
> Mata Sita came out holding alms, and you took her away in a chariot.

or:

> The babu says "tiger-tiger; where has the tiger come from?"
> My tiger is really Bajrangbali [Hanuman]; he has eaten my heart.

Having performed at individual households, the dancers began to move through the village lanes in procession. In Sitapur the Kandaras (basketmakers) played a special role in the festival. The Kandaras worship a deity known as *bairang*, which consists of two long poles, each festooned with small triangular flags, one with white flags the other with black. When the procession arrived at the neighborhood of the Kandaras the two poles were held erect while they were worshipped by a senior man of the Kandara community. He ignited a lamp, offered incense, and broke a coconut. He grasped the poles at their base and entered a state of trembling possession. He then flogged himself over both shoulders with a spiked chain. After this the flags were braced upright against his stomach and he joined the procession as it moved through the remainder of the village. A small boy carried the spiked chain conspicuously and reverently alongside.

The procession then moved to the edge of the village, where a deity known as Saharha Dev reposes in the form of a large upright stone. Saharha Dev, a special deity of the Jaria Ravats, protects cattle from disease. Near the god a large representation of the Hill Gobardhan had been made from cowdung. The Ravats worshipped the hill, Saharha Dev, and a calf staked nearby. Then a lane was cleared through the crowd and a herd of some forty or fifty cattle was driven out of the darkness and over the fecal representation of the hill. There was then a scramble among the men as each attempted to get a fistful of the dung, after which each man applied cowdung to the foreheads of the other participants. Informants stated that this final episode of *gobardhan puja* is simply another form of *lakshmi puja*. Lakshmi is incarnate in the cow, and one of the most common words for cow in Chhattisgarhi is simply *lakshmi*. The final phase of *gobardhan puja* is a gesture of very profound humility before the goddess. Her feces, touched by her feet, are applied to the foreheads of her worshippers.

Kartik sudi 2 is apparently known over most of North India as *bhai duj* (brother second) or *yam duj* (Yama—the god of death—second). In this festival brothers and sisters exchange gifts. *Bhai duj* has some importance in Raipur, but at least in Sitapur it is eclipsed by regional festival that occurs on the same date: *matar*. *Matar*, a festival linked to a deity worshipped by the Kanaujia Ravats, has been described in detail in chapter 2 and it is enough to say here that it marks the conclusion of the *divali* sequence. However, the emotions aroused during this cluster of rites—possibly the most important, certainly the most festive, of the entire year—are strong, and the excitement tapers off only gradually. The dancing parties are to be seen for several days afterward as they move into the towns and cities to perform the *gahira nach* for money. The sight of these dancing parties moving through the streets is one of the most distinctive features of the *divali* season in Raipur.

Following closely after *divali* is *devuthni ekadashi*, also known as *jethoni*. This, it will be recalled, is the date upon which Vishnu rises from his rainy-season slumber. Informants are well aware of the association with Vishnu, but the occasion is also linked with the goddess Tulsi. The *tulsi* plant should be worshipped, and in the evening lamps should be set out around houses as they are during *divali*. Sugarcane is included among the offerings, and this is supposed to be the first night of the season when it may be eaten.

Melas

Melas are religious fairs. They vary greatly in size and importance. Some have regional constituencies, while others are of importance only to smaller areas. At the lowest level are fairlets known as *marhais*, which involve only a few cooperating villages. These too have a religious character, being presided over by a deity in the form of a tall pole topped by peacock feathers. In Chhattisgarh there are great numbers of *melas* and *marhais*, and most of them fall within the autumn-winter-spring period. The lunar month of *magh* has a particularly high incidence of *melas*. During *magh* (also during *kartik*) it is considered meritorious to take special ritual baths daily, and of all the days of the month, *magh purnima* is the most important. Accordingly, many *melas* are held on this date, most notably at Ratanpur, Sirpur, Somnath, and Rajim. Of these by far the most important is the *mela* at Rajim. It is said that every person should visit the Rajim *mela* at least once in a lifetime. Another *mela* of considerable importance in the region is the *punni mela*, which occurs on *kartik purnima* at Mahadev Ghat, just outside Raipur. This *mela* draws large numbers of people from Raipur itself and from the surrounding countryside.

Each *mela* has its own raison d'être and distinctive character, but there are certain general patterns found in all. On the day of a *mela* the roads are typically clogged with bullock carts bringing entire families from outlying villages. Near the site of the *mela* itself there is usually an area set aside as an encampment for the participants. For each participant the central religious act of the *mela* is a bath in the watercourse followed by a visit to the deity in a temple nearby. But if the principal rationale of

Punni mela: Bathing at Mahadev Ghat at Raipur

mela is religious, most of what actually takes place has little relationship to ritual bathing and worship. The atmosphere at these affairs is distinctly commercial. There is always a large temporary bazaar, where merchandise of all kinds is sold, much of which is probably not easily available in more remote villages. Entertainment is also an important part of *melas*; there may be *bhajan*-singing, sideshows, acrobatics, and the like. All of this combines to make the *mela* a rare treat for the predominantly village people who come.

Mahashivratri

Mahashivratri, or "the great night of Shiva," is celebrated on *phalgun badi* 14, and commemorates the night of Shiva's marriage to Parvati. Thus, Shiva's marriage is celebrated on two occasions in the Chhattisgarhi sacred year: once on *mahashivratri* and once at the time of *gaura*. Of the two, *gaura* seems more likely to be indigenous to the Chhattisgarh region, as it remains the more important in rural areas. *Mahashivratri* is, in Chhattisgarh, primarily an urban festival, although there are a number of country *melas* on this date.

When *mahashivratri* is celebrated in the household, a *ling* is fashioned from sand on a brass plate to provide the focus of worship. Offerings consisting of bananas, hard white candy, and cake made from white flour are presented to the deity, and *prasad* is distributed in the usual manner to the family and friends. However, the most important activities of the occasion take place not in the household, but at Shiva's temples. During the morning hours women line up outside the Shiva temples of Raipur, each with a pot of water in her hand, and each barefoot. These women—who must fast for the day—are required to walk barefoot from their houses to the temple, where Shiva is worshipped in the usual way—by pouring water over the *ling*, the conventional phallic representation of Shiva. There is variation here; some offer flowers as well as water and others pour milk over the *ling*. Informants state that married women who worship Shiva on *mahashivratri* do so for the well-being of their husbands, and that unmarried girls who participate are doing so in hopes of obtaining a "good husband." The role of Shiva in the rite of the sixteen Mondays' vow, *tija*, and *mahashivratri* suggests a special connection between this deity and the marital welfare of women. Later we shall see that Shiva plays a key role with respect to marriage as it functions in the pantheon.

In the rites of *mahashivratri* the theme of hot and cold is once again evident. By the time of *mahashivratri* the weather has again become very warm, and some informants say the hot season begins on this day. The water which is poured over the *ling* is cooling in its effects, and so is the milk. In many Shiva temples a pot of water pierced at the bottom is suspended over the *ling* in such a way that water constantly drips down upon it. This is done explicitly to keep the god "cool." In a later chapter we shall see that there is an important sense in which Shiva is a "hot" deity. Such an interpretation is consistent with these ritual attentions designed to keep the god "cool."

The consumption of *bhang* (a preparation of Cannabis sativa) is also an important feature of *mahashivratri*. Shiva's liking for this substance is proverbial, and his wedding to Parvati is said by informants to have been a narcotic revel. On *mahashivratri*, *bhang* is prepared in Shiva temples, offered to the god, and taken as *prasad*.

Holi: End and Renewal

The mood of the festival of *holi* begins to develop as the month of *magh* nears its end. After *magh purnima* the songs of *holi* are sung, and wood begins to accumulate in piles at the places where the bonfires of *holi* night are to be lighted. The actual night of *holi* falls on *phalgun purnima*, and during the two or three days preceding this date the mood of the festival becomes increasingly pervasive as young men roam the streets of the city and the countryside in search of wood for the *holi* fires. Wood is scarce in Chhattisgarh, and items made from wood are apt to disappear mysteriously unless carefully watched.

The ritual sequence of *holi* begins with the lighting of a bonfire on *phalgun purnima* night. The fire is associated with the story of Prahalad:

Once long ago there lived an extremely virtuous young man by the name of Prahalad. He was a fervent devotee of Rama (or Vishnu, depending upon the telling), and his thoughts dwelt day and night on the deity. His father, by contrast, was a wicked man who was convinced that he himself was divine. He ordered his son to worship him as a god, but Prahalad refused and persisted in his devotion to Rama. As a result, his father became exceedingly angry.

Prahalad had a paternal aunt named Holika, who had once been given the divine boon that she could never be destroyed by fire. Knowing this, Prahalad's father devised with his sister a scheme for the destruction of the pious boy. Prahalad was to be tricked into sitting on his aunt's lap while she in turn was sitting on a great pile of wood. The wood would be ignited, and Prahalad would perish while Holika would emerge unharmed. But because of Prahalad's intense devotion for Rama, the god intervened and the youth was unharmed while Holika was consumed by the flames.

The *holi* fire, which is identified with the fire in the story, should be ignited with the rising of the moon on *holi* night, though in fact the fires were lighted at various times when I observed *holi* in Raipur. In Raipur there is a separate fire for each neighborhood, and the village of Sitapur has a single fire for all of its inhabitants. Once the fire is burning briskly both men and women circumambulate it. After completing five circuits of the fire many people make an offering of five cakes of cowdung, which are thrown into the flames. As the fire is symbolically consuming the demoness Holika, it is appropriate to direct vituperation toward the blaze. This *kharab bhasha* (bad talk) is genuinely obscene and would be entirely out of order in any other context.

With this we are brought to what is one of the most interesting aspects of *holi*—the sense of catharsis and purging which seems to dominate the entire affair. Informants maintain that in *holi* the accumulated evils of the past year are swept away. The obscene songs and shouts directed at the *holi* fire are merely the beginning of this process, as we shall see shortly. It should be noted that these cathartic elements are quite at variance with norms of everyday behavior and, more particularly, with the values of the twice-born. "Terrible things go on during *holi*," an informant remarked, even as he was about to participate in the festival. *Holi* is the festival of the Shudras, as a proverb goes, and we shall see evidence that this is more than a mere figure of speech. *Holi* combines themes of pollution, heat, and license in a manner that would be highly inappropriate at any other time of year.

The mood of license is a part of *holi* in both city and village, but some of its most striking manifestations are to be seen in Raipur, particularly among the Marwaris. In 1967 the first indication of the licentiousness of *holi* was the appearance in the evenings of a statue known as Nathu Ram in the heart of Raipur's bazaar near a number of Marwari business establishments. Upon close inspection Nathu Ram turned out to be a life-sized image of a seated man dressed in the style of a raja. He was endowed with an immense phallus hinged in such a way that it could be waved about by a manipulator crouching behind the statue. He was surrounded by a court of guffawing men, and newcomers were formally introduced to him with mock solemnity.

The phallic theme is an important part of the festival. In Raipur in 1967 a number of mimeographed sheets on obscene themes were circulating around the bazaars in the days immediately before *holi*. One was drawn up in the form of a public proclamation, which announced that an unknown woman had made away with Nathu Ram's "matchless penis" and that this had resulted in great inconvenience for other ladies of the city, who held the object in great regard. The sheet went on to describe the stolen item, and concluded with a few lines of bawdy verse. During this same period young men of the city carved obscene words—usually *land* (penis)—in reverse on the faces of split potatoes, and with these they printed obscenities on the clothing of unsuspecting men. On the night of *holi* itself some men display wooden images of an erect penis. One may bow in *pranam* to these in an act of mock worship. All of this is reflected in the obscene and often phallic themes of the songs traditionally sung during the *holi* period. A favorite rallying cry for *holi* revelers—*maharaj land ki jai* (victory to the lord penis)—seems to express well one of the dominant moods of the festival.

On the morning following the burning of the *holi* fire (*chaitra badi* 1) a new phase of the festival begins, this known as *holi khel* (*holi* play). This aspect of *holi*, consisting basically of the throwing of colored water on other participants, is said by informants to be in imitation of the play of Krishna and Radha. Krishna, indeed, is regarded as the presiding deity of this aspect of the festival. Hot weather is desired for this "play." In 1967 there were unseasonable rains during *holi* in Raipur, and the air was correspondingly cool. Informants stated that this would make for a very poor *holi*.

The essentials of *holi* play are the same in villages and the city. Groups of men go from house to house picking up additional members. At each house the group raises a clamor, demanding that the man (or men) of the house emerge to join the fun. When the unfortunate man finally comes out he is usually thoroughly doused with colored water, and he may have colored powder ground into his face and hair as well. There is, however, noticeable variation in the way *holi* play is conducted. There is a minimal "core" gesture, which occurs when two men of more or less quiet and dignified disposition meet. Each simply applies a small amount of red powder to the other's forehead, and then they embrace. This, I was told, is "pure *holi*"—a gesture of amity which some informants maintained is the proper expression of the spirit of the festival. The play is ordinarily less benign. The more usual pattern is for the two individuals to throw colored water at each other, which again should be followed by an embrace.

Sometimes *holi* play carries overtones of genuine violence. *Holi*, as Marriott (1966) has pointed out, is a time when the bully is bullied and the high brought low, an aspect of the festival in perfect keeping with its cathartic aspects. The bully and the man who has the advantage at other times are sought for *holi* play, and sometimes their treatment is very rough indeed. Old scores from the preceding year can be settled on *holi*. But whatever happens, the victim must play the good sport. In the end, enemies must embrace and the issue is regarded as closed (though indeed it may not be). The victim should respond with good humor; the only time I saw this rule dramatically broken was when a Marwari acquaintance was pushed against the concrete wall of a water cistern in such a way that several teeth were loosened. His unsporting response was an embarrassment to those standing by.

Women play *holi* as well as men. In Raipur women band together in the morning to lure other women out of their houses in the same fashion as men. *Holi* play between men and women is usually confined to the household, though in villages groups of women may waylay lone men and subject them to the standard indignities of the day. During these episodes of *holi* play women display an aggressiveness entirely out of keeping with ordinary standards of feminine behavior. *Holi*, however, represents an occasion upon which ordinary norms and conventions are temporarily overturned. If Hindu culture ordinarily puts a premium on unassertiveness in women, on *holi* the reverse is entirely appropriate. Likewise, if Hindu culture ordinarily proscribes open displays of sexuality, on *holi* sexuality is one of the dominant and most obvious motifs of the day. There is a clear sense of reversal in the festival, which perhaps is in no way more vividly exemplified than by the feminine dress some men wear on the day of *holi* play

Associated with the license and frenzy of *holi* is the important role of *bhang* in the celebrations. It is consumed in considerable quantity on *holi* night and on the following day, and it is taken by many individuals who would disapprove of its use on any other occasion. *Bhang* is sold in the form of tiny leaf fragments, and these are mixed with black pepper and ground into a greenish paste on flat stones. The paste is then formed into balls about an inch in diameter. These may be broken into smaller pieces and swallowed, but it is more common for *bhang* to be mixed with food or drinks. By preference it is taken with a preparation of sweetened milk known as *thandai*. *Thandai* derives from the word *thanda* (cold), and it seems likely that this "cold" drink is preferred because it in some way balances the heat of the occasion.

Holi is an occasion explicitly associated with pollution, and in this respect its closest analogues in the ritual cycles are the periods of birth and death in the life cycle of the individual. *Holi* is a time when people who are ordinarily vegetarian may eat meat, with all of its implications of pollution. After the completion of *holi*, baths are taken; and clay pots are thrown away and new ones purchased, just as at the time of death. It is clear, in fact, that in *holi* we see themes of frenzy, license, pollution, and heat in a converging pattern. The festival comes at the beginning of the hottest time of year, and it is understood that the weather should be hot for a successful *holi*. At the same time the most conspicuous mood of the festival is one of frenzy and license, which appears in interpersonal aggression and open displays of sexuality. The link between this kind of behavior and conceptions of "heat" is not hard to find in Chhattisgarhi culture. Hot foods are associated with sexual passion, and according to the Chhattisgarhi stereotype, the meat-eating and liquor-drinking Panjabis are choleric and oversexed. Meat and liquor, the hottest foods, are also linked with pollution—meat because of its connection with bloodshed, and liquor because of its association with decay. All of these ideas seem to rotate around conceptions of the intrinsic nature of the lower castes. On *holi* license, frenzy, heightened sexuality, pollution—things that are both demeaning and "hot"—are to some degree allowable for everyone. Seen in this light the common saying that "*holi* is the festival of the Shudras" takes on considerable meaning. Indeed, on *holi* every participant becomes a Shudra.

If *holi* negates the rules of everyday life, perhaps the most important negation of all is that of status differentiation. Hierarchy is a pervasive fact of Chhattisgarhi social life. The central gesture of *holi* play, the reciprocal application of colored powder and the subsequent embrace, seem to express both closeness and equality. Equally, the elaborations on the core gesture, the throwing of colored water and other pranks, suggest a temporary erasure of hierarchical distance. In chapter 2 I tried to show that the very structure of *puja* lends itself to the masking of worldly hierarchy. In *holi* there seems to be a sense in which hierarchy is not masked but rudely shattered. Such an interpretation is quite explicit in what informants say: *holi* is a time when everyone is brought to the same level. This is precisely the visual effect produced by the festival. Everyone looks more or less the same—with face, hair, and clothing smeared with colors. In such a setting the normal patterns of hierarchy seem very remote indeed.

This is not to say, however, that *holi* is a time of *complete* overturning of the structural framework of everyday life. While a man on the faculty of a college might play *holi* with his students, a bank manager would not normally play *holi* with his office flunky. A Kurmi might play *holi* with other villagers of lower caste, but he does not play *holi* with Untouchables. In fact, where status difference is sufficiently great it is expressed directly during *holi*. On this day servants approach their employers and garland them with sugar cakes. Then they bow in *pranam* and are given gifts, usually of money. Within these outside limitations, however, *holi* is a time when the differences that hold men apart are temporarily negated and when the slate is wiped clean for the coming year. Marriott has captured the essence of the festival when he says "Each actor playfully takes the role of others in relation to his own usual self. Each may thereby learn to play his own routine roles afresh, surely with renewed understanding, possibly with greater grace, perhaps with reciprocating love" (1966:212).

Conclusion

The Chhattisgarhi sacred year is based on lunar-solar calculations and is the most complex cycle of rituals we have encountered. During the course of the sacred year the people of Chhattisgarh are drawn into a highly diverse array of ritual performances. These ceremonies constitute ritual expressions of many of the most important social units in Chhattisgarhi society: family, village, neighborhood, caste, and—in the case of the great religious fairs—even region and subregion. They also express a range of very different ritual attitudes toward the world of gods, goddesses, and other beings and powers as they affect human life.

The sacred year is not divisible into sharply defined segments. Nevertheless, it falls into three recognizable phases, which seem to respond to the physical turning of the seasons. The first phase is that of the hot season in which ritual expressions linked to various manifestations of the goddess are a dominant motif. This is the season of smallpox, and conceptions of this disease provide a particularly vivid exemplification of ideas of feminine malevolence and divine power as heat. The second phase is that of the rainy season, in which danger and hazard become ritually prominent. What I have called "rites of protection" seem to be stressed during this period. The third phase, that of autumn-winter-spring, lacks the same degree of focus, but it is during this period that village festivals and religious fairs, rites that draw from territorial constituencies, become particularly conspicuous. The sacred year begins and ends with *holi*, a time when the detritus of the previous year is swept away; a time of reversal, purging, catharsis, and finally renewal.

In the sacred year certain aspects of the differentiation of the pantheon emerge clearly. Of particular interest are the transmutations of feminine divinity, which are represented in yearly cycle. The rites of the hot season stress certain sinister goddesses who are associated with disease, possession, heat, and blood sacrifice. Elsewhere we see goddesses of a very different character—Lakshmi, Parvati, Savitri, and Tulsi—who are benevolent and who are exemplars of certain specifically feminine virtues. In the stories associated with *savitri puja* and *tija* (and in the story of the sixteen Mondays' vow), we have seen hints that the containment of the potentially malevolent side of female divinity is associated with a juxtaposition of male and female in marriage. I shall return to this idea in my discussion of the structure of the pantheon.

In a discussion of Hanuman in chapter 4 we have already encountered the idea that renunciation is a source of power. The same principle operates in the story of Parvati's marriage to Shiva, and is also reflected in the idea that fasting is a way to tap beneficent power, an idea that appears at many points in the ritual cycles. We have also seen ample evidence linking the ideas of power and heat. This is an important association, and one that we shall encounter again.

These and other themes have emerged in our examination of the ritual cycles of Chhattisgarh. It remains now to put them into some kind of relationship with each other.

6
Brahman and Baiga

I shall now turn to the roles of religious specialists. The topic is an important one because it touches directly on the question of "levels" in Chhattisgarhi religion. This question, in turn, sharpens itself into a more specific problem—that of the role of the text. By now it should be evident that this role is not a simple one. To begin with, we have seen that quite apart from the question of textual *elaboration*, there is a basic structural homology between virtually all forms of Chhattisgarhi cere-monialism that has its basis in the manipulations of *puja*. Since these manipulations are set down in texts, there is a sense in which all forms of ritual are "textual."

Nevertheless, some ceremonials employ textual ritual "styles" to a greater degree than others. Here, however, the situation becomes exceedingly complex. Higher castes tend more than others to employ textual ritual styles in domestic ceremonies and to focus religious attitudes on deities described in texts, but such styles and deities are not relevant only to the higher castes. Certain ritual events (such as the *saptashati path* described in chapter 2) are almost wholly textualized, but Chhattisgarhi ceremonialism, taken in its broadest dimensions, forms a pattern in which elements of textual and local provenance are inextricably intermingled. The festival of *gaura* provides an excellent example. The festival celebrates the marriage of the deities Shiva and Parvati, an event described in texts. However, it celebrates the marriage in a manner that is at least partially defined by local custom rather than by texts. In sum, it does not seem possible to separate textual and nontextual strata in Chhattisgarhi religion. The evidence suggests that instead of defining a "type" of Hinduism that competes with, or replaces, other religious orientations, texts are in some way drawn into a more inclusive religious system that contains both textual and nontextual elements. The question, then, becomes that of what the relationship between textual and nontextual elements is *within* a single system.

The problem of texts leads us directly to the Brahman priest, for he above all is the vehicle through which sacred literature enters the religious life of the region. This, in turn, leads us to questions concerning the roles of religious specialists more generally, for the Brahman priest coexists with another religious specialist, the Baiga, whose role complements his own. There are other types of religious specialists in the region (such as the Bairagis) but the Brahman and Baiga are the major figures.

A pattern for the analysis of the roles of religious specialists in Hinduism already exists. David Mandelbaum has proposed that a distinction be drawn between "pragmatic" and "transcendental" aspects of religion. These, he suggests, are expressed in two different "complexes" of religious belief and practice. The transcendental complex "is used to ensure the long-term welfare of society, to explain and help maintain village institutions, to guarantee the proper transition of individuals from stage to stage within the institutions. It is concerned with the ultimate purposes of man. The pragmatic complex, by contrast, is used for local exigencies, for personal benefit, for individual welfare" (Mandelbaum 1966:1175).

Mandelbaum ties these two aspects of religion to the roles of two contrasting types of religious specialists. In the Indian case, the transcendental complex is in the hands of hereditary priests, usually Brahman, who are exemplars of ritual purity. The pragmatic complex is in the hands of ritualist-exorcists, often shamanistic, whose status is achieved, not ascribed, and whose origins generally are in the lower castes. These two types of specialists do not compete; rather, their roles are complementary. Each has his own sphere in the religious life of the community.

Mandelbaum's schema provides an excellent starting point for the following discussion. In his concern with the similarity and the contrast between the roles of religious specialists, he has put his finger on a principle of great importance in the organization of religious practice in Chhattisgarh. There are two major types of religious specialists in this region. Their roles are complementary, not competitive. Textual and nontextual religious styles intermingle in religious practice, but when seen in relation to the roles of these religious specialists, differences in religious style acquire functional significance. This, in turn, is linked in fundamental ways to the structure of the pantheon and to the view of reality embodied in Chhattisgarhi religion.

Brahman Priests

In Chhattisgarh a Brahman priest is known as a *pandit*, and by convention is addressed as *maharaj*, "great lord." He is Brahman by definition—in this region usually a Kanaujia Brahman (a branch that traces its origin to the city of Kanauj). His role has two aspects. One is a particular kind of knowledge, the other is purity; and I shall discuss each of these in turn.

Knowledge

Brahmans are not always priests; indeed, most Brahmans are not. A Brahman priest possesses a certain kind of knowledge and expertise, as the designation *pandit* (learned man) implies. A Brahman priest is a specialist in certain kinds of ritual—specifically, the performance of rites that involve, refer to, or derive from sacred literature. Rituals of this sort demand knowledge, and to perform his function the Brahman priest must be well-versed in the manipulations required, and must have at least a putative knowledge of Sanskrit and the textual tradition.

Brahman priests are often called upon to preside over life cycle rituals. When they do so, they perform the rituals in a manner sanctioned by texts. This style has great prestige, as does the presence of the Brahman; indeed, the presence of Brahman priests is a traditional mark of high caste, and among the twice-born they are virtually required. Among middle-ranking castes their presence is certainly desired, but is not always possible, often for reasons of cost. At least in theory they will not serve Untouchables in this fashion, whatever the inducement. While no Brahmans live in Sitapur, Brahman priests are available from nearby communities. Nevertheless, most of the life cycle rites I saw in Sitapur and nearby villages were conducted by the principals themselves without Brahmanical assistance. This is important, for it shows that Brahmans are not essential to the rites as such. Such rites have generally the same purpose and structure whether or not they are presided over by a Brahman priest. However, if they are done with such assistance they are textually elaborated to a very high degree, elaboration that involves the recitation of Sanskrit *mantras* and complicated ritual manipulations in accord with textual formulas.

Brahman priests also preside over domestic rites other than those of the life cycle. Again, when present they conduct these rites with a high degree of textual elaboration. Such rituals might be performed in conjunction with festival occasions, or they might be performed at other times for some specific purpose. In the *saptashati path* we have already seen an example of such a rite. A more common "occasional" domestic rite is the *satynarayan katha*, a ceremony honoring Vishnu (Satynarayan) in which a text of (apparently) Puranic origin (the *katha*) is read by the officiating priest. The important elements of the ceremony are the recitation of the text, a *homa*, and the distribution of *prasad*. It is important to note that the rationale for sponsoring this ceremony, or others like it, is not necessarily "transcendental" in what I take to be Mandelbaum's sense. Rather, the desire for business success, good health, children, and the like, are the usual motivations. One may either hold the ceremony in hopes that the deity will fulfill the request or vow to sponsor the ceremony after the request has been honored. More abstract benefits such as religious "merit" (*punya*) are sometimes said to be consequences of sponsorship, but were never presented to me as reasons for a specific ceremony. The text of the *katha* read during the ceremony relates how performing the ritual "wipes away sorrow, multiplies prosperity, is beneficial to women, will bring about the birth of children, will bring happiness and *moksha* [salvation]." The role of the Brahman priest is not necessarily divorced from "pragmatic" concerns.

The presence of a Brahman priest is, strictly speaking, not essential for the performance of domestic ceremonies. Ceremonies of any kind can be conducted in the home with or without the assistance of a Brahman priest. However, to perform the rites in a textually elaborated style requires the presence of the priest, unless the sponsor himself is well-versed in the specific requirements of ceremonial of this type. Prestige attaches to the rites as done by the Brahman. Prestige is also imparted by the Brahman's presence at the site of the ritual. As we shall see, the fact that the Brahman can enter the household suggests that the household is relatively pure, with concomitant implications of high status. In addition, the presence of the Brahman priest evokes the ancient textual paradigm of priest serving prince; the sponsor symbolically assumes the royal role of the supporter of the sacrifice as presided over by the Brahman priesthood.

The Brahman priest might or might not play a role in village or neighborhood festivals. The festivals celebrated in Sitapur generally involve relatively simple manipulations, and their performance is quite within the competence of their sponsors. In some cases, however, a Brahman priest may be called upon to preside over some more elaborate segment. The rites of *javara*, for example, may be conducted throughout without the assistance of a priest. However, the sponsors might decide that at some point during the nine-day sequence it would be appropriate to have a *homa*. Anyone can perform a simple *homa*, but if one desires to have it done with full textual elaboration a priest might be engaged to preside. Also, on festival days it is common for certain ceremonies not directly connected with the festival to be added. Thus, on the day of a given festival a village, neighborhood, or other group might sponsor a session of recitation and singing from the *Ramayana*. Again, though not strictly necessary, a Brahman priest would probably be engaged to preside.

Purity

A Brahman priest is a man of knowledge, but he is not merely this, for he must also be a Brahman. If the book is an important component of his role, it is not the only one; caste clearly plays a part too. This, in turn, is directly related to the question of purity.

In chapter 2 we saw that an essential element in the performance of *puja* is the requirement that the object of worship, the deity, be surrounded by a protective zone of purity. Purity is an essential condition for beneficial contact between human beings and deities. It is now necessary to look more closely at the implications of this requirement. An important fact about the pantheon is that the requirement for the zone of

Temple images of Lakshman, Rama, and Sita at the Dudhadhari Math, Raipur

purity that must surround the deity may be more or less stringent depending on the nature of the deity involved. Obviously the household deities of Untouchables cannot be so demanding of purity that they are prevented from receiving food offerings from Untouchables. Just as obviously caste deities cannot be so fastidious that they exclude their own worshippers from their altars. There are, however, certain deities for whom the requirements of surrounding purity are very stringent indeed. These are the deities who are housed in temples served by Brahman priests.

A temple (*mandir*) is a place where a deity, or a group of deities, is permanently situated. This should be understood in a nearly literal sense. The image (*murti*) of the deity is lifeless stone until the ceremonies of installation in the temple are performed. Once these rites have been completed the image *is* the deity, and those responsible for the operation of the temple are under an obligation to see that the image is treated with all of the consideration due to the deity himself. Thus, as a matter of routine, the image must be fed, bathed, clothed, flattered, even amused by the recitation of texts or song. Above all, those who are responsible for the deity's welfare must make certain that his or her immediate environment is pure. Given the ubiquity of pollution in the world, this means that the temple must be essentially a place of protection or shelter, a place from which much that goes on in the world must be excluded. Therefore, a temple is, in effect, a place where the zone of purity that is a prerequisite for *puja* is permanently maintained, and where the manipulations that constitute *puja* are continuously performed. In other words, it is possible to say that a temple is the act of *puja*, permanently sustained. Or, conversely, one might say that the creation of the zone of purity for ordinary *pujas* is the creation of a temporary temple, necessary if the deity is actually to be present to accept the offerings of his human worshippers.

The essential nature of a temple, then, is provided by the paradigm of *puja*. This suggests further implications. As we have seen in chapter 2, stripped of its potential elaborations *puja* is at its heart a ritual "statement" about social relationships, which is expressed in terms of a hierarchical opposition between the congregation and a deity. In theory the same should be true of temples. In fact the same principle applies, though here its operation is not always clear-cut or precise. An act of *puja* has a constituency: those who sponsor it and, in the language of the rite, those who receive *prasad*. Likewise, a functioning temple has a constituency: those who are responsible for its upkeep, and, (in ritual terms) those who worship (i.e. receive *prasad* from) the deity or deities the temple contains. Thus, just as objects of worship in *puja* are deities "of" particular groups, so too objects of worship in temples acquire definition in relation to, and in turn impart identification to, particular social groups or territorial units.

Hindu temples are ubiquitous in Chhattisgarh. The largest and most important are actually complexes of temples, which serve as major regional religious centers. The Rajivlochan Temple at Rajim and the Dudhadhari Math at Raipur are examples of these. They are the nuclei of the sacred geography of the region, and have undoubtedly played a major historical role in the diffusion of textual religious styles in Chhattisgarh. Somewhat below these major centers in importance are smaller centers that nevertheless have regional reputations. Most of these are located at well-known pilgrimage sites such as Ratanpur (a Mahamaya temple, as well as others), Rajim (several important Shiva temples), Sirpur (an important Shiva temple), or Mahadev Ghat in Raipur (a Shiva temple). *Melas* are held at all these centers at specific times of the year, drawing large numbers of people from extensive areas of the surrounding countryside.

The deities housed in these major temples cannot be said to be the deities of any particular group or section of society; they are the gods of the whole rather than any part. Their constituencies lack clear-cut outer boundaries, and are essentially regional. They also seem to be associated with human welfare in the socially and territorially most inclusive senses. Historically sophisticated informants have told me that the goddesses housed in three major temples—the Danteshwari Temple at Jagdalpur (in Bastar), the Mahamaya Temple at Ratanpur, and the Kankali Temple at Raipur—were collectively responsible for the fact that the Muslims never ruled in Chhattisgarh. At the Dudhadhari Math in Raipur there is a large, stone-lined pit, which was once used for great sacrifices. The head priest told me that at one time thousands of rupees worth of *ghi* was burned in this pit during years of scarcity, the cost being borne by the great landholders of the region. Sacrifices on this scale are no longer held, but it seems clear that when they were they were premised on the idea that the greatest deities are concerned with the fortunes of great collectivities, even on a regional scale. These great deities can, of course, be worshipped by individuals for their own purposes, but there is also a sense in which these deities are responsible for human welfare in its least parochial or individuated aspects.

Below the level of the great regional temples one encounters strata of temples that have increasingly localized or socially specified constituencies. Some have constituencies which, while not regional or even subregional, are large, highly variegated, and lack clear outer boundaries. For example, in Neora, only a few miles from Sitapur, there is a major Rama temple, which is patronized by the townspeople and by villagers from within a radius of several miles. There are several major temples in Raipur, including temples of Rama, Krishna, Kankali (Kali), Mahamaya, and Jagannath. These have citywide patronage, though most of it tends to be in their immediate vicinity. Other temples are much more "localized" either territorially or socially. Some temples serve particular castes. For example, the Satnamis have a temple at the village of Bhandar (about thirty miles northeast of Raipur), which serves all the Satnamis of the region. The Lohars (blacksmiths) have a temple housing their patron deity (Vishvakarma, the architect and builder of the gods) at Rajim. Temples may serve villages or sections of villages, locally resident groups of castemates, or particular neighborhoods or residential colonies in towns and cities. Most numerous of all are household shrines, which are "temples" on a diminutive scale.

In *puja* a group, potentially of any size or composition, is defined as a group in hierarchical opposition to a particular object of worship. Cleavages within it are symbolically reduced—although they may then be reasserted—within the far wider hierarchical gap between the group as a whole and the deity. A temple, as we have seen, may be regarded as an act of *puja* in fixation. Hence, a temple may be regarded as an expression of the social reality of the group or territorial entity with which it is associated. If the group is defined in opposition to the deity, then there is an equivalent sense in which the deity is defined in opposition to the group. Just as any deity may be regarded as the divine reflex of the group that worships it in *puja*, a deity placed in a temple may be regarded as a fixed divine embodiment, in the restricted sense I have indicated, of the group with which the temple is associated. Some deities—specifically those having the widest patronage—are expressive of the social order in its widest dimensions, while others—those with narrowly defined constituencies—are expressive of portions or fragments of the larger whole.

Thus, embedded within the temple organization of Chhattisgarh is a hierarchy of objects of worship associated with the social and territorial segmentation of Chhattisgarhi society at various levels, the lowest being that of the individual household. It can hardly be said, however, that temple organization presents a precise map of the social and territorial organization of the region. Above the level of family, neighborhood, village, and caste, temple constituencies are poorly defined. One can only speculate that the "match" between temple organization and the territorial segmentation of the region was much clearer in the past, before Maratha and British rule disrupted the indigenous political system of the region. The important point, however, is that even today it is possible to speak of deities as objects of worship of ascending and descending degrees of social and territorial "spread."

There appears to be a relationship between this hierarchy and one important aspect of the role of the Brahman priest. Deities with more inclusive constituencies are likely to be served by Brahman priests, and deities with the broadest constituencies of all are invariably served by Brahmans. Family shrines are served by members of the family. Caste temples are tended by members of the castes with which they are associated. The deities represented in temples serving villages are linked with the role of the Baiga, a religious specialist whom we shall examine in greater detail shortly. (He is not, however, the officiating priest in these temples, for in them people may make offerings to the deities without a human intermediary.) But in the greatest temples, those associated with territorially broad and socially inclusive constituencies, the deities are usually served by Brahmans. This is not a universal rule but a tendency; as a tendency, however, it is very marked.

The Brahman pujari of a Hanuman temple at Raipur

These are the purest deities. Brahmans are the purest of men. The presence of a Brahman priest in a temple is an expression of the need of the deity housed in the temple for an environment free of pollution. Thus, when Brahmans serve as temple priests (*pujaris*) it is purity, not knowledge, that is stressed, although temple priests must of course know something of the ceremonial conventions appropriate to the deities housed in such temples.

All deities, as we have seen, require a pure environment as a condition for beneficial contact with human beings, but the stringency of this requirement is quite variable. The shrine of the village goddess in Sitapur may be entered by all villagers but Untouchables, provided they are clean and unshod. Those who enter may touch the stones representing the goddess and may make offerings, including food, without mediation by any other party. However, in temples where Brahmans serve as priests the protection is far more elaborate. Untouchables may enter the outer compound of the temple, but not the temple building itself. From there they may receive *prasad* brought out from the temple. Ordinary worshippers may enter the temple building, but not the inner enclosure where the deity is located. Only the Brahman priest actually approaches the deity. In this situation he serves as a key element in an insulating barrier between the deity and the population at large. It is the priest who dresses the god, bathes him, and places gifts before him. It is through the Brahman priest that offerings are given, and from his hand that *prasad* is received.

In all of this we may note again a closure between the social order and a more strictly religious logic. These highest gods are those with the greatest social and territorial spread. Not only "must" they be served by a Brahman because of their own vulnerability to pollution, but a similar necessity applies in reverse, for it is only from the Brahman's hand that everyone may receive *prasad*. Thus, the universality of the highest deities is matched by the universality of their priesthood.

The highest gods are the purest gods. One function of the Brahman priest is to protect their purity by serving as a mediator between them and their human constituencies. On the basis of data from Mysore in South India, Edward Harper (1964) has

proposed a theory of caste in which the caste hierarchy is interpreted as a system of ritual interdependence necessitated by the
hierarchical differentiation of the pantheon (see also Harper
1959). According to this view, castes acquire rank as an outcome
of their ritual interaction with each other, and especially with
the Havik Brahmans who, in the region with which Harper is
concerned, constitute the apex and keystone of the system. His
model is based on the assumption that the pantheon is ordered
along a purity-pollution continuum in a hierarchy that mirrors
the hierarchy of castes, and that the pantheon as a whole is
vitally important to the welfare of the society with which it is
associated. All the gods must be worshipped for the well-being
of society, but different gods must be worshipped in different
ways. The highest deities must be worshipped in a context that
is kept as pure as possible, while the inferior deities are worshipped in a fashion that involves a degree of pollution the
highest deities would find intolerable—by blood sacrifice. These
circumstances necessitate a ritual division of labor in the society
as a whole. Different groups must worship different gods for the
benefit of the whole, and all groups must cooperate in the protection of the purity of the Brahmans, who worship the high
gods, by performing polluting services. Each group therefore
has a necessary function in a ritual complex that serves to order
the society's relations with a differentiated pantheon. To deal
adequately with the pantheon as a whole, the society must itself
consist of a hierarchy of groups of differing degrees of pollution.

Leaving aside the question of whether caste is merely a
ritual division of labor, it is clear that Harper's model highlights
an important feature of Chhattisgarhi Hinduism—the relationship between the stratification of the pantheon and the special
role of the Brahman priest. The highest deities are the most pure.
Since the world is pervaded by pollution, there must be a group
of men set apart, a group whose purity is protected, to serve as
mediators between the highest deities and the generality of men.

In this requirement lies one of the most important dimensions of the role of the Brahman priest in Chhattisgarh.

Having said all this, however, it remains to be pointed out that the question of hierarchy in the pantheon is by no means so simple as it might at first appear. In stressing the purity of the highest gods, I have set aside the fact that deities have characteristics other than relative purity. Deities have different sexes, different personalities, different sorts of powers, and different kinds of impact on the lives of their worshippers. I have said that the highest deities are found in temples served by Brahman priests. I must now establish in a more precise sense who these superior deities really are.

Initially the matter seems quite straightforward. The superior deities, the deities typically represented in temples served by Brahmans, are the gods and goddesses celebrated in sacred literature, the "textual" deities. A great many textual deities are worshipped in Chhattisgarh, but a few figures tend to stand out as the most important. Shiva is a major deity in the region. So are Vishnu and his two principal *avatars*, Rama and Krishna. Indeed, Rama is probably the most widely venerated of all the textual deities in Chhattisgarh. Also important is Devi, "the goddess," who appears in a variety of forms: Durga, Kali, Mahamaya, Chandi, and others.

These deities tend to have very distinctive characteristics and personalities. Associated with each of them is a particular body of scripture, which describes their histories, attributes, and relationships with the other deities. In this they contrast with the nontextual deities. The latter are deities of regional or even more localized tradition. Their attributes are defined by folklore, not by texts, and in some cases even folklore is silent. Rama is a great king, a great warrior, an ideal son; these attributes, and many others, are described in the *Ramayana*. Since his pictures are displayed everywhere, everyone knows what he looks like. Thakur Dev, the godling who protects Chhattisgarhi villages,

Rama: A popular print
  The god is surrounded by ancillary figures. Note Hanuman in a devotional attitude in the
  lower left corner.

cannot be described in comparable detail. His formal attributes
are few, and to my knowledge he is associated with no iconographic tradition. The attributes of certain other minor deities
are virtually nonexistent, consisting in some instances of little
more than rules concerning when, where, and how they should
be worshipped.

The superior deities, then, are the deities of the texts. However, this assertion leads at once to a rather puzzling difficulty.
Thakur Dev is a parochial deity. He is the protector of villages,
and is worshipped in village shrines. In this he contrasts with, to
take a particular example, Vishnu. Vishnu is a textual deity, and

is represented in some of the largest and most important temples in the region. His attributes suggest the very reverse of parochialism. Far from being a protector of mere villages, in the texts he is described as the "preserver" of the entire universe. Nevertheless, there is no reason why Vishnu, or some identifiable form of Vishnu, cannot be worshipped in a village shrine or, for that matter, on a family altar. Indeed, it is quite common to place images of textual deities on family altars, particularly in urban areas. If the textual deities are the superior deities, how is it that they can appear in the same ritual contexts as lesser deities? If the highest gods are the purest gods, how is it that they can be worshipped without Brahmanical mediation?

The apparent contradiction arises because there are actually two senses in which we may speak of "a deity." This distinction is vital. First, we may speak of a deity in the sense of a *specific object of worship* in a particular temple or in a particular episode of *puja*. A deity, in this "operational" sense, exists permanently in a temple and ephemerally in an act of *puja* outside it. Second, we may speak of a deity in a "nominal" sense. A nominal deity is not an actual object of worship, but rather consists of a name and a cluster of attributes and conventions of worship linked with that name. In other words, a nominal deity is a complex of characteristics, an "identity," which may be *assigned* to various operational deities—i.e., specific objects of worship. Such a nominal deity is Rama, who fought and defeated Ravana, whose wife is Sita, whose servant is Hanuman, whose power is great, and who is worshipped with vegetarian food. This identity is assigned to the objects of worship in many temples and in innumerable episodes of *puja*. Thakur Dev, who guards villages, who likes the meat of goats, and who (as we shall see) is associated with the goddess, is also such a deity, and this identity too is assigned to various objects of worship.

Likewise, it is possible to speak of the pantheon as a hierarchy in two senses. First, one may speak of a hierarchy of objects of worship, an "operational" hierarchy. The rank of a deity in this sense is determined by the relationship of the deity with a constituency, and at the apex of this hierarchy are the objects of worship in the major temples of the region. These are the purest deities, surrounded by the most elaborate forms of protection from polluting intrusions.

It is also possible to speak of a hierarchy of deities in the nominal sense. This is a different kind of hierarchy, existing on a different plane of cultural reality. It is this sort of "rank" that is meant when Vishnu is said to be a higher god than Thakur Dev. It must be noted that purity is not a property of deities in the nominal sense, but an "operational" fact, something that emerges only in the relationship between a specific object of worship and the human world. However, it should also be noted that power, as opposed to purity, can indeed be a property of nominal deities. Power can reside in words; hence the power of *mantras*. The repetition of Rama's name alone (*ram nam*) is said to be sufficient to invoke the power of this god. Thus, when informants say that "Rama," as opposed to any particular ex-emplification of Rama, has great "power" they may be taken to mean exactly what they say. When the identity of Rama, or of any other deity, is assigned to a particular object of worship, this would appear to determine the context of application of the deity's power, which might be narrow or broad depending on the scope of the constituency of the object of worship.

It must also be recognized that although purity cannot be a property of a deity in the nominal sense, it is nevertheless true that the conventions of worship that form part of the identity of any nominal deity may well have implications with regard to purity and pollution. For example, an appetite for blood sacrifice carries strong suggestions of pollution. If such an appetite is to be fully satisfied, then the identity of the deity cannot be assigned to an object of worship of great vulnerability to pollution without certain ritual adjustments (ch. 7). Thus, there seems to be a degree of "resonance" between certain nominal divine identities and certain kinds of status as objects of worship.

In any event, the highest deities in the nominal hierarchy are the deities described in texts. They are said to be more powerful than the gods and goddesses of nontextual tradition. Their worship carries more prestige. As we have seen, they possess attributes that are more elaborated and more finely drawn than those of the lesser deities. They also have greater "attributional" spread than the lesser deities, just as the superior objects of worship have greater territorial and social spread. By this I mean that these deities are typically associated in the texts with issues, values, and principles that have a cultural relevance extending far beyond questions concerning the immediate welfare of individuals or groups, though these deities may well be concerned with human welfare in this more limited sense too. These are "exemplary" as well as "presiding" deities, a theme to which we shall return in the next chapter.

In addition, these deities tend to be associated with particular kinds of ritual conventions, specifically the incantations and physical manipulations prescribed by texts. Indeed, these ritual conventions constitute an integral part of their identities, for there are specific manipulations and *mantras* associated with each of the more important textual deities. This in not to say that textual ritual styles may be employed only in the worship of textual deities. To some degree such styles have infiltrated virtually all Chhattisgarhi ceremonialism. The point to be stressed here is that textual ritual styles have a special relationship with textual deities. That this should be so is consistent with the high status of these deities. This is a ritual style of great complexity and formality, a courtly style, which is appropriate before the great and the mighty. It is also a ritual style that confers prestige on those who can use it with facility or, as in the case of those who patronize Brahman priests, those who can have it employed on their behalf. With this we are brought back to the question of priesthood, for expertise in textual ritual styles is one of the most important aspects of the Brahman priest's role. He is a specialist in these modes of ceremonial, which provide access to the highest and most powerful gods and goddesses.

In Chhattisgarh the operational and nominal hierarchies tend to match, but never perfectly; this is the source of many apparent anomalies. There is clearly a "fit" between high operational and nominal status. Deities high in the operational hierarchy are invariably high in the nominal hierarchy as well—superior objects of worship always carry the identities of textual deities. However, superior nominal identities may appear at a very low level in the operational hierarchy. An image of Vishnu may be placed on the family altars of those who would never be allowed to approach the image of Vishnu at the Rajivlochan Temple. Are these two images in fact the same deity? By now it will be seen that the answer is both yes and no. The constellation of assigned attributes is the same. However, the two images are in actuality two totally different objects of worship. One is a powerful regional god. The other is a family deity, in this sense a minor god, to whom a particularly prestigious identity has been assigned.

The assignment of prestigious identities to lesser objects of worship is, of course, a major aspect of the process which Srinivas calls "Sanskritization." It should be noted that the assignment of such identities is only a claim, a hopeful assertion which has as its goal the raising of the prestige of the family (or other group) associated with the object of worship. The validation of such a claim depends ultimately on a single factor—the willingness of a Brahman to preside at rites sponsored by the family. His presence constitutes a twofold affirmation. His use of fully elaborated textual styles lends prestige to the family and confirms the nominal identity of the deity being worshipped; his presence also suggests the imagery of kingly sacrificial sponsorship. Also, by merely entering such a household the Brahman is stating, in effect, that the pollution of the household is sufficiently low to be innocuous to him. This is a direct validation of the high status of the family. To the degree that the purity of the household is affirmed, the analogy between the family shrine and a major temple becomes increasingly credible, though as objects of worship the family deities remain quite distinct from others. Only in a nominal and analogical sense does the family worshipping Vishnu in its own shrine worship the same deity as that located in major temples.

I shall return to questions concerning the nature and structure of the pantheon later. For the present it is sufficient to note that the pantheon has important hierarchical dimensions, and that the Brahman priest's role is related to them. Speaking in the broadest terms, the Brahman priest is the human instrument of access to the uppermost regions of the pantheon. This is true in two distinct senses, a fact that is in turn reflected in the two most important aspects of the priest's role: purity and knowledge. He mediates between his fellow men and the purest objects of worship, the highest deities in the operational sense. He does so by virtue of his purity as a Brahman. He is also an expert in ritual styles most appropriate for the highest deities in the nominal sense, the textual deities. Thus, in combining purity and knowledge, the Brahman priesthood effects closure between the nominal and operational aspects of the pantheon.

The Baiga

The role of the Brahman priest is complemented by that of the Baiga. The word "Baiga," as it is used in Chhattisgarh, probably derives from the name of a tribe, the Baigas, who coexist with the Gonds in the tribal regions of Madhya Pradesh. Among the Gonds the Baigas have a considerable reputation as sorcerers and are employed by them in this capacity. In Chhattisgarh the word refers specifically to a type of priest-exorcist who specializes in diagnostics, healing, and the worship of village deities. In theory Baigas may belong to any caste. There is a general feeling, however, that Gonds make the best Baigas—reflecting, possibly,

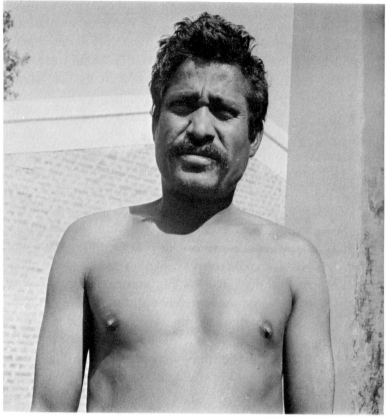

A Baiga

a time when most Baigas were Gonds. In fact, Baigas belong to
many castes, and the most important and widely patronized
Baiga of the Sitapur area is a Ravat. The only clear rule seems
to be that Baigas never come from the twice-born castes.

The Baiga, like the Brahman priest, uses a special kind of
knowledge for the benefit of his clients. He has knowledge of
special *mantras*, which give him access to, and a degree of control
over, certain benevolent and harmful deities and spirits. He
knows how to deal with human problems, particularly illness,
that result from misalignments of human relationships with
these powers. Yet to this an important qualification must be

added. While informants insist that his knowledge of *mantras* lies at the basis of the Baiga's powers, it is equally clear that a Baiga's professional efficacy, his power in the eyes of his clients, depends on factors that have largely to do with the imponderables of individual personality. The successful Baiga—that is, the Baiga with a large and flourishing clientele—seems to radiate an aura of easy familiarity with the world of minor gods and goddesses and malevolent spirits. He seems to have a reassuring confidence in his ability to deal with matters that produce awe and fear in others. A Baiga's success in his calling seems to depend far more on these aspects of character than on more formal qualifications, as in the case of the Brahman priest.

All villages have Baigas. The Baiga is the priest, though in an informal sense, of the village deities. While people may worship these deities without priestly mediation, the Baiga often worships them on behalf of others, and the village shrines are regarded as his special province. He is conceived to have a special relationship with these deities. They appear to him in dreams to warn of disease or other misfortune coming to the village, and he prescribes appropriate countermeasures on the basis of such warnings. When trouble has already come, it is the Baiga who indicates which deities are involved, and what kind of palliative action should be taken. He is also a diagnostician and curer of the ailments of individual clients, and on a day-to-day basis this is his most conspicuous function. Some Baigas specialize in particular types of ailments. Thus, in Sitapur there is a *bichu ka baiga*, a "scorpion Baiga," who knows a *mantra* that will cure a scorpion sting. More generally, however, a Baiga's jurisdiction includes a wide variety of human afflictions, particularly those attributed to "nonempirical" causes.

A great variety of diseases and ailments are understood in terms of man's relationships with deities, minor spirits, ghosts, and other malignant beings. Of these, we have already examined one, smallpox, in some detail. There are other types of illness that are also attributed to malignant feminine deities or spirits.

Apparently any of an assortment of diseases that involve red eruptions on the skin may be attributed to a goddess, and illness in young children is often said to be due to the influence of the demoness Churalin, the composite spirit of women who have died in childbirth. There is in addition a sizable residue of illnesses attributed to witchcraft or possession by malignant ghosts, and the diagnosis and curing of these seems to be the Baiga's special métier.

Techniques for the diagnosis of such illnesses are variable and sometimes ad hoc. Smallpox, for example, is quite easily diagnosed, and the cure is standard. Other ailments are more subtle, and require a certain degree of judgment. Madness is often attributed to witchcraft, ghosts, or both. Otherwise, long illnesses that are resistant to other modes of treatment are often ultimately assigned to this category. According to the Baiga who acted as my principal informant in these matters, it is difficult to point to any particular symptom as decisive. The patient often has a kind of sadness in his demeanor that the Baiga is able to see. Beyond this, there are certain tests that may be applied to the patient. In one of them a string is tied around the toe of the patient and the other end is tied around his head in such a way that it is drawn tight when the leg is at a right angle to the torso. The string is then measured seven times. If the patient is under attack by a witch, the string will appear to measure shorter each time.

Witches and malevolent ghosts are sources of immense fascination to the people of Chhattisgarh, especially the rural population. Stories about instances of confrontations with witches and ghosts are legion, and from them a great deal can be learned about the nature of these beings and their role in Chhattisgarhi Hinduism. The following tales, collected from informants in Sitapur and Raipur, are typical of the genre:

1

A boy from Tilda [a village near Sitapur] went to a distant village to visit relatives. After he returned to Tilda he became weak and feverish. His parents knew about the reputation of the village the boy had visited [these things always seem to go on in distant villages], and they concluded that some sort of *jadu* [magic, what witches do] was involved. To make sure, the boy's mother performed a simple test. She sprinkled some dry chillies on a fire [a traditional test]. A sharp smell, the kind that makes you sneeze, did not come, so the boy's parents knew that witchcraft was involved. The parents then called the Baiga, who used his *mantras*. The boy recovered.

2

The father of a local schoolmaster [my informant was the schoolmaster] was engaged to be married. When time came for the marriage he was seated under the marriage pavilion with his bride-to-be. Saying nothing, he suddenly arose from his seat and left, leaving consternation behind him. He returned to his home. He said that something had forced him to leave the wedding; that he simply couldn't help himself. So he called a Baiga who used certain of his *mantras*. The Baiga told the schoolmaster that he was possessed by some ancestor who did not agree with the proposed marriage, and who came in the form of a ghost.

3

In Brahman Para in Raipur [one of the older sections of town] a young bride was taken to a Dhobi's (washerman's) house in preparation for her marriage. A witch attacked her from the watching crowd. When she returned to her house for the marriage ceremony she became sick, and ultimately she went mad. She cried and raved and never recovered. The marriage, of course, never occurred.

4

A newly married couple in Neora happened to walk by the house of a witch one night. The witch saw them and became angry. Knowing nothing of this, the couple went home to bed. Later that night the witch came in the form of a cat. She climbed on the roof of the house and hung a string down through a hole so that the end touched the young man. She then began to suck his blood up through the string. The young man woke up, saw the string, and immediately realized what was happening. He brought in a pot of water and put the end of the string in it, and, as he watched, the level of the water went steadily down. The pot finally became empty. When the witch's stomach was filled with water she returned to her human form. Then she fell down and died.

5

Once in Simga there lived a Muslim lady who sold bangles. She had a son about 12 years of age. She died one day leaving her son very despondent. He finally went to a river near Simga and hanged himself from a fig tree on one of its banks. He then turned into a *jin* [the ghost of a Muslim] and became notorious for his evil tricks.

Now the spot where the boy hanged himself happens to be very popular fishing place. One day some boys from Tilda went there for fishing. One of them ventured near the fig tree. While he was fishing a very attractive girl came with a water pot to the bank near him. She was very pretty, but very dark, and had long hair. She filled her pot and then asked the boy to help her put it on her head. He thought that she was just a village girl from nearby, so he helped her without thinking about it. It turned out later that she had chosen him because he was the strongest of all the boys who had come for fishing that day. While he was lifting the pot to her head she playfully flicked some water in his face with her fingertips. He thought at the time that this was just some girlish playfulness. After she left he wanted to get one more look at her and ran up the embankment. But she had completely disappeared.

The boy returned to his home in Tilda. The next day he became weak and feverish. His sister prepared some food, but he was unable to eat it. He began to say some peculiar things: "she is coming," "I see her," and so forth. He then began to strike his chest very hard with his fist.

His parents, now fully alarmed, took him to the nearby mission hospital. There he was examined by the doctors, but they could find nothing wrong with him. Yet he continued to rave and beat his chest. He was kept in the hospital for the day, but that evening he was taken home again.

The neighbors suggested that a certain Baiga be called. The Baiga came and applied his *mantras* and the boy got well immediately. The next day, however, he was sicker than ever. He had a severe fit in his brother's house, and he had to be forcibly restrained from hitting himself. At this point the *jin* began to speak through the boy's mouth. The boy said a certain person was coming to the house, even though he had no way of knowing this. Later this person, who was an Ayurvedic doctor, actually arrived. The patient was asked, "who are you?" The *jin*, through the mouth of the boy, gave the name Gulmohammad, which was the name of the Muslim boy who had committed suicide. The *jin* said that he customarily sat in the fig tree, and that he lived in a hole nearby. It was now evident that the girl carrying water was, in fact, the *jin*. The boy was becoming progressively weaker, and everyone present begged the *jin* to withdraw. But the ghost refused and said that not even the Baiga had the power to dislodge him.

Once again the Baiga was called and all of this was related to him. The Baiga then applied new and more powerful *mantras*, and also performed a *homa*. The result was a complete and permanent cure.

Several important themes emerge in these tales. Most striking is the distinctly feminine overtone that seems to pervade witchcraft lore (see also Harper 1969). Even a male ghost attacks his victim in a feminine guise. In fact, the concept of witchcraft seems distinctly feminine in its associations. Every concrete instance of witchcraft brought to my attention was attributed to a woman or a girl. The word for witch in Hindi and its Chhattisgarhi dialect is *tonhi*, a feminine noun. The word can be masculinized to *tonha*, but one rarely hears the word in this form in any but the hypothetical sense. Informants said that a man could have similar powers, but that he would be a *guniya*, a priest-sorcerer who uses his powers in the service of victims of witchcraft.

It is said that by day a witch is indistinguishable from other women in appearance and manner. She may, however, give herself away by staring at people in a peculiar fashion. By night the witch takes on the attributes of a supernatural being, having extranormal powers of perception, movement, and attack. A witch may harm her victims in a variety of ways: she may send ghosts to possess them, or put poison in their food. She may even cause an epidemic in a community by magically poisoning a water source. She may attack individuals by means of the evil eye (*nazar lagna*).

During the night (especially on the night of *hareli*, which is considered a witches' Sabbath in Chhattisgarh) witches are said to congregate at cemeteries or burning grounds, where they perform a kind of dance. Informants liken this dance to possession, and suggest that it is a way of worshipping certain malignant deities. The witches loosen their hair and dance nude. As their hair swirls around their heads, saliva drips from their mouths and glows like fire. One hears many stories about people who have actually seen—from a distance—the glow of the witches' saliva as they dance on *hareli* night. In the image of the dancing witches there are, again, suggestions of the more general link between malevolent witchcraft and the feminine or, at least, with feminine divinity. Some informants told me that the witches dance in worship of the goddess. Interestingly, this image has an almost exact textual counterpart. The goddess as Kali is attended by the *dakanis*, "female imps, eaters of raw flesh" (Danielou 1964:288). There is the implication here that witches stand in a similar relationship to the goddess, for as we shall shortly see they too are "eaters of raw flesh" in the sense that witches are insatiable drinkers of human blood. An alternative version holds that the witches go to the burning grounds to make a special pact with Bhairav—a fierce manifestation of Shiva who is associated with the goddess (see ch. 7.) The witches, the tale goes, dance nude before Bhairav. Bhairav is pleased by this and asks them what they want. The witches tell the deity that they wish to take a specified number of lives. A bargain is then struck: Bhairav allows them to do as they want if in return they agree to give some of the blood to him.

Blood is an important integrating theme in Chhattisgarhi images of witchcraft. Many informants insisted that the ultimate object of the witch is to drink her victim's blood. Witches are believed to quicken the dead in order to drink their blood, and stories centering on this theme are among the most common of the witchcraft tales in circulation in Chhattisgarh. One such tale, told in Sitapur, goes as follows: A boy had died in Bilaspur about three months before. Witches came to his grave one night, dug him up, and brought him back to life. They were preparing to drink his blood when they discovered that they had forgotten to bring a knife. While they were searching, the boy ran back to his home and hid there the remainder of the night. In the morning he emerged from his house to tell his tale.

The associations between witchcraft and blood provide a conceptual bridge between witchcraft and the more general cultural themes of heat and pollution. Blood is both hot and polluting. Thus, the idea that witches are drinkers of human blood carries the suggestions of both heat and deep pollution. In this connection it may be recalled that in one of the tales cited above a witch was killed when water (cold) was substituted for the blood she was drinking. The tale thereby suggests a basic antipathy between witches and coolness. The witches dance, we are told, on the burning grounds and near cemeteries. Such places are at once both deeply sinister and associated with intense pollution. Here the witches dance, and their dance is likened to possession. As we have seen, possession is a phenomenon conceived in terms of heat. In the image of the witch, then, ideas of malevolence, pollution, and heat converge.

Malignant ghosts are closely associated with witchcraft in Chhattisgarhi thought. Like witches, ghosts are associated with burning grounds and graveyards. They are sometimes said to be the servants of witches. Witches are said to ride on ghosts from place to place, and to use them as instruments to attack their victims. It is also said that witches have the ability to manufacture ghosts. A Baiga told me that if a witch falls in love with a man during his lifetime, then after his death she may dig his body from the grave. She then gives her victim the shadow-life of a ghost, letting him wander the earth forever in envy of both the living and the dead. Such a victim, my informant told me, might be the best of men. His fate would not be a consequence of misdeeds in life, but simply the ill luck of falling under the eye of a witch.

Concrete accusations of witchcraft sometimes occur, and one hears from time to time about beatings of suspected witches. Nevertheless, it is my impression that actual accusations of specific persons are by no means so common as the general concern about witchcraft would suggest. In most communities there seem to be a few individuals who are under suspicion most of the time. An old widow living alone or the only Muslim woman in an otherwise all Hindu community are the sorts of marginal women who tend to attract suspicion. The wives of barbers are also thought to be prone to witchcraft. Barbers' wives often assist other women in dressing and with other details during weddings, and in so doing may see them in a state of partial undress. Exposure of this sort is thought to leave one especially vulnerable to "the glance" (*nazar*) of witches. But despite these notions, most instances of illness diagnosed as the results of witchcraft are attributed to persons unknown or to chance encounters with strangers. It is quite possible that specific accusations were more common in the past, but have been suppressed in recent times because of the legal consequences of the persecution of alleged witches. Baigas can describe traditional techniques for the detection of witches, but the most important Baiga of the Sitapur area explained to me that he simply did not like to become involved in such matters. "What good would it do?" he asked. Under existing circumstances, very little good indeed.

In chapter 3 we examined some of the conditions of extreme vulnerability to witchcraft. We saw that childbirth, childhood, and marriage are episodes in the life cycle during which special precautions against witchcraft and other malevolent super-natural forces are necessary. It will be recalled that envy of a peculiarly feminine cast is associated with the dangers of these periods. Children and marriage lie very close to what life is all about for women, and it is no coincidence that they constitute nodal points around which ideas of witchcraft cluster. This theme of feminine malice is central to witchcraft beliefs and, as we shall see in the next chapter, is an aspect of the structure of the pantheon.

But vulnerability to witchcraft is by no means confined to small children and the about-to-be-married. Chhattisgarhi culture provides what amounts to a psychological theory of vulnerability. In general, it is said, "weak" people are especially liable to attack from witches. It is clear that "weakness" here refers primarily to the psychological disposition of the victim, not to the physical condition. Weakness in this sense, it was explained, means a tendency to "fear" things. A weak person is sometimes described as having a "light" as opposed to a "heavy" or "salty" shadow. A person with a heavy shadow is strong-hearted and is feared by witches. A person with a light shadow is especially vulnerable to witchcraft because, as one informant put it, "These people are fearful, and the witches can only harm those who fear them." The "weight" of a person's shadow can be tested by making it fall over oil that is being heated. If the shadow is heavy, then a froth will form on the surface of the oil, otherwise not.

The Baiga uses his *mantras* primarily to combat witchcraft and possession by ghosts and other malignant beings. The Baigas learn their *mantras* from their *gurus*, other Baigas, to whom they must pay a fee. The *mantras* are generally thought to be highly esoteric. Different *mantras* are applicable to different types of illness, and most Baigas have an armory of several. The *mantras* I was able to collect from a Baiga turned out to be invocations to long lists of deities, both local and textual, ending with pleas to cast the affliction out. The *mantra* is conventionally applied to the patient in a form of exorcism known as *jhara-phunka*. The Baiga and his patient squat on the ground facing each other. The Baiga then takes a pinch of cowdung ash in his right hand and, holding it before his face, begins to intone the *mantras*. At the conclusion of each stanza he blows the ash onto the patient in such a way that it settles over the patient's body. Presumably the efficacy of the *mantra* is thereby transferred from the lips of the Baiga to the body of the afflicted person.

While the *mantra* is the specific instrument of the Baiga's therapeutic abilities, his powers derive generally from his special relationship with the gods. Although his *mantras* may contain invocations to all the gods, this relationship is primarily with the local gods and goddesses. If the Brahman priest is the mediator between man and the highest deities, the Baiga's main concern is with the lower regions of the pantheon. It is the local deities who warn him of impending trouble, and it is he who has a special responsibility for their worship. In particular, there seems to be a special connection between the Baiga and one specific deity, Thakur Dev. Thakur Dev is the protector of villages. He is said to station himself on their outskirts, from which point he can resist the intrusion of sinister forces. The best-known Baiga of the Sitapur area identifies himself with this god. He considers himself to be a devotee (*bhakt*) of Thakur Dev, and he keeps the god in his home in the form of a few *sindur*-stained pebbles. Originally, he says, there was only one pebble in the box in which the deity is kept, but over the years this original stone has given birth to several others. This, the Baiga claims, is a sign of the god's special favor. The Baiga is a human agent, Thakur Dev is a god; but there seems to be an overlap, and even a degree of identity, in their respective roles. Each is an agent of protection. Thakur Dev receives offerings, the Baiga is paid cash (nowadays), and each stands between his clients and the dangerous and malignant forces that are so important a feature of life as it is understood in Chhattisgarh.

Renunciation

There are important differences between the Brahman priest and the Baiga, but when contrasted with another figure in the religious life of Chhattisgarh they look very much alike. This third figure is the renouncer (see Dumont 1960:43ff). Renunciation is, of course, a central value in philosophical Hinduism. We have seen evidence that it is also a very important principle in popular Hinduism in Chhattisgarh. Renunciation, especially sexual renunciation, is associated with the acquisition and control of power. Scripture validates the efficacy of renunciation in countless stories, of which the tale of Parvati's winning of Shiva is but one example. Renunciation is an integral part of the character of one of the most popular deities, Hanuman, and is directly associated with his great strength. The idea of renunciation is also the operating premise of one of the most common types of religious observances in Chhattisgarh, the fast.

However, if the concept of renunciation permeates Chhattisgarhi Hinduism, the act of full renunciation is far from common. Few men truly step out of life and the social order to seek salvation in any of the classical philosophical senses. Yet at the same time the figure of the renouncer is omnipresent in the region in the persons of mendicants known as Sadhus. Their appearance reflects, or at least suggests, lives of genuine renunciation. Wearing or bearing symbols of their various orders, they dress in the simplest clothing, sometimes in rags, and wander from house to house in the countryside and city seeking alms. The attitude of the people of Chhattisgarh toward these figures seems generally ambivalent. The ideal they represent is greatly admired, but it is known—indeed it is proverbial—that many of them are frauds. It is often said that while most Sadhus are scoundrels it is best to give equally to all, because it is difficult to distinguish the fake from the real. The admiration for the genuine article is mixed with fear. The blessing of a Sadhu is to be sought, but the curse of a Sadhu is very dangerous. The following incident, reported to me by an informant, illustrates what seems to be the general feeling.

One day a Sadhu came to R. S. Shukla Road in Raipur. This is at the heart of Raipur's business section and beggars do well here, especially on Mondays, the day the Hindu businessmen of Raipur have reserved for beggars to come to their shops. But this was not Monday, and the Sadhu was not getting as much as he had hoped. He began to shout that if each of the merchants would give him twelve annas (far more than beggars usually get) he would leave. The merchants refused, at which point the Sadhu began to walk up and down the street hurling curses. "Rise Chandi," he shouted, and with his invocation to this fearsome goddess the shopkeepers began one by one to pay. They knew, as everyone does, that many Sadhus are charlatans, but the curse of a real Sadhu is dangerous, and in the present instance it was worth twelve annas not to take a chance.

The figure of the renouncer contrasts strikingly with that of the Brahman priest and the Baiga. The Brahman priest is a "technician" (Berreman 1964:60) of ritual. He is a master of learned techniques who, because of his knowledge of text and his innate purity, can serve as an intermediary between his clients and the gods. Also the Brahman priest must be a Brahman, and the very fact that caste is a prerequisite for serving in his role inevitably binds him to the world and the social order. The true

Renunciation exemplified: A Sadhu at the Rajim mela

renouncer, the *sannysi*, must renounce his caste along with all other social bonds. He leaves the orders of society and stands quite apart from normal worldly life. The Brahman priest, by contrast, marries, has children, owns property, and moves through the world as most men do. The Baiga, too, is a man of this world, and in no way stands apart from it. He too is a kind of technician of ritual, and although his qualifications are somewhat different from those of the Brahman priest, like the Brahman he practices his speciality within the framework of social institutions. The renouncer, in his very being, represents an idea of basic importance in Chhattisgarhi religious thought. He is, in a precise sense, a living symbol. The Brahman priest and the Baiga are specialists in the arcana of ritual and are mediators between gods and men. They are not exemplars of more basic truths.

Varieties of Priesthood

The attributes of the Brahman priest and the Baiga merge or are differentiated according to the context in which they are viewed. Seen in opposition to the renouncer, they are very similar figures. Seen in relation to each other, they are quite distinct. The Brahman priest fuses textual knowledge and ritual purity. He serves as a mediator between man and the upper levels of the pantheon. These are the deities most demanding of purity, and so it is necessary for a class of men of protected purity, the Brahman priests, to stand between them and the rest of humanity. The conventions of worship most appropriate for them, the ritual styles of texts, are of an intricacy that virtually demands a specialist. For mankind to deal with the upper strata of the pantheon, the Brahman priest is the indispensable bridge.

The role of the Brahman priest is complemented by that of the Baiga. The Baiga deals with the lesser deities, who as objects of worship are less demanding of purity. As nominal entities they tend to be gods and goddesses defined in local tradition, not in texts, and may be dealt with in simple, relatively unelaborated ritual styles. Finally, the Baiga deals with yet another, even lower, category of beings—the malevolent ghosts, minor spirits, and witches. The Baiga serves as an important instrument of defense against these malignant beings. As in the case of the Brahman priest, a part of the Baiga's ability to fulfill his role is a special kind of knowledge, in his case the knowledge of protective and curative *mantras*. In part, too, it is his personal ability to inspire confidence in his clients.

Following Mandelbaum, it is possible to speak of the roles of these two specialists as the institutional foci of two analytically separable "complexes" of religious idioms and practices. One is a "textual complex," which is connected with the role of the Brahman priest. It centers on the deities and ritual styles of sacred texts. I shall avoid using Mandelbaum's term, "transcendental," because as we have seen this complex is often put to uses that are distinctly "pragmatic" in Mandelbaum's sense of the term. Nevertheless, this complex does involve issues and principles of more than merely pragmatic concern, a matter we shall explore in greater detail in the next chapter. The textual complex is opposed by a "local complex," which is linked with the role of the Baiga. In using the term "local" I do not mean to imply that this complex is unique to any particular locality, or that the phenomenon more generally is unique to the Chhattisgarh region. It is found in every locality, and it falls within a pattern that is probably pan-Indian in distribution. Rather, I have in mind the essential parochialism of its manifestations and functions. It is concerned with divine immanence on a scale that is local and restricted; with deities who, as objects of worship, are associated with social and territorial units at the most parochial level, and who, as nominal entities, tend to be defined in terms of relatively simple, unelaborated attributes, and tend to be associated with relatively simple ritual conventions. Both as objects of worship and as divine identities, these deities tend to be narrower in their spheres of jurisdiction and relevance than their textual counterparts.

In a more general context of observation, these two complexes do not emerge as discrete entities, but appear only as identifiable tendencies. In most ceremonial activity textual and nontextual elements intermingle. Under most circumstances textual and nontextual elements are set free, as it were, in such a manner that they find mutual association in combinations and permutations that are almost as various as the total range of Chhattisgarhi ceremonialism itself. It is here that relative prestige becomes an important organizing factor. Textual religious styles carry high prestige, and the use of such styles in domestic or other kinds of ceremonial is a marker of the high status of the sponsoring group, or at least of the desire for high status. The result is a situation in which the ceremonies of some groups are highly textualized, and in which the greater part of Chhattisgarhi ceremonialism is at least to some degree "Sanskritized" in the sense that some textual elements are present in virtually every ceremonial event. Seen in this context, textual and local elements constitute different ritual styles, which provide alternative ways of "saying the same things" (Dumont and Pocock 1959b:45), the textual style being the more prestigious of the two, just as "pure" Hindi carries more prestige than its Chhattisgarhi dialect.

However, textual and local elements are drawn into distinguishable complexes in relation to the roles of the Brahman priest and the Baiga. This suggests that in certain respects differences in religious style may have functional significance beyond the mere difference in prestige value. No longer a matter of saying the "same things" in different ways, it now becomes a matter of saying the same things in different ways for different purposes. But for what purposes? At least part of the answer seems already at hand. The local complex is directly connected with illness and therapeutics. Indeed, this seems to explain why it has not been "Sanskritized" out of existence. Illness, like the weather, has no respect for human hierarchy, and despite the lower prestige of the local complex, it is patronized by high castes as well as low. In this functional role the local complex persists in Chhattisgarh. Questions remain, however, concerning the functional role of the textual complex and the nature of its relationship with the local complex. To answer these questions it is necessary to look more closely at the symbolism of the pantheon.

7
Divine Hierarchy: The Pantheon

I shall now shift attention from ritual behavior to religious ideas as such—to the concepts that are presupposed by ritual action. These ideas have been discussed in previous chapters, and my present purpose is to draw them into some kind of coherent set of relationships. My vehicle for this will be the pantheon. The pantheon is not a haphazard congeries of gods and goddesses but a system of symbols that formulate a view of reality. The pantheon symbolizes a world, the world in which ritual action takes place. It is a world that has both benign and malevolent aspects, a world that includes sources of order and disorder. It is a world inhabited by the people of Chhattisgarh and by a great number of highly varied extramundane powers. Many of these affect human life, some for good and some for ill. Most are only marginally under the control of human beings. They are various, and must be dealt with variously. It is the necessity of dealing with them all, and the inherent difficulties of doing so, that constitutes the central religious problem in Chhattisgarh.

The pantheon resists simple modes of analysis. From a distance it appears orderly and stable, but with closer scrutiny the picture becomes far less clear. There are obvious differences between deities, but they tend to merge, and distinctions that seem obvious and sharp from one perspective often disappear when viewed from another. The resulting configuration is one that can maintain seemingly limitless diversity under an over-arching unity. Ultimately, as the most casual student of Hin-duism knows, all the gods and goddesses are "one." This is a doctrine of genuine significance, and not merely an extravagance of bookish philosophers. It is a doctrine that is reiterated fre-quently in the texts, but illiterate villagers are equally fluent in maintaining that although there are many deities, and although they have different and sometimes contradictory characteristics, in the end all are the same and all are one. In a sense, the very lack of surface structure permits a deeper structure of another kind. A shifting, ultimately monistic, pantheon tolerates differentia-tion and even contradiction, and can couple these with its first premise of unity. Form and particularity can be permitted be-cause they are contingent; the underlying substance is real.

We start with the simple fact of differentiation. Divinity ap-pears in many different forms in Chhattisgarhi religion. Sophis-ticated informants speak of *paramatma*, the all-pervasive, un-differentiated world-soul of philosophical Hinduism. But this is a notion that rarely intrudes into popular religion; *paramatma* is seen, by those who understand it, as inert—an object of con-templation not of worship. Divinity becomes active in the affairs of the universe and men only when it is differentiated into particular divine entities. With this differentiation we move into the world of everyday religious practice.

Of all the different kinds of differentiation found within the pantheon, one seems to be particularly stable, that of sex. Divin-ity seems to have two basic qualities or transmutations. One is essentially protective and benevolent, the other is the very em-bodiment of malevolence when unrestrained or unappeased. At the most abstract level these doubtless represent two different aspects of the same thing, a notion of potential "power" intrinsic to the sacred. However, in myth and ritual these emerge in the form of a sex-linked opposition, a distinction between *devta* and *devi*, between "god" and "goddess."

The importance of goddess-worship in the religious life of the Chhattisgarhi Hindus should by now be quite evident. Some of the region's most important temples are dedicated to various forms of the goddess, as are innumerable village temples and shrines. There is hardly a village without such a shrine, and in Sitapur the main temple of the village houses an image of the goddess. One part of the sacred year, the hot season, is dominated by goddess-worship, and various goddesses play roles in ceremonial events taking place throughout the year. We have also noted a link between the goddess and smallpox. It is clear, therefore, that the goddess in her numerous manifestations plays a vital role in the religious life of the region, and at this point it is appropriate that we examine the nature of her role more closely.

In the previous chapter I distinguished between local and textual complexes of religious usages and practices that emerge in relation to the roles of the Brahman priest and the Baiga. The figure of the goddess appears within both complexes, and I shall argue that she at once differentiates and unites the two. I shall discuss the textual delineation of the goddess first, and then move to a consideration of her role in the local complex.

The Goddess of the Text

It is possible to speak of "cults" that center on the nominal identities of certain textual deities. These cults often have physical centers in certain major temples, and usually there are particular festivals in which they find direct ritual expression. One such cult centers on Rama and his ancillary deities: Sita, Lakshman, and Hanuman. Its basic text is the *Ramayana* of Tulsidas, and in Chhattisgarh its primary physical center is the Dudhadhari Math in Raipur, a major regional religious institution. It has certain major festivals as well, specifically *ramnavmi* and *dassehra*. One of its principal ritual expressions is the ubiquitous *Ramayana*-singing session.

Similarly, there is such a cult focusing on a series of goddesses, each considered to be a separate manifestation of Devi, "the goddess." Its main foci are a central body of texts and an array of festivals and ceremonials, the most important being those of the *navratra* or "nine nights" periods of the lunar months of *chaitra* and *kunvar*. Although the goddess appears in other contexts as well, it is in her own texts and ceremonials that she emerges with the finest degree of definition.

In Chhattisgarh the most important text of the goddess is the *Shri Durga Saptashati* (or *Devi-Mahatmyam*), a book of 700 Sanskrit stanzas devoted to the goddess in a number of particular forms. This text, as we have already seen, is chanted in temples of the goddess and in private homes on appropriate ritual occasions, especially during the *navratra* periods. It is an essential item in ritual connected with the goddess in her textual forms.

It is important to realize that the *Saptashati*, like all Hindu texts, has two distinct kinds of religious significance. It has, first of all, a kind of intrinsic potency as a collection of sacred utterances. The chanting of the *mantras* of which it is composed is a way of pleasing the goddess and tapping her great powers. But the *mantras* have meaning of another sort, for together they constitute one of the principal scriptural delineations of the goddess. The text is to be understood as well as chanted, and consequently in the editions available in the Raipur bazaar the Sanskrit stanzas are given together with their Hindi translation. The text explains the goddess, and provides a context for her in the pantheon as a whole. When I asked the head priest of the principal goddess-temple of Raipur (the Mahamaya Temple) for "the story of the goddess," he recommended this text.

Apart from a leavening of more or less standard pieties, the text is an account of how and under what circumstances the goddess came into existence. We learn that she originated at a time of great crisis in the affairs of the gods—at a time in the very remote past when the supremacy of the gods, and the world order they upheld, was threatened by the rise of a race of powerful demons, the *asuras*. Many battles were fought, the advantage going this way and that, until it finally became clear that the gods were the weaker of the two contending groups and faced imminent defeat. Thus, to preserve the world order, it was necessary for the gods to awaken a kind of terrible force with which to confront the demons. This force took the form of a succession of goddesses, the first of which was formed from the tangible anger of Brahma, Vishnu, and Shiva—anger that appeared as a blinding light emanating from their faces.

The battle between the gods and the demons was a protracted one and lasted, intermittently, for many ages. On successive occasions, when the gods were on the point of being overcome by the demons, the goddess manifested herself and came to their aid. Her various manifestations all embodied an irresistible power. The most terrible of her forms was Kali: "Bearing the strange skull-topped staff, decorated with a garland of skulls, clad in a tiger's skin, very appalling owing to her emaciated flesh, with gaping mouth, fearful with her tongue lolling out, having deep-sunk reddish eyes and filling the regions of the sky with her roars" (*Shri Durga Saptashati*, ch. 7, lines 7–9, from Jagadisvarananda 1953:95).

The notion that the essence of the goddess is a kind of force is explicitly expressed in one of her most common names, *shakti*, which means literally "energy" or "force." It is in the Hindu tantric tradition especially that this idea receives its most elaborate development. Hindu tantrism identifies the goddess as one member of a male-female polarity. The "female principle" is conceived as the active, dynamic component of reality, while

Kali

the male principle is regarded as static and passive (see Agehananda Bharati 1965: esp. 200–224; also Woodroffe 1951).

Quite apart from philosophical elaboration, it seems clear that in the texts a significant distinction is made between the qualities of masculine and feminine divinity. While the gods of scripture could hardly be called passive, their collective character is different from that of the goddess of the *Saptashati*. The goddess represents a terrible and almost sinister force, all the more sinister by comparison with the gods. While the gods are very powerful beings themselves, they seem at the same time to be essentially magnifications of human beings—

human beings who make mistakes, who can be defeated, and who are often motivated by their emotions, often to anger, but often to mercy and benevolence as well. As she is represented in the *Saptashati*, the only discernible emotion of the goddess is anger—black, implacable, and bloodthirsty. She is something emerging from the highest gods; she is the very essence of their anger. But once unleashed this *shakti* seems to achieve an identity of her own, and she seems more powerful, certainly more terrible, than her creators. Yet we must carefully note that although the goddess emerges in differentiation *from* the gods, in the end she is *of* the gods, an idea suggesting that the goddess is ultimately controllable.

In fact, if approached in the correct fashion the goddess, even in her most terrible manifestations, will serve the ends of men as she did the ends of the gods, and the *Saptashati* includes many hymns designed to flatter her into cooperation with her devotees. But beyond this, there appear to be circumstances under which the *shakti* the goddess embodies is restrained or redirected into something really different. The *Saptashati* describes the goddess in all her manifestations as follows: "She indeed takes the form of the great destroyer at the [proper] time; she, the unborn, indeed becomes this creation. . . . she herself, the eternal Being, sustains the beings at [another] time. In times of prosperity she indeed is Lakshmi, who bestows prosperity in the homes of men; and in times of misfortune, she herself becomes the goddess of misfortune, and brings about ruin" (*Shri Durga Saptashati*, ch. 12, lines 39–40, from Jagadisvarananda 1953:159–60).

This is perhaps the central mystery of Devi—that the goddess is at once Kali (the destroyer) and Lakshmi (the bestower of wealth and happiness), and even Mata, the mother (the giver of life). What, we must now ask, is the context in which the goddess truly becomes Lakshmi?

There is a widely known story that seems to indicate in what direction the answer might lie. It is said that after her defeat of the *asuras* Kali went on a bloody rampage, a mindless spree of killing that threatened both gods and men alike. She could not be stopped until Shiva lay in her path. She was on the point of killing him when she recoiled in horror, suddenly realizing that she had almost killed her husband. This brings us to a critical feature of the relationship between god and goddess, that of marriage, and to a critical pairing in the Hindu pantheon, that of Shiva and Parvati.

The Hindu pantheon is a fluid array of supernatural beings, and tends to alter in form as one context is replaced by another. In some contexts particular deities are seen as discrete entities, but under other circumstances deities merge with one another and their characteristics blend. At the most abstract level differentiation disappears altogether, as is suggested in the frequently heard Hindu truism that "all gods are one."

It is thus possible to say that the goddess, in the most abstract sense, is both married and not married. That she is married follows from the premise that all goddesses are one, as indeed all gods are one, and the fact that in some of her manifestations she is quite explicitly married. Kali, informants say, represents a form of Parvati who is Shiva's wife, and is in addition all the goddesses, whether explicitly married or not.

Yet is it clear that there is a sense in which we may speak of the goddess as having both married and unmarried—or at least not explicitly married—forms. The criterion is the ritual and iconographic context in which various manifestations of the goddess appear. The goddess as Parvati or Sita appears in popular iconography in a matrimonial context, standing beside and subordinate to her husband. While Lakshmi usually appears alone, she is explicitly understood to be Vishnu's wife. But the goddess as Durga, Mahamaya, Kali, etc.—the bloodthirsty goddess of the *Saptashati*—never appears in a matrimonial context, but rather alone, and surrounded by the paraphernalia of killing. Further, we shall see shortly that the goddess in these forms is identified directly with the parochial goddesses of Chhattisgarh, who are never thought of as married. It is in these "unmarried" manifestations that the goddess may, in Chhattisgarh and presumably elsewhere, receive blood sacrifice, quite in keeping with her combative and bloodthirsty nature. But as the consort of any of the gods the goddess seems to undergo a kind of transformation into what is almost the antithesis of the goddess of the *Saptashati*. As Parvati, Lakshmi, Sita, or Savitri she becomes a benevolent goddess, a giver of wealth and progeny, and an exemplar of passive devotion to her husband. In Chhattisgarh the goddess in these manifestations never receives blood sacrifice. In this context it is worth recalling the story of *tija*. Parvati, in an unmarried state, threatened the gods with her *tapasya*. The gods attempted to reduce her power, but the threat to their supremacy was not finally ended until her marriage to Shiva.

Involved in the transformation from the sinister to the domesticated goddess is an intriguing reversal of the male-female pairing. The substance of this reversal finds particularly clear expression in certain aspects of temple architecture. In a Rama-temple, Sita appears standing beside her husband in the attitude of the dutiful wife. Shiva and Parvati are not worshipped in anthropomorphic form in Shiva-temples, but when they are pictured together in lithography, Parvati, again, is standing beside her consort in a submissive attitude. But when the goddess stands in her terrible aspect in a temple, there is no god by her side. Rather, in the Mahamaya Temple, Raipur's largest and most important goddess-temple, the two deities associated with the goddess are Lal Bhairav and Kal Bhairav (Red and Black Bhairav). These are two rather sinister looking images standing outside and to either side of the door leading into the goddess's inner shrine. Bhairav, the Pujari of the temple says, is none other than Shiva in a *krodh rup*, a "terrible form." Here Shiva is subordinate to the goddess. He is no longer portrayed as her husband, but, in the Pujari's words, as "her bodyguard." He is also described as "field guard" (*kshetrapal*), which is consistent with his role as guardian of the goddess for, as we have seen, in the rites of *javara* there is an apparent identification between the goddess and crops growing in the fields. No longer ascendant, Shiva here becomes the instrument of the goddess, and his characteristics become submerged in hers. In this form he takes blood sacrifice. As Shiva he never does.

At this level in the pantheon, then, we can see two pairings of god and goddess, the union of Shiva and Parvati being the apparent medium of transformation between them. In one pairing god and goddess appear unambiguously as husband and wife. In this pairing the god is represented as dominant, the goddess as dutifully subordinate, and the goddess—indeed, the pairing as a unit—is benign. The Rama-Sita pairing is, to be sure, very powerful, but power here seems to have a different quality from that exemplified by Kali or Mahamaya. These are vegetarian deities; they never receive blood sacrifice, insisting instead on "pure" offerings of flowers or vegetarian foods. Even though Rama is represented as a great warrior, the element of ferocity and bloodthirstiness is strongly muted.

Of equal significance, it seems to me, is the fact that deities of this kind seem to embody certain key values of Indian civilization. It is as if the imposition of a basic vehicle of social order—marriage—on the relationship between god and goddess creates the possibility for the elaboration of divine attributes in accordance with basic order-producing values—hence the great variety in this sector of the pantheon. Shiva is the divine exemplar of renunciation, among other things. Vishnu, in his role of world "preserver," seems to represent order in the most inclusive sense. The figure of Krishna carries the values and imagery of devotional religious attitudes. Above all Rama, who is certainly the most important textual deity in Chhattisgarh, is the supreme example of the "exemplary" deity. His cult is a veritable encyclopedia of social values. He himself stands for the Kshatriya ideal: a brave warrior and a good king. In popular imagination his kingdom, as described in the *Ramayana*, represents the ideal of the benevolent and just polity. Because of his devotion and obedience to his father, he is regarded as the type of the ideal son. His relationship with his brothers represents ideal fraternity. His wife, Sita, is the very model of wifely virtues. His servant, Hanuman, represents service in the most ideal form, and this is extended and amplified into a form of religious devotion; Hanuman emerges as the ideal religious devotee (*bhakt*) as well.

This elaboration seems to dissolve away in the opposite pairing. Here the goddess is ascendant. If the god appears at all, it is not in the role of husband but of henchman and servant, and the pairing as a unit takes on the sinister attributes of the goddess herself. The goddess in this form is not conceived primarily as an exemplar of values and principles, but as the embodiment of an impersonal force—one that can be used, but that may be dangerous to the user, as indeed it endangers the gods themselves until it is contained. She may be induced to aid her devotees, but an important theme in her worship is the appeasement of her blood-thirst. "The Devi likes blood," informants say, and even in vegetarian houses when the goddess is worshipped in this form she is given red flowers in recognition of her appetites. Most important of all, there is an explicit identification of the goddess in this form with certain agencies of misfortune, which is not true of the Rama-Sita pairing or others like it. I shall return to this point shortly.

Thus, we seem to be at a point of intersection between social and religious symbolism. Within the pantheon a very dangerous force is symbolized, but this is a force that seems to undergo a basic transformation into something almost antisinister, the loving wife, the source of wealth and progeny, when placed within the context of a restraining social relationship, that of marriage. An appetite for conflict and destruction is thus transformed into the most fundamental of social virtues, that of wifely submission which, on the premises given in Hindu culture, makes the continuation of society possible. The basis for this transformation is a dual notion of divinity, a duality that in turn is linked to the opposition between male and female. When female dominates male the pair is sinister; when male dominates female the pair is benign.

The Goddess of Experience

A shrine or temple housing a goddess is an apparently indispensable part of the village scene. The goddesses represented in these shrines have many different names. In Sitapur the village goddess is called Mahamay, a contraction of the textual Mahamaya. In the closest neighboring village she is called Mauli Devi, and in other villages she is designated by a variety of specific names. There are certain generic names applicable to all local goddesses. Shitla is one. Mata, meaning simply "the mother," is another. She is often called "the seven sisters" or "the twenty-one sisters." However, the specific names are not really very important, for these goddesses have basically the same attributes whatever they are called.

Perhaps the most important fact about the local goddesses is that whether or not they are given textual names and attributes they are identified directly with the goddess of the texts in her sinister forms. Informants state explicitly that the Mata is really just the same as Durga, Chandi, or Mahamaya, who, in turn, are merely different forms of the same goddess. Furthermore, all of these goddesses share certain symbols. In Raipur the main temple of Shitla is decorated with pictures of lions. The lion is also Durga's vehicle (*vahan*) and ally in battle. The *trishul* is iconographically associated with the goddess in her sinister forms as well as with Shiva. It is also almost invariably drawn on the walls of the temples of village goddesses. One of the most important rites of the village goddesses is the *javara* sequence of the *navrata* periods. The same rites, including the growing of wheat seedlings, are also performed at the Mahamaya and Durga temples in Raipur.

The local goddess, whatever her particular name, has a multiplicity of associations, as does her textual counterpart, although the formal elaboration of her attributes is finally less rich. She is clearly linked with the fertility of the fields. As we have seen, she plays a role in marriage ceremonial. She will aid her worshippers if they give her the ritual attentions she regards as her due. But in addition to this she is associated with some of the darkest areas of human experience, and in abstract terms she may be said to embody the forces that underlie certain particularly feared and intractable forms of human misfortune, especially diseases. This being so, the local goddess plays a pivotal role in what I have called the local complex which, as I have tried to show, achieves its most precise definition in relation to diagnostics and therapeutics.

The most obvious link between the goddess and disease is, of course, smallpox. Smallpox is a direct intrusion of the goddess into the body of her victim. She is manifest in the patient's body in the form of heat, the fever; and the various therapeutic measures employed to combat smallpox—i.e., applications of cool water and *nim* leaves—are ritual acts designed to "cool" the goddess and effect her withdrawal. The goddess is also implicated in other areas of human misfortune, though here, perhaps, her involvement is less direct or obvious. In the last chapter we saw that witchcraft and malevolent ghosts are regarded as substantial dangers in Chhattisgarh. Here too there seems to be a diffuse association with divinity in its feminine forms. Witchcraft, as we have seen, is strongly feminine in its general associations, and seems to be linked with a concept of feminine malice. Also, witches are sometimes said to be "devotees" (*bhakts*) of the goddess, and they are described as dancing for the goddess on burning grounds, just as demonesses do for Kali. Witches are also said to dance for Bhairav, who is directly associated with the goddess. Malevolent ghosts are drawn into the same complex of ideas. Witches use ghosts as vehicles and as instruments of attack. Moreover, there is an identification between malignant ghosts and Bhairav. Bhairav, a Baiga told me, is himself a ghost, in fact "the *sardar* [chieftain] of ghosts." Finally, the most malevolent of all ghosts is female. This is Churalin, the composite spirit of women who have died in childbirth.

Human beings are not helpless before these sinister entities. The principal resource for dealing with them is, of course, the Baiga. He has a special relationship with various local deities, chief among them Thakur Dev, the protector of villages. The latter is a *devta*, a male deity. His relationship with the goddess is fraught with contradiction, and this very contradiction, I would suggest, provides a basis for the essential realism of the view of life presented by Chhattisgarhi religion. In Sitapur, Thakur Dev is physically represented by a small heap of stones lying directly in front of the door leading into the shrine of the goddess. Here Thakur Dev stands in a relationship with the goddess which is analogous to the relationship between Lal and Kal Bhairav and the goddess in the Mahamaya Temple in Raipur. But at the same time Sitapur informants maintain that Thakur Dev protects the village, and that he stands outside the village, from which point he can guard it from malignant intrusions. "Thakur Dev," one informant said, "is like the peon of the Mata. Just as the Sahib's peon [meaning the peon of any important official] will come to warn us that the Sahib is coming, so will Thakur Dev warn us that the Mata is coming and that we must worship her." Thakur Dev will protect people, the same informant went on to say, if he is worshipped himself. But people are forgetful, and remember him only in times of trouble. Thus sickness and other misfortune come to the village.

It seems clear that the opposition between male and female is an important integrating principle in the pantheon.

It appears in both the textual and local complexes, and in so doing unites the two. In both complexes divinity is manifest in male and female forms, as god and goddess. In general, masculine divinity seems to act as a restraining factor while feminine divinity is associated with a potentially destructive force that must be restrained. From the perspective of the texts, the goddess is ultimately the subordinate member of the pair, her more sinister aspects apparently subdued by marriage. In the local complex the goddess is not represented as married. Here she is ascendant, standing alone in her shrine, and here she is the master of the protective god. Thakur Dev and the Baiga can protect their clients from the forces associated with the goddess, but this is never a sustained control. That their protection is ephemeral is surely an accurate reflection of the uncertainties of life in rural Chhattisgarh.

The symbolism of the pantheon provides for disruptive and harmful forces and allows them a zone of ascendancy. In so doing it accounts for aspects of the human experience that, however they may be regretted, can never be denied. At the same time it ultimately contains these forces, and by doing so seems to say that although they may have a degree of free play in man's most immediate situation, in a wider context, that represented by the textual deities, they are transcended by basic values of society. It is vital to note, however, that if the pantheon contains these sinister forces, it does not negate them. Indeed, it cannot, for in the final analysis the benign and malevolent aspects of divinity are simply different faces of the same thing. Rather—to borrow both an expression and a concept from Dumont—the pantheon manipulates its symbolic apparatus in such a way that malevolent aspects of divine power are "encompassed" (Dumont 1970:78) within a wider order. Never fully suppressed, hazard and disorder retain existence in the form of the sinister goddesses, and are potential in the gods themselves from whom the goddesses ultimately came.

Heat and Divine Power

That sex is such an important differentiating principle in the pantheon leads to the more general consideration of concepts of sexuality as they apply to the deities. This, in turn, brings into play ideas of heat, renunciation, and power, and unites several themes that emerged in our previous discussions of the ritual cycles.

In the *Puranas* ideas about divine sexuality seem to cluster around the figure of Shiva. This god combines sexual attributes that at first glance seem glaringly contradictory. He is the lover and the spouse of Parvati, but is also renowned as an ascetic. Indeed, in his ascetic aspect he is regarded as the archetypal anchorite. He is described as "the perfect ascetic (Maha Yogi), in whom is centered the perfection of austerity, penance and meditation, through which unlimited powers are attained" (Danielou 1964:202). Shiva's great powers are directly associated with his sexual abstinence. Recent work by Wendy O'Flaherty has made the nature of this relationship clear. "Siva," she writes, "is the natural enemy of Kama [the god of sexual desire] because he is the epitome of chastity, the eternal brahmacarin, his seed drawn up, the very incarnation of chastity" (1969b:17). The power resulting from Shiva's chastity is understood as a kind of heat. By "drawing up" his semen Shiva generates heat within himself, a heat that can be released creatively or destructively, but is in all events a very powerful force. This internal heat, generated by continence, is the same as erotic heat, the heat of sexual desire; "yogic fire" is Kama denied, and thereby transmuted. It is clear from O'Flaherty's analysis that Shiva's chastity is not a negation of sexuality, but a mode or aspect of sexuality: "he does it [sexual union] but he does not enjoy it. Physical involvement without emotional involvement makes him even a greater yogi than he would be if he merely remained forever in his meditation. For this reason, Siva is said to have conquered

A shiv-ling enshrined at the base of a tree
Facing the god is Shiva's vehicle, the bull.

Kama, not in spite of the fact that Kama first stirred his senses greatly, but *because* he was so greatly aroused" (1969a:334).

The image of Shiva in Chhattisgarhi Hinduism is consistent with this Puranic delineation. In the most common of his pictorial representations, Shiva is shown in a meditative pose, seated upon a tiger's skin, the traditional seat of the ascetic. By his side is the begging bowl, a symbol of asceticism. But most important of all is the conventional form Shiva takes as an object of worship, the *ling*. The *shiv-ling* is a phallic representation, but it is not, as O'Flaherty points out (1969b:309–10), a libertine symbol. The *ling* may be seen as chaste, as symbolizing sexuality in a contained and potential state rather than sexuality in release. But even more important, it is a symbol of restraint in the context of active and aroused sexuality. Shiva's heat-power is generated by this transmutation of his sexuality. Such an interpretation is consistent with the principal way Shiva is worshipped in Chhattisgarh. Water is poured over the *ling*. Water is regarded as "cooling" in its effects, and the role of water in Shiva worship suggests that the *ling* itself is ritually "hot." The worshipper pours cooling water over the heated *ling*, an act that—in the context of similar applications of cooling things and substances in other ritual settings—suggests containment and control of the heat-power symbolized by the *ling*.

If Shiva epitomizes the association between sexual restraint and power, the same principle is illustrated elsewhere in the pantheon. The story of *tija* tells how Parvati's austerities almost made her more powerful than the gods themselves. Significantly, Indra sent Kama, the god of sexual desire, to divert the energies she was accumulating, but this measure failed. Only by marriage was her power contained. But in Chhattisgarh it is Hanuman who most explicitly exemplifies the link between chastity and power. Hanuman is absolutely chaste in his devotion to Rama, and as a result of this he has become a deity who presides over chastity. As the model of the *brahmacharin*, it is Hanuman whom young men should worship if they need help in maintaining chastity. One is struck by the contrast between Hanuman's physique, as portrayed in popular iconography, and the bodies of other masculine deities. The musculature and features of the other gods are usually softened, and this gives them an almost androgynous appearance. Hanuman is very different. His face is simian, and his body is emphatically masculine, with muscles bulging on his arms, torso, and legs. He is celebrated as being immensely strong. That in addition to this he should be the very model of chastity is in no way inconsistent. Strength is dissipated in uncontained sexuality; power results from the seed drawn up. Aggressively and vividly masculine, chaste Hanuman becomes a symbol of male power.

This association between sexual restraint and power is important because it points to a more general link between divine power and heat. By drawing up his seed, Shiva accumulates great heat (*tapas*), and it is this heat with which Shiva once destroyed Kama and will ultimately destroy the world at the end of the present creation (O'Flaherty 1969b:19ff). Heat seems to be closely identified with Shiva's power, and I think we have seen a good deal of evidence that suggests a more general identification between the power of the deities and heat. There is a sense in which divinity is "hot" in relation to the world of human experience.

The most palpable intrusion of divine power into the human world is, of course, possession, either as illness (smallpox) or in ritually controlled circumstances (the rites of *javara*, *gaura*, etc.). Possession of either type is understood as a kind of heat. In illness the heat of divine presence is manifest as fever, and is dealt with by means of the worship of the occupying deity and the application of "cooling" things and substances to the patient's body. Ritual possession is also considered a fever, but here it is deliberately cultivated as a special sign of the deity's favor. Under these circumstances, divine heat is controlled by the surrounding symbols of coolness. It will be recalled that in the rites of *javara* the "cold" leaves of the *nim* tree are kept nearby during the episodes of possession. Lemons, regarded as extremely cold, are cut before the feet of the goddess and are impaled on the ends of the flesh-piercing rods as if to suggest containment of the frenzy associated with possession. Constraint descends with finality at the end of the ritual as the goddess is cooled by immersion and the manifestations of possession fall away. In the final, "cool" state the congregational aspects of the ritual emerge strongly, as seen in the exchanges of "cooled" *javara* seedlings and the exchanges of gold and silver leaf from the images of Parvati and Shiva at the conclusion of the rites of *gaura*. Thus, the heat of ritual possession differs from the heat of illness in that it is subject to ritual control. It is actively sought by the worshippers, occurring, as it does, in a setting in which it is believed to signal a salutary relationship between the deity and the worshippers. It is not, in sum, the uncontrolled, unsought, and manifestly harmful heat-of-possession that characterizes smallpox.

In most ceremonials divine power does not enter the world so dramatically, yet the same theme of divinity-as-heat is echoed in a broad array of ritual performances. As we have seen, the "cooling" sequence at the termination of ritual is a general pattern in Chhattisgarhi ceremonial. The materials of the ritual, often including images of the deities, are assembled within the required zone of purity. A *kalash* may be present; if so, it is regarded as the material seat of divinity during the ceremony. These material items constitute the foci of worship for the duration of the ritual. At the conclusion of the sequence they are removed from the protected zone and taken (often in public procession) to a body of water where they are immersed and usually allowed to remain submerged. Again, this procedure is known as *thanda karna* (to cool).

The pattern of terminal "cooling" is seen in a variety of ostensibly very different rituals. The procedure is typical of ceremonies that specifically involve the worship of deities. It is also present in funerary rites. There is great variation in the way funerals are conducted, but in instances where the dead are cremated, the ashes are ultimately disposed of in water. Here the symbolism of cooling stands in striking contrast to the heat of the funeral pyre. The same pattern is even found in certain Muslim ceremonies in Chhattisgarh. The high point of the festival of *muharram* in Raipur comes at the end when the *tazias*, representations of the tomb of the martyred Hussain, are taken through the streets of the city in procession. The processions end at the city's tanks, where the *tazias* are cooled by immersion.

These terminal "cooling" sequences suggest that a kind of heat is generated in ritual. Moreover, the evidence suggests that this heat has something to do with the presence of the extramundane forces with which ritual deals. In the ritual context divinity intrudes momentarily into the phenomenal world and becomes accessible to the purposes of men. The deity is present at the altar and "tastes" the offerings of the worshippers. At the end of the sequence divinity withdraws, and with this departure the devices of the altar are "cooled." At the conclusion of funerary rites the animating spirit of the deceased has likewise withdrawn, and has crossed the barrier that separates the living from the dead. The remains, now devoid of spirit, are "cooled." Finally, in smallpox the goddess enters her victim's body and is manifest as fever. As she is "cooled" with *nim* leaves and water she withdraws, just as the possessing deity withdraws when the seedlings are immersed in water in the rites of *javara*. A single premise seems to unify these diverse occurrences: when "spirit" unites with substance, heat results—the warmth of life, the heat of the altar, and the fever of smallpox. Divested of "spirit," substance is cooled.

The opposition between heat and cold appears to be an ordering conception operative in an extensive domain of human concerns, which includes such seemingly unrelated matters as the classification of foods and mankind's experience of divinity. Heat is associated with power. Through the concept of heat the powers of renunciation and the powers of the deities are united. Likewise, the concept of heat provides a link by means of which the diffuse notion of divinity and its powers can be brought into relation with sensory aspects of human life. The experienced heat of fever (and indeed the blazing month of May) exemplifies and validates a far more general and abstract conception. Heat, then, is a truly multifaceted concept. Its ambit includes aspects of human temperament—the malevolent impulse of witchcraft, the frenzy of ritual possession, and the saturnalian excesses of *holi*. Divine power, sexuality, and even illness are drawn together within the semantic range of this single powerful symbol.

We might even speculate that the polarity of heat and cold represents an implicit ontological postulate in Chhattisgarhi Hinduism. This would seem to be a kind of thermal Manicheanism. Hot and cold, as modalities of existence, are in perpetual contention. A balance exists between the two that is stable in nature as a whole (at least at the present time), but that is subject to momentary local disturbances. It is in such disturbances that hot and cold become factors to be dealt with in human life. Beck has shown that in South India the heat that is represented in ritual symbolism is regarded as essential for human life, but is seen as dangerous if not contained within surrounding symbolic coolness (1969:565–66). The same pattern appears in the Chhattisgarhi data. Heat is necessary for life, but uncontrolled heat is dangerous and is associated with illness and violence, just as imbalance in the opposite direction, cold to excess, also has negative associations.

Implicit in the heat-cold polarity seems to be a distinction between substance and animating energy as basic principles of existence. The quality of coldness seems to imply inert and inanimate corporeality. It may be glimpsed in the corpse divested of spirit and the cold altar from which divinity has withdrawn. In heat there is the suggestion of a dynamic component of existence, a vital force that kindles life, is present in divinity, and lies at the heart of some of the most vivid episodes in Chhattisgarhi religious experience—namely, divine possession. It suggests an equation between divine power and the spirit in man, and this in turn seems to say that men *may* be deities in more than a metaphorical sense. We have seen that human beings are often worshipped as deities; in this there seems to be a consistency between religiously founded ontology and the ritualizations of social life. The "sacred," it would seem, is without precise boundaries, and is found within man himself. In any event, life as men know it combines both heat and cold, and human welfare—in the most immediate sense—rests upon a balance between the two.

The Divine Hierarchy

If men share something with the gods, this is not to say there are no gods. They exist, and they exist on a plane in some way removed from that of human existence. For this reason mediating ritual acts are necessary. It is said that all the gods are one, and yet the gods are also many. As we have seen, sex is a crucial differentiating factor, but not the only one; the pantheon is also a hierarchy. Some deities are superior to others: they are more powerful; their worship is more prestigious; their range of divine responsibility and jurisdiction is greater. All of this seems fairly clear, and yet the precise nature of the hierarchy of the pantheon remains elusive. Why is it a hierarchy? Why are the identities of the local deities not fully absorbed by the superior deities whose worship carries more prestige? Why, in turn, are the superior deities present when the lesser deities seem to be far more directly concerned with the immediate interests of human beings?

Obviously the answer cannot be a simple one, and a complete answer is not within the compass of this study. Nonetheless I would like to suggest that at least part of the answer may lie in a feature of Chhattisgarhi religion that we have already touched upon—the role of the symbolism of the pantheon in overriding or transcending a basic contradiction in Chhattisgarhi life, that posed by the necessity for order and the fact of immanent disorder, the necessity for safety, and the fact of pervasive hazard. We have already seen that the pantheon mutes the contradiction by drawing an equivalence between ultimate safety and immediate danger; they are simply different aspects of the same thing. Now I would like to suggest that in order to pose this equation in a way that is both affirmative and consistent with the realities of experienced life, it is necessary for distance to be a factor in humanity's relationships with the gods. This, in turn, implies a divine hierarchy.

The deities regarded as the most powerful are those of sacred literature. Their power is such that they can preside over the welfare of great collectivities, and is thus consonant with the fact that the identities of these deities are assigned to superior objects of worship. The greatest among them are also "exemplary" deities, who seem to embody certain important values in Indian civilization. More broadly, the manipulation of divine sexuality at this level of the pantheon seems to constitute an affirmation of the ultimate validity of social values in general, as opposed to the contingent reality of disorder and danger. Consistent with this, these deities—even those with more sinister attributes—play a role of general benevolence in the lives of their worshippers. By this I mean that they may be approached for help in various matters, and that people rarely, if ever, attribute instances of misfortune directly to them.

These deities seem to be connected with general welfare as opposed to specific advantages, with general principles as opposed to immediate exigencies, with the encompassing order as opposed to the encompassed realities of everyday life. This, however, is not to say that these deities are not worshipped by individuals for individual benefit. That they are the most powerful deities, and that their worship carries the greatest prestige, is enough to ensure a constant pressure for the substitution of their identities for those of the lesser deities. But at the same time there is a countervailing tendency, one occasioned by the very superiority of these deities. If they are the greatest deities, they are also the most remote. They are much too high to have any great concern with the petty affairs of ordinary human beings. As we have seen, it is for this reason that Hanuman is often worshipped instead of Rama, for the more lowly Hanuman can serve as a mediator between his human worshippers and benevolent but distant Rama. Thus, although the superior deities may be the most powerful, their great power does not seem to be equally applicable in all contexts. From the standpoint of the most immediate exigencies of life, their benevolence and power is very abstract and distant.

Nor is this only a metaphor. The remoteness of the highest deities has a tangible ritual dimension. These are the deities who, in terms of ceremonial requirements, are the least accessible to most human worshippers. This is true in two senses. As nominal entities, these deities are associated with conventions of worship which, if undertaken to the fullest degree, virtually require specialized knowledge—knowledge that is the special responsibility of the Brahman priesthood. But also the identities of these deities are associated in a special way with objects of worship that are extremely vulnerable to pollution; these identities, we might say, are fully "realized" only when they are assigned to objects of worship that occupy the inner sancta of major temples served by Brahmans. Under such circumstances ordinary worshippers cannot approach them directly, but must worship them through the medium of the Brahman. Thus, both operationally and nominally the highest gods are the most remote. At its heart the role of the Brahman priest is that of bridging the gap between these deities and the world of their human worshippers.

There is a great profusion of local deities. Most of them are relatively featureless gods and goddesses associated with particular families, castes, festivals, and localities. While technically a textual deity, Hanuman is frequently represented in village shrines. It is probable that with the diffusion of *Ramayana* lore in Chhattisgarh, Hanuman has come to replace certain local deities while absorbing some of their attributes. He is in an excellent position to do so. Celibate Hanuman is neither married to the goddess nor subordinate to her; he is the perfect mediator between the local and textual complexes. Interestingly, some village informants state that Hanuman is the goddess's brother. However, the most important of the local deities are the local goddesses (who are directly identified with the sinister goddesses of the texts) and the godling Thakur Dev (who is conceived as both the guardian and servant of the goddess and the protector of the village). This pair stands at the center of what I have called the local complex.

The local deities lack the power of the great deities. They also lack the richness of attributes characteristic of the superior deities. They are not exemplary deities; they are essentially "presiding" deities, usually associated with socially and territorially localized constituencies. Unlike the great deities, they are not conceived to be remote from their human worshippers. They are ritually more accessible than the great deities. They do not ask for elaborated ritual styles. As objects of worship they, like the superior deities, must be dealt with in a context of ritual purity, but in their case the requirement is greatly attenuated. They need not be insulated from the world by a priesthood of protected purity. Consistent with all of this is the apparent willingness of these deities to enter directly into the world and affairs of human beings. Thakur Dev appears unbidden in the dreams of the Baiga to warn of impending trouble. These deities, unlike most of the great deities, are quite likely to possess their worshippers during certain ceremonies, and when they do so they often make oracular pronouncements through the mouths of their possessed devotees. The goddess, as we have seen, often voluntarily enters the bodies of human beings in the form of smallpox.

The disposition of these deities toward the affairs of humanity seems to have a significantly different tone from that of the superior deities. Sinister elements are present at all levels of the pantheon, including the top. Nevertheless, at the uppermost level of the pantheon, the textual stratum, these are contained within a wider ordering. Even as the textual goddess is allowed her potentially malevolent and destructive characteristics, these are harnessed in the service of the preservation of the world-order represented by the gods (for, after all, the goddess was created to fight for the gods), and are ultimately constrained by the fact of divine marriage. At this level the "encompassing" of the goddess permits divine power to be modulated into a profuse array of exemplary attributes. This seems consistent with the fact that the superior deities are not directly implicated in the everyday troubles of men.

At the level of the local deities the constraining factor is lifted away, and here there is a far more ambiguous relationship between divine intention and human welfare. Under the right circumstances—when they are worshipped properly and regularly—these deities help and protect their worshippers. But they are jealous of their prerogatives. Regular attention and flattery are necessary to ensure their continuing goodwill, and neglecting them may result in reciprocal neglect, or even angry retaliation. The potential malevolence of these deities seems consistent with their appetites. Generally they are fond of blood sacrifice. In this we may note a basic consonance between their attributes and their usual characteristics as objects of worship. As objects of worship, these deities *must* be less pure than the superior deities if their appetites are to be satisfied, for animal sacrifice is an activity that yields pollution. Put another way, there seems to be an essential harmony between potential malevolence and greater ritual accessibility at this level of the pantheon.

This, however, raises an interesting question with regard to the goddess in her textual forms. These goddesses also "want blood." It is, indeed, this very characteristic that allows them to provide a link between the upper levels of the pantheon and the strata below. How, then, can these goddesses be concretized as objects of worship of great vulnerability to pollution? How can they exist in temples served by Brahmans? The situation is one of apparent contradiction. The dilemma is solved by using symbolic substitutes for meat (red flowers, red cloth, the cutting of a cucumber or gourd instead of a goat) or by insisting that actual animal sacrifice be conducted by low-caste menials outside the temple. The apparent incongruity disappears when the identity of the sinister goddess is absorbed by Parvati, and, through Parvati, by the other benign goddesses. In these forms she has no appetite for meat; her malign attributes are contained by marriage.

We may note a similar ambiguity in the case of Shiva. There seems, in fact, to be a basic symmetry between the roles of Shiva and the goddess. On the one hand, Shiva is a superior god. Some of the most important temples of the region contain representations of Shiva, and he is commonly portrayed iconographically together with the supreme deities Vishnu and Brahma (the latter is of no significance in Chhattisgarh). He is, like his peers, strictly vegetarian. But even so there is a sense in which his attributes echo themes that are much stronger at lower levels in the pantheon. In the texts he is linked with destruction; he will destroy the universe by fire at the end of the present cosmic cyle. Furthermore, in the rite of *gaura*, Shiva (with Parvati) is associated with ritual possession. Nor is the frenzy of possession inconsistent with his character. His wedding procession was accompanied by drunken demons, and Shiva himself is quite fond of *bhang*, which, in turn, is linked with the frenetic activities of *holi*. Shiva is worshipped with *bhang* on *mahashivratri*. Thus, the image of Shiva, like that of the goddess, seems to contain tendencies that bridge the gap between upper and lower levels of the pantheon. One element, however, is missing; Shiva is vegetarian, the goddess is not. It is perhaps because of these ambiguities in Shiva's character that ritual accessibility seems less of an issue in his case than with the other superior gods. He, with Hanuman, is one of the most commonly "localized" of the textual deities. While he is often enclosed in major temples behind the Brahmanical screen, he is also represented in small, local shrines beside virtually every body of water in the region.

Shiva's apparent ambivalence is explained by his close connection with the goddess. Just as the character of the goddess shifts as her relationship with the male deity alters, so too the character of the male deity depends on his relationship with the goddess. The Shiva-Parvati pair function as the basis for this transformation. So it is that Shiva, like the goddess, has two different identities; he is either husband or subordinate of the goddess, depending on the context in which he appears. There are inconsistencies in the textual image of the goddess; these are shed when her identity is fully absorbed by the married goddesses. Just so, the apparent inconsistencies in Shiva's character disappear when his identity is absorbed by the other superior gods, most importantly by Vishnu and his *avatars*. Conversely, ambiguity vanishes when the goddess appears at the local level; here her attributes are in harmony with her status as an object of worship. The same is true in Shiva's case when his identity is absorbed by Bhairav, and, through Bhairav, by Thakur Dev, whose relationship with the goddess falls into the same paradigm. Here, like his female counterpart, he is fully parochialized. No longer vegetarian, he wants blood sacrifice, and is in a position to accept it. Having said all this, however, it is important to note again that there is a crucial point of asymmetry between the role of Shiva and that of the goddess. Shiva, when dominant, is vegetarian; his contrast with the goddess in this respect points to the controlling function of male divinity in relation to the feminine, a theme duplicated at lower levels in the pantheon in the protective functions of Thakur Dev, the local god.

There is yet another level in the panthon, one lower than that of the local deities. It consists of entities who in almost every respect are the opposites of the highest deities. These are the malevolent ghosts, malignant spirits such as Churalin, and the witches. If the highest deities are aloof and difficult of access, the reverse is true here. Far from requiring elaborate ritual pre-conditions for contact with human beings, these entities avidly seek contact on their own volition, and it is up to their potential victims to apply appropriate measures to keep them at bay and to minimize the unfortunate consequences of inadvertent encounters. If the highest deities should be enclosed within a zone of purity, these beings are associated directly with pollution. Death is a source of severe pollution, and malignant ghosts (unlike the benign *pitris*) exist on a plane only just removed from death itself. Witches drink human blood, an image with powerful implications of pollution. Purity is a condition for contact with the deities. By contrast, these beings are removed by means of what amounts to a form of purification. They are dealt with by the Baiga, who applies his *mantras* using cowdung ash as a vehicle. Cowdung is both pure and purifying, and the Baiga's procedure may be seen as a form of purification.

These beings exist on a plane that is very close to that of human life, and are separated from it by the frailest of membranes. The malignant ghosts are spirits of the dead who have not yet managed to break away completely from the attachments of their previous existence. The witches would seem to have a foot in both worlds, sharing, as they do, both human and non-human abilities and characteristics. At this bottommost level of the pantheon, then, we seem to be at a point of direct contact, and even interpenetration, between the world of extramundane beings and the world of men. Pollution seems to be a characteristic of this zone. In pollution man is born, as his spirit moves into flesh, and in pollution he dies as his spirit struggles to escape the entanglements of the world.

As we move from the upper to the lower levels of the pantheon we see a shift in the disposition of divine entities toward human affairs. At the uppermost levels the deities regard humanity with general—if abstract and distant—benevolence. The deities at the middle levels are less dependably benevolent, but more accessible and more directly involved in the immediate affairs of their worshippers. At the base of the pantheon involvement in the human world is both intimate and characterized by unmitigated malevolence. At this level of the pantheon jealousy—a dark, disruptive human emotion—emerges: the jealousy of the dead for the living and, as we have also noted, the jealousy associated with the frustration of certain feminine aspirations, which stand out most clearly in the contexts of childbearing and marriage.

Life in Chhattisgarh, like life anywhere, presents a seemingly irreconcilable contradition. Human affairs rest on the premise of order, but real life too often denies this premise. Life is full of hazards and obstacles. In part these are foreseeable, and hence assimilable to a wider order, because they respond to the rhythm of the seasons and the phases of growth and development of the individual. In part they are unforeseeable and fortuitous. The pantheon, seen in all its aspects, seems to express and assess man's situation. To do so it must accommodate the necessity for order and safety with the fact of disorder and hazard. As objects of worship in *puja* the deities embody the structure of the society with which they are associated, and their worship is a continuing affirmation of the particular features of this structure. In their nominal aspects the deities conceptualize the relationships between ordering values and potential disorder, between safety and hazard. Divine power is "refracted" (Evans-Pritchard 1956) into entities of varying sex, character, accessibility, and disposition toward men. Some embody general malevolence or specific dangers; others provide the possibility of safety and countermeasures. Still others, the greatest gods, provide the promise of an encompassing order in which society, and the enduring values upon which it is based, are sustained despite the greater immediacy of value-negating aspects of life.

As an assessment of humanity's situation Chhattisgarhi Hinduism tends toward a kind of resigned realism. The reality of the less pleasant facts of life acquires full recognition in the concept of distance as a feature of man's relationships with the gods. The entities most closely associated with human misfortune are metaphorically and ritually the closest and most accessible to mankind. The deities who seem to be the ultimate guarantors of ordering values are the least accessible and most distant from humanity. Arrayed in this way, the pantheon evaluates the human prospect in a way that, while not wholly pessimistic, is at least realistic given the facts of life in Chhattisgarh. The pantheon cannot deny these facts; instead it seeks to make them consistent with the wider order it affirms. The pantheon achieves a consistency which is wide indeed. Given the key role of renunciation as a value in Indian civilization, and as a basis for soteriology, it is with a sense of wonderment that one sees the concept of feminine divinity providing an equation in which prosperity (Lakshmi), the creation of life (Mata), and the fecundity of the fields (the goddess in *javara*) are linked with destruction (Kali), disease (Shitla and the other lesser goddesses), and finally with illusion (Mahamaya, which may be translated as "the grand illusion").

In the texts the distance between man and the great deities is given a temporal character. Ages ago there was a time, known to us through scripture, when the great deities lived and warred with the enemies of man and the gods alike on the very ground men inhabit today. But this was a time when the great questions were being decided—issues of far greater moment than humanity's petty troubles. High divinity and the world of human experience have subsequently separated. In this *kali yug*, this present age of darkness and evil, divinity touches the world hesitantly, and not always to the advantage of mankind.

Glossary

achhut	untouchable
adivasi	aborigine, tribesman
Agni	god of fire
amavashya	new moon
arti (*arati*)	mode of worship in which a flame is moved in a circular fashion before the deity
asharh	June–July
ashirvad	blessing
ashivan (*kunvar*)	September–October
asura	demon
ata	coarse wheat flour
avatar	incarnation of a deity
Ayodhya	Rama's capital
Ayurvedic	traditional Indian system of medicine
badi (*krishna*)	dark fortnight
Baiga	priest/diagnostician/exorcist; a non-Brahman religious specialist

baisakh	April–May
Bania	merchant or moneylender
barat	groom's wedding party
bel	the wood apple
bhadon	see *bhadrapad*
bhadrapad (*bhadon*)	August–September
Bhagavata Purana	best known of the *Puranas* which includes an account of Krishna's life
Bhairav	a fierce form of Shiva
bhajan	devotional song, devotional singing
bhakt (*bhakta*)	devotee
bhakti	devotion
bhang	a preparation of marijuana (*Cannibis sativa*)
bhut-pret	malevolent ghosts
Brahma	creator of the universe, not an important deity in Chhattisgarh
brahmacharya	celibacy, the first of the four *ashramas*, or stages of life among the twice-born
Brahman	first of the four *varnas* in rank, priests and teachers
Burha Dev	a deity associated with the Gonds
chaitra	March–April
Chamar	caste of leatherworkers
Chandi	a form of the goddess
channa	gram
Churalin	a demoness regarded as the composite spirit of women who have died in childbirth
churi pahanana	"putting on the bangle," secondary marriage rite

darshan	view, glimpse, royal or divine audience
dev (*deva*)	a god
Devar	swineherding and begging caste
Devi	the goddess
devi	a goddess
devta	a god
dharm (*dharma*)	duty, religious duty, righteousness
Dhobi	washerman caste
dhoti	a man's garment (loincloth) worn around the waist
dhup	incense
dulha	bridegroom
Dulha Dev	the "bridegroom" god, a deity associated especially with the Ravats
dulhin	bride
Durga	a form of the goddess
Ganda	caste of musicians and dancers
Ganesh	elephant-headed son of Shiva
gayatri mantra	verse from the *Rig Veda*, taught to twice-born youths as part of the investiture of the sacred thread
ghat	see *kalash*
ghi	clarified butter
Gond	a tribal people of Central India
gotra	patriclan
gur	jaggery
guru	teacher, spiritual guide
Hanuman	monkey-faced servant and devotee of Rama, a major deity in Chhattisgarh
havan	see *homa*

hom (*homa*; also *havan*)	ceremony in which offerings to the deity are burned
ishta devta	personal deity
jadu-tona	witchcraft
Jagannath	epithet of Krishna
janeu	the sacred thread worn by the twice-born
Jaria Ravat	Ravat subcaste believed to be indigenous to Chhattisgarh
jati	birth, parentage, kind, breed; caste or subcaste
jhara-phunka	technique by which Baigas apply their *mantras* to patients
jiv (*jiva*)	the soul, the spirit
jutha	leavings, garbage
jyeshth	May–June
kajal	lampblack
kalash (*ghat*)	a pot, the physical locus of the deity in some *pujas*
Kali	a form of the goddess
Kama (*Kamdev*)	god of sexual desire
Kanaujia Ravat	*Ravat* subcaste which traces its origin to the city of Kanauj
Kandara	basketmaking caste
Kankali	a form of the goddess
karm (*karma*)	act, deed, destiny; the influence of past acts
kartik	October–November
katha	story
Kevant	fishing caste
Krishna	*avatar* of Vishnu and one of the most important deities in the tradition of devotional Hinduism

Kshatriya	second of the four *varnas* in rank, rulers, and warriors
Kumhar	potter caste
kunvar	see *ashivan*
Kurmi	farming caste
Lakshman	brother of Rama
Lakshmi	Vishnu's consort, goddess of wealth
ling (linga)	phallic representation of Shiva
Lohar	blacksmith caste
magh	January–February
Mahadev	epithet of Shiva
Mahamaya	a form of the goddess
mandap	marriage pavilion
mandir	temple
mantra	incantation
Marar	gardener caste
margashirsh	November–December
Marwari	group of merchantile castes from Marwar in Rajasthan
Mata	the mother, an epithet of the goddess
mata	mother
Matar	deity associated with the Kanaujia Ravats
mata seva	"the service of the mother," small-pox therapy
maya	illusion, fraud, jugglery; the creative power of a deity
Mehar	shoemaking caste
Mehetar	sweeper caste
mela	religious fair
mitan	friendship, ceremonial friendship
moksha (mukti)	release, salvation

muharram	a Muslim festival
mukti	see *moksha*
Nai	barber caste
Narad	an ancient sage
Narayana	Vishnu
navratra	"nine nights," a ritual period occurring during the bright fortnights of the lunar months of *chaitra* and *kunvar*
nazar	the glance, the evil eye
nim	the margosa tree
Painka	watchman caste
pak (*paksh*)	lunar fortnight
pan	a preparation of betel leaf and areca nut
panchang	almanac
Pandit	learned man, a Brahman priest
pap	sin
Paramatma	the oversoul
Parvati	Shiva's wife
path	recitation of a text
paush	December–January
phalgun	February–March
pinda	offerings to the dead
pipal	the sacred fig tree (*Ficus religiosa*)
pranam	literally "salutation," a bow of obeisance
prasad	sanctified food, food retrieved from the altar and distributed to worshippers in *puja*
pret-yoni	a ghostly form of existence
puja	worship, homage
Pujari	temple priest

punya	merit
Purana	old story; together with the Epics the 18 principal *puranas* are the main texts of popular Hinduism
purnima (*punni*)	full moon
raja	king
Rajput	group of castes of Kshatriya status
Rama	hero of the *Ramayana*, *avatar* of Vishnu, exemplar of perfect rule
Ramayana	epic of 24,000 couplets attributed to Valmiki; describes the abduction of Rama's wife, Sita, by the demon Ravana, and the subsequent war in which Ravana is killed and Sita recovered
Ravana	demon king who abducted Sita in the *Ramayana*
Ravat	herding caste
Sadhu	ascetic mendicant
Saharha Dev	deity associated with the Ravats
Saligram	Vishnu in the form of a small stone
sanskar (*sanskara*)	life-cycle rites
sannyasi	homeless ascetic
Satnami	sectarian caste, ex-leatherworkers
savan	see *shravan*
Savitri	wife of Satyavan, exemplar of wifely devotion
Shakti	energy or force, an epithet of the goddess
Shankar	Shiva
Shitla	the goddess of smallpox
Shiva	one of the principal Hindu deities, god of destruction and creation

shiv-ling	see *ling*
shravan (*savan*)	July–August
Shri Durga Saptashati	
(*Devi Mahatmyam*)	a text on the goddess
Shudra	fourth and lowest of the *varnas*; once- as opposed to twice-born
sindur	red lead
Sita	wife of Rama, model of wifely virtues
Sonar (*Soni*)	goldsmith caste
sudi (*shukla*)	bright fortnight
tapas	penance, self-mortification, heat generated by asceticism
tapasya	penance, self-mortification
taviz	amulet
tazia	representation of Hussain's tomb carried in procession during *muharram*
Teli	oil-pressing caste
Thakur Dev	protective god of rural Chhattisgarh
thanda karna	to cool
til	sesamum
tilak	mark made on the forehead
tithi	date in the Hindu calendar
tonhi	witch
trishul	Shiva's trident
tulsi	basil plant
twice-born	the three highest *varnas*; so designated because males of these *varnas* undergo an initiation regarded as a "second birth"
urad	horse bean

Vaishya	third of the four *varnas* in rank, merchants
varna	one of the four traditional categories of Hindu society; *Brahmans, Kshatriyas, Vaishyas,* and *Shudras*
Vishnu	one of the principal Hindu deities; he is regarded as the preserver of the world order
vrat	religious vow, fast
yagya	sacrifice
Yama (Yam)	god of death

References

Agehananda Bharati
1965 *The Tantric Tradition.* London: Rider and Company.

Babb, Lawrence A.
1970a "The Food of the Gods in Chhattisgarh: Some Structural Features of Hindu Ritual." *Southwestern Journal of Anthropology,* 26: 287–304.
1970b "Marriage and Malevolence: The uses of Sexual Opposition in a Hindu Pantheon." *Ethnology,* 9: 137–148.
1972 "The Satnamis—Political Involvement of a Religious Movement." In *The Untouchables in Contemporary India,* ed. J. M. Mahar. Tucson: University of Arizona Press, 143–51.
1973 "Heat and Control in Chhattisgarhi Ritual." *The Eastern Anthropologist,* 26: 11–28.

Beck, Brenda E. F.
1969 "Colour and Heat in South Indian Ritual." *Man,* 4: 553–72.

Berreman, Gerald D.
1964 "Brahmans and Shamans in Pahari Religion." *Journal of Asian Studies,* 23: 53–69.

Carstairs, Morris G.
1961 *The Twice-Born: A Study of High Caste Hindus.* Bloomington: Indiana University Press.

Census Operations, Superintendent
1961 *District Census Handbook: Raipur District.* Bhopal: Govt. of Madhya Pradesh (1964).

Cunningham, Alexander

1884 "Report on a Tour in the Central Provinces and Lower Gangetic Doab in 1881–82." *Archaeological Survey of India*, 17: entire.

Danielou, Alain

1964 *Hindu Polytheism*. New York: Pantheon Books.

De Brett, E. A.

1909 *Chhattisgarh Feudatory States*. Bombay: Times Press.

Dubey, K. C., and M. G. Mohril

1965 *Fairs and Festivals of Madhya Pradesh*. Delhi: Manager of Publications.

Dumont, Louis

1960 "World Renunciation in Indian Religions." *Contributions to Indian Sociology*, 4: 33–62.

1970 *Homo Hierarchicus: An Essay on the Caste System*, trans. Mark Sainsbury. Chicago: University of Chicago Press.

Dumont, Louis, and David Pocock

1959a "On the Different Aspects or Levels in Hinduism." Contributions to Indian Sociology, 3: 40–54.

1959b "Possession and Priesthood." *Contributions to Indian Sociology*, 3: 55–74.

1959c "Pure and Impure." *Contributions to Indian Sociology*, 3: 9–39.

Evans-Pritchard, E.

1956 *Nuer Religion*. London: Oxford University Press.

Freed, Ruth S. and Stanley A.

1964 "Calendars, Ceremonies and Festivals in a North Indian Village: The Necessary Calendric Information for Fieldwork." *Southwestern Journal of Anthropology*, 20: 67–90.

Harper, Edward B.

1959 "A Hindu Village Pantheon." *Southwestern Journal of Anthropology*, 15: 227–34.

1964 "Ritual Pollution, as an Integrator of Caste and Religion." *Journal of Asian Studies*, 23: 151–97.

1969 "Fear and the Status of Women." *Southwestern Journal of Anthropology*, 25: 81–95.

Jagadisvarananda (trans.)

The Devi-Mahatmyam or Sri Durga-Saptasati. Mylapore: Sri Ramakrishna Math.

Jay, Edward J.

1973 "Bridging the Gap Between Castes: Ceremonial Friendship in Chhattisgarh." *Contributions to Indian Sociology*, n.s., 7: 144–158.

Kavyopadhyaya, Hira Lal

1921 *A Grammar of the Chhattisgarhi Dialect of Eastern Hindi*. Calcutta: Baptist Mission Press.

Leach, Edmund R.
   1964 *Political Systems of Highland Burma; A Study of Kachin Social Structure.* London: London School of Economics and Political Science.

Mandelbaum, David
   1966 "Transcendental and Pragmatic Aspects of Religion." *American Anthropologist,* 68: 1174–91.

Marriott, McKim
   1966 "The Feast of Love." In *Krishna: Myths, Rites and Attitudes,* ed., M. Singer. Honolulu: East-West Center Press, 200–212.
   1968 "Caste Ranking and Food Transactions: A Matrix Analysis." In *Structure and Change in Indian Society,* eds., M. Singer and B. Cohn. Chicago: Aldine Publishing Company, 133–71.

Mauss, Marcel
   1967 *The Gift,* trans. Ian Cunnison. New York: Norton and Co.

Mayer, Adrian C.
   1960 *Caste and Kinship in Central India.* Berkeley and Los Angeles: University of California Press.

Needham, Rodney
   1972 *Belief, Language, and Experience.* Chicago: University of Chicago Press.

Nelson, A. E. (ed.)
   1909 *Central Provinces District Gazetteers. Raipur District.* Vol. A, Descriptive. Bombay: British India Press.
   1910a *Central Provinces District Gazetteers. Bilaspur District.* Vol. A, Descriptive. Allahabad: Pioneer Press.
   1910b *Central Provinces District Gazetteers. Drug District.* Vol. A, Descriptive. Calcutta: Baptist Mission Press.

O'Flaherty, Wendy D.
   1969a "Asceticism and Sexuality in the Mythology of Siva, Part I." *History of Religions,* 8: 300–337.
   1969b "Asceticism and Sexuality in the Mythology of Siva, Part II." *History of Religions,* 9: 1–41.

Redfield, Robert
   1960 *Peasant Society and Culture.* Chicago: University of Chicago Press.

Russell, Robert Vane
   1916 *The Tribes and Castes of the Central Provinces of India,* 4v. London: Macmillan.

Singer, Milton
   1972 *When a Great Tradition Modernizes.* New York: Praeger.

Sinha, Surajit
   1962 "State Formation and Rajput Myth in Tribal Central India." *Man in India,* 42: 35–80.

Srinavas, M. N.

  1952 *Religion and Society among the Coorgs of South India.* London: Asia
     Publishing House.

Staal, J. F.

  1963 "Sanskrit and Sanskritization." *Journal of Asian Studies*, 22: 261–75.

Stevenson, Mrs. Sinclair

  1920 *The Rites of the Twice-born.* London: Oxford University Press.

Underhill, M. M.

  1921 *The Hindu Religious Year.* London: Oxford University Press.

Wills, C. U.

  1919 "The Territorial Systems of the Rajput Kingdoms of Mediaeval
     Chhattisgarh." *Journal and Proceedings of the Asiatic Society of Bengal*,
     15: 197–262.

Woodroffe, Sir John

  1951 *Shakti and Shakta: Essays and Addresses on the Shakta Tantrashastra.*
     Madras: Ganesh and Company.

Index